Routledge Revivals

Superpower Intervention in the Middle East

Strategically placed on the global chess board, as well as controlling vast oil resources, the Middle East was one of the main theatres of Cold War. In the 1950s the Soviet Union had taken advantage of Arab Nationalists' disillusion with British and French Imperialism, along with the emerging Arab-Israeli conflict, to establish relations with Egypt, Syria and Iraq. The United States responded by moving in to shore up the Western position. Confrontation was inevitable. *Superpower Intervention in the Middle East* was written in 1978, when this confrontation was at its height. The book's main theme focuses on how the superpowers became competitively involved in local Middle East conflicts over which they could exercise only limited control, and the risks of nuclear confrontation of the kind which occurred at the end of the 1973 Arab-Israeli war. The threat to Western oil supplies is also examined. This is a fascinating work, of great relevance to scholars and students of Middle Eastern history and political diplomacy, as well as those with an interest in the relationship between the Western superpowers and this volatile region.

Peter Mangold has worked in the Foreign and Commonwealth Office Research Department and the BBC World Service, and is currently Senior Associate Member of St Antony's College, Oxford. He has written widely on international affairs and is the author of *National Security and International Relations* (Routledge, 1990; *Routledge Revivals*, 2013).

Superpower Intervention in the Middle East

Peter Mangold

Routledge
Taylor & Francis Group

First published in 1978
by Croom Helm Ltd

This edition first published in 2013 by Routledge
2 Park Square, Milton Park, Abingdon, Oxon, OX14 4RN

Simultaneously published in the USA and Canada
by Routledge
711 Third Avenue, New York, NY 10017

Routledge is an imprint of the Taylor & Francis Group, an informa business

© 1978 Peter Mangold

Publisher's Note
The publisher has gone to great lengths to ensure the quality of this reprint but points out that some imperfections in the original copies may be apparent.

Disclaimer
The publisher has made every effort to trace copyright holders and welcomes correspondence from those they have been unable to contact.

ISBN 13: 978-0-415-83096-6 (hbk)
ISBN 13: 978-0-203-49615-2 (ebk)

SUPERPOWER INTERVENTION IN THE MIDDLE EAST

PETER MANGOLD

CROOM HELM LONDON

© 1978 Peter Mangold
Croom Helm Ltd., 2-10 St John's Road, London SW11
ISBN 0-85664-543-5

British Library Cataloguing in Publication Data

Mangold, Peter
    Superpower intervention in the Middle East.
    1. Near East - Foreign relations – Russia
    2. Russia - Foreign relations – Near East
    3. Near East - Foreign relations – United States
    4. United States - Foreign relations – Near East
    I. Title
    327.56'047   DS63.2.R9

    ISBN 0-85664-543-5

CONTENTS

INTRODUCTION

'Beneath the nuclear umbrella, the temptation to probe with regional forces or proxy wars increases'.[1] Thus Dr Henry Kissinger, speaking in 1976. His argument, as might have been expected from an American Secretary of State, drew heavily on the growth of Soviet conventional and naval power, and on the Soviet Union's expanding 'global reach'. Had he sought doctrinal justification, he would no doubt have been able to draw on the writings of the Commander-in-Chief of the Soviet Navy, Admiral Gorchkov. Gorchkov and other Russians would however add a further perspective to the argument, and point in turn to the size of American conventional mobile forces and to the long history of American interventionary politics going back to the early days of the Cold War. Yet whatever the rival perceptions of where the interventionary initiative may lie, the behaviour of both superpowers provides ample evidence for Dr Kissinger's basic contention that various modes of military policy continue to remain open to the superpowers. This despite the very real constraints imposed by the nuclear balance of terror and, outside Europe, by the growth of Afro-Asian nationalism.

The scope for military policy beneath the nuclear umbrella is perhaps most readily evident in the Middle East. This is a region with a long history of domination by external powers, domination the nature of which has also undergone significant change during the twentieth century. In the wake of the collapse of the Ottoman Empire at the end of the First World War, Britain and France acquired League of Nations mandates over Iraq, Palestine, Syria and the Lebanon. A series of bilateral treaties imposed restrictions on the foreign, and by extension also the domestic, policies of Middle Eastern governments, ranging in size and importance from Egypt and Iraq to the sheikhdoms of the Persian Gulf. These restrictions were largely determined by imperial strategic interests. They were enforced by garrisons and locally recruited levies, which in emergency could be reinforced from strategic reserves. As late as 1942 the British Ambassador could surround the Abdin palace in Cairo with armoured cars, and present King Farouk with the choice of installing a pro-British government or of abdication.

Fourteen years later however a major Anglo-French expeditionary force failed ignominiously to overthrow the government of President Nasser. By 1956 the balance of power between Arab nationalism and European imperialism was shifting decisively in favour of the former, undermining the governments on whom the British Empire by treaty system had rested,[2] and, through a combination of political pressure and guerilla harassment, making British land and air bases untenable. The process however was a long and uneven one and it reflected not only the strength of Arab nationalism, in itself an unequal force, but the weakness of the imperial powers of postwar Europe. It began in the eastern Mediterranean, where the French had in 1946 been forced to concede independence to Syria and the Lebanon. The following year Britain abandoned primary responsibility for Greece and Turkey, as well as the Palestine mandate. In 1956, after years of harassment, British troops left the Suez Canal Zone base, and the British effort was henceforth largely concentrated on the conservative Arabian peninsula and Gulf region. Only in 1967 did British troops leave Aden, and in 1971, for reasons which had more to do with domestic economic weakness than immediate Middle Eastern politics, the British presence was largely withdrawn from the Gulf.

The British military withdrawal did not however mark the end of external military involvement in the Middle East, a development any listener to Cairo radio in the mid 1950s might well have anticipated. Rather it meant a change in the identity of the interventionary powers, and in the nature of external military involvement. Soviet-American rivalry, which had begun immediately after the defeat of Germany, made it impossible for an area as strategically important as the Middle East to avoid being drawn into the Cold War. And the acute instability of the Middle Eastern political system as it emerged from imperial tutelage, was such that there were few states which did not quickly begin to look outside the region for arms and protection. These included not only the still numerous conservative states which sought some form of replacement for erstwhile British support but also those nationalist regimes, including Nasser's Egypt, which feared Western intervention and also became directly embroiled in the Arab-Israeli conflict.

The Americans, and subsequently the Russians, thus made their postwar military debut in the Middle East in the guise of armourers and protectors. Major bases and 'unequal treaties' had gone and, as the Soviet experience in Egypt showed, proved impossible to re-establish permanently. Direct military intervention became a rare and dangerous phenomenon, and was never undertaken without regional allies. The superpowers were heavily dependent on the availability of *military access,* i.e. local actors—states, alliance groupings and insurgency movements, with whom they shared a common interest, and through whom various forms of military influence could be channelled into the region. This was most frequently effected indirectly by the transfer to these local recipients of military resources in an attempt to manipulate the regional balance of power. In the first place this meant the transfer of arms.[3] But it involved also the transfer of military skills and technology, the provision of economic aid for security-related purposes, the establishment of military infrastructures and the supply of intelligence. The recipients included virtually every independent state in the Middle East, the main concentration being on key regional powers, whom the superpowers were anxious to develop as local military proxies, as well as the other confrontation states in the Arab-Israeli conflict, and the non-Arab Moslem states lying directly on the Soviet periphery. Given the level of regional instability, the fact that only Israel had a significant arms industry, and that few countries had societies readily capable of operating sophisticated weapons, the demands made on the superpowers for all forms of military resources were very high. In some cases military resource transfers were so structured to enhance the real military capabilities of the recipients. In others they were of an essentially symbolic character, designed to reassure local governments, or to deter or intimidate their adversaries through a demonstration of support or a manipulation of the balance of power on paper, but of only limited military value.

While many Middle Eastern countries welcomed the military commitments which sometimes were implicit, and sometimes were hoped to be implicit in a *military resource transfer* relationship, they were frequently unwilling for these to be augmented by a permanent external military presence. Nor were the superpowers, and in particular the United States, always anxious to extend their global military commitments and involvements. But the gospel of military self-help often proved as much aspiration as achievement, and the superpowers were therefore also compelled to deploy their own armed forces in support of their Middle Eastern policy objectives. The exercise of military power, that is the use of force to attack or to engage in armed combat with regional states or military movements, proved infrequent, Soviet control over the Egyptian air defence system from 1970 to 1972 notwithstanding.

Much more important was the exercise of military influence by means of the threat of military intervention or the promise of support. Its most permanent manifestation was a series of security treaties, declarations or doctrines and implicit or assumed defence commitments.

as well as the presence of some relatively small locally-stationed forces. During the periods when local military conflict appeared imminent or threatened to take a course fundamentally detrimental to a client, the superpowers resorted to more immediate warnings of possible military intervention. These warnings were usually underscored by the readying of forces outside the Middle East. Through the movements of ships, troops and aircraft, and through the upgrading of the alert status of various conventional and also nuclear forces, the United States and the Soviet Union sought to convey to each other, as well as to regional states, the seriousness of their military interventionary intentions should their specific political demands not be met. The rationale of these *minatory deployments* is explained by Admiral Radford:

> Since good military planning requires that the capabilities of the opponent be the primary consideration in determining one's courses of action, the Soviets are required to evaluate their options within the shadow of our shifting military presence. Prudence would dictate that they be alert to all the possibilities inherent in our changing dispositions, and to guide their own actions accordingly. Even changes in geographical positions, courses and speeds may be used as conscious indicators to establish without ambiguity just what degree of interest we attach to specific cases of rising tensions.[4]

Yet not all exercises in minatory diplomacy involved superpower confrontation or the movement of military forces and, *pace* Admiral Radford, the signals which could be transmitted ranged from the highly specific to the deliberately ambiguous, and allowed for a certain element of bluff. Hence this form of diplomacy, which depended on the threat to coerce, provided the superpowers with a particularly effective and flexible instrument of policy, an instrument which, carefully used, paid high political dividends at the cost of fairly manageable risks.

Thus despite the growing ascendency of local nationalism and the withdrawal of the European military presence and the risk of nuclear confrontation, interventionary powers continued to play a prominent military role in the Middle East. The superpowers did not control the policies of the regional states as their European predecessors had done: no Pax Americana or Sovietica replaced the Pax Britannica in the Gulf in the 1970s. The United States and the Soviet Union tended to exercise influence rather than power. But both superpowers did make substantial use of military policy in the Middle East. Why they did so, how effectively they succeeded in furthering their own and their clients' interests, and how they were constrained by regional and extra-regional factors, is the subject of this study of interventionary politics under the nuclear umbrella.

Notes

1. The 1976 Alastair Buchan Memorial Lecture, *Survival,* September-October 1976, pp.196-7.
2. The title of a book by M.A. Fitzsimons.
3. Military resource transfer however excludes the sale of arms for primarily commercial reasons, although it is of course frequently difficult to disentangle political and economic motives.
4. *New York Times,* 16 February 1971.

1 THE IMPORTANCE OF THE MIDDLE EAST

The importance of the Middle East is one of the commonplaces of writings on international politics, a function of oil, strategy and regional instability. Stated in these bald terms, the proposition was as true at the end of the Second World War as in the mid 1970s. But closer examination shows that the role of the region in the international system, as well as the rationale for interventionary politics, had undergone significant changes over the thirty-year period. Outside the region, these were the results of shifts in the loci of international power, changes in weapons technology and the growing importance of oil as a source of energy. Within the Middle East they resulted from the rapidly shifting kaleidoscope of regional tensions, as well as from the growing economic and political strength of the major oil producers.

The most dramatic of these changes has been the emergence of Middle Eastern countries as independent actors in world affairs, as countries which needed to be courted for their independent influence, instead of as in the past being dominated and exploited for their economic resources or for their strategic real estate. The political basis for this development had its roots in the emergence of nationalism. Its economic origins are found in the spectacular growth of world oil consumption. In 1938 the Middle East produced 16.2 million metric tons of oil, representing 7.7 per cent of world production. In 1963 production was 390.4 million tons – 34.7 per cent of world production. Ten years later production had trebled to 1,210.2 million metric tons, which now represented 51.3 per cent of world production.[1] These figures come into clearer perspective when viewed not only against the high economic growth rates of the 1950s and 1960s, which had in large measure been made possible by the availability of cheap Middle Eastern oil, but also against the increasing use of oil as a source of energy. Whereas in 1960 oil represented 39 per cent of total energy consumption in OECD, in 1973 the figure was 53 per cent.[2] Moreover the Middle East contained the bulk of world proven oil reserves. In 1974 the figure was 60.85 per cent. Saudi Arabia alone accounted for 24.2 per cent of world proven oil reserves, Kuwait for 11.4 per cent and Iran for 9.2 per cent.[3]

With the growth of oil production came a build-up of wealth. Already in the mid 1950s Kuwait had amassed large foreign currency holdings, the existence of which had become a matter of some concern to the authorities in London. In 1961 the sheikhdom established the Kuwaiti Fund for Arab Economic Development. Kuwait's example presaged what would happen throughout the Gulf in the 1970s. After remaining stable for more than fifteen years, the price of oil began to rise in 1970 and then quadrupled in the wake of the Yom Kippur War. The result was a sudden and initially highly destabilising transfer of wealth from the oil consumers to the producers, the latter amassing a balance of payments surplus of some $60 billion in 1974.[4] After the initial panic it began to appear as though the shift in the economic balance of power between consumers and producers was in fact manageable without a world economic crisis. But the Middle East had dramatically demonstrated its capacity for undermining the international economic order, and the future standing of many of the oil producers had been revolutionised. Those Gulf states whose revenues outran their own development and military budgets, most notably Saudi Arabia, had suddenly acquired important international leverage.[5] They enjoyed the means to influence political and economic developments both in and outside the Middle East – in the Third World, through the provision of aid,[6] in major international economic institutions, and also in the industrialised world, whether as a result of economic investment, or through the deployment of the so-called 'money weapon'.[7]

As of the mid 1970s, however, the emergence of the Middle East as an independent actor in the international system had largely been confined to economic affairs and much of the producers' oil wealth was in the process of being invested in development projects. While substantial military expansion programmes were also under way, few Middle Eastern countries had as yet emerged as military powers of anything more than regional significance.[8] And in contrast to the economic importance of the region, its strategic significance had probably suffered some decline since the end of the Second World War. In 1947 the British Chiefs of Staff argued that in the event of a major war the Middle East would be a strategic theatre 'second only in importance, or perhaps equal in importance, to the United Kingdom'.[9] But the British were still envisaging a conventional war, and the importance of the Middle East in the nuclear era was more uncertain. The rapid pace of the arms race soon rendered obsolete the generation of Anglo-American bombers and American missiles which had made use of Middle Eastern bases in the 1950s and the early 1960s. Only a small number of ballistic missile submarines were deployed in the Mediterranean or the Arabian Sea, which after 1964 became a potential, although

in practice a rarely used, deployment area.[10] As a subsidiary element
in the central nuclear balance, the United States operated a number
of important electronic intelligence facilities in the Middle East. These
included a key link in the American early-warning radar system, as well
as a number of listening posts which provided the primary source of
American intelligence data on Soviet missile developments and Soviet
compliance with the 1972 SALT agreement.

Similarly the Middle East played only a secondary role in the East-
West conventional balance, viewed in terms of the defence of NATO
and of the southern borders of the Soviet Union. External military
incursions into the region were of inevitable concern to both Soviet and
Western defence planners, although it is doubtful whether the Soviet
Union ever faced any real conventional threat from the Middle East.
The Baghdad Pact, the culmination of some years of attempts by
Britain and the United States to organise an anti-Soviet military alliance
system in the Middle East, proved stillborn. NATO may have had more
cause for concern with the establishment in the 1960s of the Soviet
squadron in the Mediterranean, and the attempted build-up of a Soviet
base infrastructure along its south-east littoral. This had both political
and military significance. The Soviet presence created a sense of encirclement among some of the southern European members of the
alliance,[11] and brought into question the capability of the Sixth Fleet
to reinforce these countries in time of war. It threatened to erode the
credibility of the NATO guarantee to Greece, Turkey and to some
extent Italy, and hence to weaken the whole alliance. Even under normal
peacetime conditions the Turkish, Greek and Italian air forces were
considered to be outmatched by Soviet aircraft deployed in Egypt and
attached to Warsaw Pact units in Bulgaria.[12] In war or crisis it was
assumed that additional Soviet aircraft could be rapidly deployed to
airfields in Egypt and North Africa, thereby offsetting the advantage
enjoyed by the Sixth Fleet over the Soviet Mediterranean squadron of
an integral air component, and necessitating the dilution of NATO's
limited air cover through the diversion of aircraft from the northern
and central to the southern flank.[13] But the threat was acknowledged
to be potential rather than immediate, and it receded with the expulsion
of Soviet forces from Egypt in 1972.

Of more immediate significance were the lines of military communications to Africa, Asia and the Indian Ocean. The Middle East had
been a vital communications route for the British Empire, and remained
so in British military thinking so long as there was a presence 'east of
Suez'. But for the Americans the Middle East was a deadend rather than

a highway. The sea route from Pearl Harbour to the Persian Gulf is only 1,100 miles longer than that from the east coast of America via the Suez Canal, and even when in the early 1970s the United States navy began to show greater interest in the Indian Ocean, it did not envisage reinforcement from the Mediterranean.[14] With the British withdrawal from 'east of Suez' and the development of the Soviet long-range interventionary capability in the late 1960s, the strategic lines of communication through the Middle East shifted from an east-west to a north-south axis. Much Western attention centred on the Suez Canal, the reopening of which in 1975 cut twenty-four days off the sailing time between the Black Sea and the Arabian Sea, and reduced the sailing time between Odessa and Bombay from forty-one days via the Cape to sixteen.[15] The Suez Canal was the preferred route for the reinforcement of the Soviet Pacific fleet[16] and it also provided the Soviet Union with an alternative communications route to Far Eastern Russia, the only land routes being vulnerable to possible Chinese interference.[17] As of the mid 1970s however there was evidence to suggest that the Black Sea fleet might not be large enough to service the Indian Ocean,[18] and Soviet defence planning would always have to take into account the ease with which the canal could be blocked in emergency. Of more immediate note has been the use made since the early 1960s of Middle Eastern air staging posts and stockpiles in support of Africa[19] and the Indian Ocean area. Military facilities in Egypt were used during Soviet airlifts to the Yemen – 1968[20], the Sudan – 1971[21] and India during the Indo-Pakistani war of 1971.[22]

At a rather more technical level, the Middle East has come to exert a significant impact on the development of conventional weapons systems and military thinking. This was a result of the size of orders for military equipment being placed by Middle Eastern countries, and the increasing sophistication of the weaponry being deployed on the Middle Eastern battlefield. Already in the 1950s the French took advantage of the Arab-Israeli conflict to test their equipment under combat conditions against Soviet weaponry and to reduce the unit price of their own armaments; Israeli orders cut approximately one-third off the price of some French aircraft.[23] The Americans followed suit a decade later, some weapons being specifically developed for Israeli use on the condition that the US would be provided with detailed information about their combat performance.[24] Western countries also gained valuable information as a result of Israeli capture of much advanced Soviet weaponry. In 1973 the Yom Kippur War provided a remarkable demonstration of the performance of the whole range of new military technology which had been brought into service over the past decade, and its 'lessons' were the subject of wide international debate in both East and West.[25] Some of the results of this debate were being reflected in NATO tactics and force structure less than two years later.[26]

The broader political significance of the escalation of the Arab-Israeli conflict after the mid 1960s lay in the emergence of the region as the primary theatre of superpower rivalry. Both superpowers began to give their Middle Eastern clients priority in the matter of weapons delivery at the expense of their European allies[27] and to pay serious attention to the possibility that the Middle East might draw them into a nuclear confrontation. Indeed the 1972 Brezhnev-Nixon 'Statement of Principles'[28] laying down procedures to try to avert the development of crisis situations, was reportedly drafted with the Middle East specifically in mind.[29] The Middle East could thus be viewed as one of the major testing grounds for detente, and the Soviet failure before the Yom Kippur War to abide by the principles laid down the year previously, raised serious questions about the concept in the United States. It underscored the basic Soviet dilemma of having to weigh up the political risks of failing militarily to support existing clients as well as 'progressive' movements generally, against the broader risk of undermining the modus vivendi which Moscow needed to work out with Washington in order to minimise the danger of nuclear war.

At stake in every round of the Arab-Israeli conflict were the credibility of commitments — the willingness and the ability of Washington and Moscow to support their clients. These were essential psychological components of the East-West balance of power, and were closely monitored in the two superpower capitals for indications about the adversary's mood, determination and future intentions, and for the implications about these which might be drawn by others. The latter was a point of particular sensitivity, and one which lent itself to over-reaction. During the Yom Kippur War, the actions of most European governments suggested that they did not accept the view of a British journal which argued that the war had become much more than a local Middle Eastern issue when its outcome seemed to depend on which side's protector would ensure that it had the military means to stay in the field, and went on to draw a parallel between Israeli and European dependence for survival on the United States.[30] But the view of *The Economist* certainly coincided with that of Washington, and Dr Kissinger subsequently stated in an interview with the Egyptian newspaper *Al Ahram*, that for reasons 'directly related to the balance of power between the two superpowers' the United States 'cannot . . . .

allow Soviet arms to achieve a great victory – although it may not be a decisive victory – over American arms'.[31] Similarly the continual defeat of Soviet-equipped forces by American-equipped forces between 1967 and 1970 reflected badly on Soviet training, and suggested that in certain key branches of military technology the Soviet Union lagged behind the United States.[32] Such evaluations had serious implications for the central European theatre,[33] and raised doubt in the Third World on the desirability of seeking Soviet in preference to American military resources. Superpower prestige, in the sense of the image of power, was thus heavily involved in the Arab-Israeli conflict, and the Middle East proved a useful barometer of the fortunes of superpower rivalry.

There are therefore few countries whose interests are not to some degree involved in the Middle East. The economic and ultimately also the political structure of the international system is heavily dependent on the continuous availability of Middle Eastern oil supplies, and to a lesser degree on the price at which that oil is available. The overall balance of power between East and West is bound up with the level of conflict between, and international alignments of, a number of key Middle Eastern states. Nevertheless the level of external dependence is far from uniform. All oil importing countries are directly affected by changes in price levels, changes which the Middle Eastern members of OPEC have played a crucial role in promoting. Not all industrialised and industrialising states however are critically dependent on Middle East oil. In addition there is no uniformity in the ability of economies to adjust to price changes or disruptions in supply, nor in the impact of such disruptions on political systems. Some can be assumed to be able to stand a higher level of unemployment and greater depth of recession than others, though the level of disruption experienced in the wake of the Yom Kippur War was insufficient to put these assumptions to the test.

In discussing the Middle Eastern interests of individual states or groups of states, it is therefore useful to make a number of distinctions. The distinction between direct interests, i.e. day-to-day dependence on Middle East oil supplies, and indirect interests, i.e. the vulnerability in a period of high economic and military interdependence, to loss or damage as a result of links with other states having direct interests in the Middle East, has already been implied. Few countries, for instance, could have hoped to have escaped the repercussions of the international banking crisis feared by some in 1974 as a result of the problems caused by the need to recycle petrodollars. Secondly, some interests are obviously more important than others. There is a distinction between those interests often described as vital, and those which are not. Vital interests are those essential to the fulfilment of the functions basic to the raison d'etre of the state – security, the maintenance of law and order, the survival of a particular social or political system. Non-vital interests, which one may call 'wants', include the augmentation of a state's assets or international position for reasons of expanding wealth or the pursuit of status, or the pursuit of the benefits of minority groups. In addition, there are derivatory interests, primarily prestige or reputation, which are a function of prior commitments or involvements in the region.

Countries with vital interests in the Middle East are not confined to the obvious group of Western Europe and Japan. Many of the developing countries of the Third World are particularly sensitive to the level of oil prices, and it has been estimated that countries in Africa, Asia, Latin America and the poorest countries in southern Europe were in 1975 paying around $10 billion per year more for their oil imports than they had been before the 1973 price rise, a figure which represented around 1.7 per cent of their combined GNPs.[34] In addition a number of Third World and southern European countries have both direct and indirect security interests in the region. The Arab-Israeli conflict has exerted a military influence on some states in Africa, beginning already in the 1960s when Israel began to cultivate close relations with Ethiopia and Israeli intelligence was reported to have started operations in a number of newly independent black African states.[35] In 1976 a minor but highly dramatised incident demonstrated that Entebbe was within the reach of Middle Eastern airpower. Middle Eastern countries have also been involved in the complex of rivalries in the Horn of Africa, while to the east the military build-up in Iran has exerted an influence on the rivalries of the Indian sub-continent. Many other countries can be said to have an indirect security interest in the Middle East, in that their security and independence are dependent on the overall East-West power balance and, more immediately in some cases, on the freedom with which the Soviet Union and the United States can, or may wish to, make use of the Middle East for purposes of military transit and forward deployment. Concern on this score has been particularly evident among Mediterranean countries and is reflected in the proposal supported at one time or other by every Mediterranean country except Greece, Turkey and Italy to exclude both the Sixth Fleet and the Soviet squadron. Particular concern has been shown by Yugoslavia. Although Belgrade supported Soviet Middle Eastern policy after the Six Day War, for fear that the downfall of Nasser would impair the effectiveness of its policy of non-alignment,[36] the Yugoslavs, like the Rumanians, and even the Hungarians, have shown concern lest superpower confrontation in the Middle East should cause them to be subjected to greater Soviet pressure. Rumania and Yugoslavia both conducted military readiness exercises during the Yom Kippur War period, apparently because of nervousness regarding Soviet intentions.[37]

What distinguishes the Middle Eastern interests of the industrialised countries like Japan and West Europe from those of Third World countries[38] and also from those of the superpowers, is the high level of their dependence on Middle Eastern oil supplies. Both Western Europe and Japan have vital and direct interests in the Middle East, interests which are in the first place economic, but which also have a significant strategic element. The Japanese case is particularly dramatic. In 1962 oil imports from the Middle East and North Africa constituted 32 per cent of Japan's total energy consumption; in 1972 the figure was 57.4 per cent.[39] Comparative figures for Western Europe were lower, but nevertheless substantial: 27.2 per cent of Western Europe's total energy consumption came from Middle Eastern and North African oil imports in 1962; 47.4 per cent in 1972.[40] The degree of dependence varied within Western Europe, particularly in the mid 1970s with the onset of British and Norwegian oil production. In 1973 however oil represented, in ascending orders of magnitude, the following percentages of primary sources of energy: Britain 52.1 per cent, Netherlands 54.2 per cent, West Germany 58.6 per cent, Belgium-Luxemburg 62.1 per cent, France 72.5 per cent and Italy 78.6 per cent.[41] It was however the two countries at either end of the spectrum with the weakest economies, Britain and Italy, who experienced the greatest balance of payments difficulty as a result of the 1973 price rise, although only in Italy were the political repercussions significant.

American interests in the Middle East on the other hand were until the mid 1970s largely indirect, and hence relatively less important than those of its allies. By virtue of its size and distance from the Middle-East, American strategic interests in the region can be considered smaller than those of Greece, Italy or even West Germany. Being for many years the world's largest oil producer, the United States was only marginally dependent on Middle Eastern oil imports. These constituted 1.5 per cent of total American energy consumption in 1962, and only 2 per cent a decade later.[42] But by the mid 1970s the situation was beginning to look rather different. By 1976 the United States had become the world's largest oil importer, and the percentage of its oil imports coming from the Arab world had increased from 7 per cent in

1973 to 34 per cent in 1975.[43] In January of that year it was officially estimated that in the event of imported oil supplies being totally cut off, American oil production would be inadequate to provide for even a wartime economy, a development whose effect on national security was described as 'immediate', 'direct' and 'adverse'.[44] Already the Yom Kippur War had affected the American services, like those of its allies, with pilots for some time afterwards being restricted to short flight training and the number of steaming days of frontline warships drastically reduced.[45]

Yet well before the 1970s the United States had defined its Middle Eastern interests in primarily politico-strategic and indirect terms. Washington quickly recognised that with the emergence of the Soviet Union as its primary adversary in the wake of the Second World War, the global balance of power was partially dependent on the regional balance within the Middle East. The region was important to the United States because it was important to the members of the alliance system of which it became the leader. In consequence the United States accepted an active military involvement in the region, thereby of course establishing an additional and important derivatory element to its interests, since the reputation of its power was henceforth at stake in regional conflicts.

In contrast to the United States, the Soviet Union is geographically close to the Middle East. It shares a common border with Turkey and Iran, and is near to the Mediterranean. Yet other than security, the Soviet Union has no vital interests in the region. Southern Russia, including the highly industrialised Donets basin, is potentially vulnerable to attacks from the Middle East and from naval forces operating in the eastern Mediterranean and the Black Sea. For reasons of geography and history the Russians have long been acutely sensitive over all matters of security, and the consequent instinctive concern about the vulnerability of southern Russia may have been reinforced by experience of threats to this section of the Soviet periphery during the Civil War, the Second World War and the earlier stages of the Cold War. The latter point is evident from the exertion of Soviet pressure on Iran during the 1950s and the early 1960s in an attempt to prevent too close an Iranian alignment with the United States,[46] and also in Khruschchev's complaint during the Cuban missile crisis over the American military presence in Turkey.[47] The Middle East must remain an area of concern to Soviet defence planners in the 1970s simply because it is close to the Soviet Union, because some Western forces continue to operate there, and because it is unstable and highly armed.

But the threat from the south has receded with the withdrawal of
British nuclear V-bombers from Cyprus and American Jupiter IRBMs
from Turkey, and except in so far that the Middle East is the possible
catalyst for a superpower conflict, the threat from the south is secondary to the threat from the west and from China in the east.

The Soviet Union wants, but does not need, limited quantities of
Middle East oil. Imports from the region began in 1967, and oil agreements were concluded with a number of countries, the most important
of which was Iraq, where the Soviet Union is involved in the exploitation of the northern Rumalia field. In the mid 1970s Iraqi exports to
the Soviet Union totalled some 2 million tons per year, and were
scheduled to increase.[48] But this figure must be compared with an
annual Soviet oil production rate of well over 500 million tons,[49] and
the fact that by 1975 the Soviet Union had become the world's largest
oil producer. The import of Middle East oil is clearly a matter of
advantage rather than necessity, largely because, at a period of expanding Soviet oil consumption, the Soviet Union still wishes to continue
to export oil to Eastern and Western Europe.[50] Reserves in Siberia are
substantial, but they are either very expensive or very difficult to
exploit with existing extraction technology.

Perhaps the main Soviet interest in the Middle East is therefore a
'want'. It derives from the growing Soviet aspiration to seek political
parity with the United States and to establish a world role. This has
resulted in an increasing Soviet politico-military involvement in the
Third World of which the Middle East is an important part. Hence the
Soviet Union has an interest in supporting 'progressive' regimes in the
region, in particular those such as Nasser's Egypt, which played a
major role in the non-aligned movement, as well as in the establishment
of permanent military facilities and transit rights for operations further
afield from the Soviet Union. These developments would also allow the
Soviet Union to weaken the United States and to achieve a favourable
shift in the 'correlation of forces' in a region regarded as constituting
an important factor in the struggle against 'imperialism'.[51] The pursuit
of these objectives however involved an inevitable commitment of
prestige, and in particular the prestige of arms, which in turn created
a new derivatory Soviet interest in the region. Already by the time
of the Six Day War the Soviet Union had an important interest in
maintaining the viability of its substantial investments in the Middle
East, an interest it did not have some fifteen years earlier.

The importance of the Middle East therefore varies very much
according to which of the major or indeed the minor capitals of the

world it is viewed from. The perspectives from Moscow, Washington and Rome are very different. Moscow has important wants in the Middle East because the Soviet Union is a revisionist Power. Washington has vital interests because it is the leader of a status quo alliance, but the interests are largely indirect ones. Not so Italy's. Italy depends directly and heavily on Middle Eastern oil, its economy experienced great difficulty in coping with the balance of payments deficit caused by the rise in oil prices of the early 1970s, and it was directly threatened by the build-up of Soviet forces in the eastern Mediterranean. Nevertheless it was in Washington and Moscow, not in Rome or any of the other countless capitals where decision-makers were faced by the existence of direct and vital interests in the Middle East, that the critical military decisions were taken.

Notes

1. *The Middle East and North Africa,* 1974-5, p.83, 1973-4, p.75.
2. *The Economist,* 17 January 1976. 51 per cent in 1974.
3. Only 4.8 per cent of published proven reserves were in North Africa. Figures for proven reserves are 52.65 per cent excluding North Africa and Iran. Hanns Maull, *Oil and Influence,* p.37.
4. $45 billion of the 1974 surplus was accounted for by the Arab countries and Iran. In 1975 the surplus was estimated at between $35 and 40 billion, of which some 90 per cent accrued to the eight Middle East members of OPEC and roughly two-thirds to four Arab producers, Saudi Arabia, Kuwait, the United Arab Emirates and Qatar. *Financial Times,* 29 March 1976.
5. By the end of 1975 Saudi monetary reserves were second only to those of West Germany. *International Herald Tribune,* 3 March 1976.
6. In practice however the recipients of Arab economic aid were largely restricted to the Islamic countries.
7. The threat of the money weapon however soon came to be discounted. See Klaus Knorr, 'The limits of economic and military power', *Daedalus,* Fall 1975, p.235.
8. Indications of Soviet concern at the military build-up in Iran began to appear in 1973. *Times,* 7 August 1973, *Guardian,* 13 August 1973 and *Financial Times,* 23 November 1976. Soviet defence planners would also have to take into account the possibility that an Israeli nuclear capability might under certain circumstances be directed against the Soviet Union.
9. *The Foreign Relations of the United States, 1947,* vol. 5, The Near East and Africa, p.566.
10. Ninety per cent of Polaris submarines were normally outside the Mediterranean. According to reports in 1974 the Arabian Sea was being made more frequent use of by American missile submarines. James Cable, *Gunboat Diplomacy,* pp.138,139. United States News and World Report, 24 June 1974.
11. This was particularly relevant to Turkey which had always faced a threat along its eastern land and northern sea borders, and whose confidence in

the United States as a military guarantor had already been damaged by the Cuban missile crisis and American pressure exerted to prevent a Turkish invasion of Cyprus in 1964.

12. *Aviation Week,* 5 June 1972.

13. *Journal of the Royal United Service Institute for Defence Studies,* June 1972, p.6. In January 1971 the Chief of Staff of the Italian air force was quoted as saying that the Soviet military threat was currently limited by lack of adequate air cover, shortage of reconnaissance capability and inadequate logistic support. However the network of Soviet airfields 'makes it possible to deploy air forces powerful enough to encircle Italy from the south and actually outflank the alliance; track nearly all shipping en route to Italy or in transit in the entire Mediterranean; attack — at low altitudes — all targets in southern and central Italy; create and supply a real front in the south through airtroops landing and support actions for amphibious operations, commandos and units for subversive actions'. *Flight,* 14 January 1971.

14. Admiral Zumwalt, 'Proposed expansion of United States military facilities in the Indian Ocean', Hearings, House of Representatives, p.139. The two American aircraft carriers belonging to the Sixth Fleet are too large to go through the Suez Canal.

15. The closure of the Suez Canal in 1967 during the Vietnam war doubled the distance from the Soviet Union to North Vietnam, and the number of Soviet cargo ships reaching Haiphong fell from 47 to around 22-25 per month. Donald Mitchell, 'The Soviet naval challenge', *Orbis,* Spring 1970, p.151.

16. R.D. McLaurin, *The Middle East in Soviet Policy,* p.42.

17. Ibid., p.42.

18. According to the Director of the CIA, Mr William Colby, speaking in early 1975, the opening of the Suez Canal was expected to increase the overall flexibility of Soviet deployment in the Indian Ocean, but not significantly to increase the Soviet presence. It would facilitate the use of logistic support ships in the Indian Ocean and reduce Soviet dependence on littoral states. However the Pacific fleet would continue to be the main source of surface combatants because of the greater priority afforded to Mediterranean operations and the need to maintain a strategic reserve in the Black Sea. Congressional Record, 22 March 1975.

19. During the civil wars of the 1960s Soviet weapons supplied to Egypt were transferred to the Congo and Nigeria.

20. SIPRI, *The Arms Trade with the Third World,* p.568.

21. John Erickson, *Soviet Military Power,* p.80.

22. Not only were Soviet aircraft taking arms to India reported to have refuelled at airports in Upper Egypt, but Soviet-piloted Mig 21s then stationed in Egypt were reported to have been sent to India to replace Indian losses. Arnold Hottinger,'The Great Powers and the Middle East' in William Griffith (ed.) *The World and the Great Power Triangles,* p.138, and *New York Times,* 31 March 1972.

23. Sylvia Crosbie, *A Tacit Alliance: France and Israel from Suez to the Six Day War,* pp.156,216. Later Iran financed the development of one version of the British Rapier SAM missile, and provided a loan to the American Grumman aircraft company building the F14, which the Iranians ordered. *Guardian,* 23 July 1975.

24. Including reconnaissance drones and warheads specially developed for the Shrike air-to-surface missile against Soviet SAM 3s. *Aviation Week,* 18 January 1971. Conversely of course the loss of sophisticated arms to the West via the Middle East concerned the Soviet military and this, according

to an Egyptian account, was one of the reasons why Podgorny's visit to Egypt shortly after the Six Day War went badly. Mohamed Heikal, *The Road to Ramadan*, p.47.

25. The tactical implications of the Yom Kippur War, and in particular the future viability of armoured vehicles on the modern battlefield, were the subject of two major military conferences held in the Soviet Union in November 1974 and January 1975. These were followed by a major debate in Soviet military journals about the implications raised by the effectiveness of anti-tank weapons during the war. It was not however the tank but the infantry combat vehicle which the Soviet army perceived as being most threatened by the antitank weapon. Philip Karber,'The Soviet Anti-tank debate', *Survival*, May-June 1976, pp.105,106.

26. *Spectator*, 13 December 1975. According to this report, the problem causing greatest concern to NATO was the fact that the war had shown that stockpiles of ammunition could be exhausted much more quickly than had previously been supposed. Among other results of the war, one of the United States brigades rotated from the United States to West Germany in 1975 was given an increased number of anti-tank missiles, while the West German Bundeswehr decided to reduce the number of tanks under one commanding officer from 18 to 10 *Financial Times*, 17 June 1975.

27. This was particularly evident in the willingness of both superpowers to draw on European stockpiles during the 1973 War. But in the spring of 1971 the Soviet Union for the first time relegated its commitment to modernise the armed forces of the Warsaw Pact countries below the active defence needs of a non-Communist, non-allied country. Lawrence L. Whetten, *The Canal War*, pp.162, 166. See also chap. 10.

28. 'These principles contained the following mutual constraints on engaging in "local" adventures:
    Prevention of the development of situations capable of causing a dangerous exacerbation of Soviet-American relations.
    Doing the utmost to avoid military confrontations.
    Recognition that efforts to obtain unilateral advantage at the expense of the other, directly or indirectly, are inconsistent with these objectives.
    Special responsibility to do everything in their power so that conflicts or situations will not arise which will serve to increase international tensions.'
    Theodore Draper, 'Appeasement and detente', *Commentary*, February 1976, p.30.

29. George Ball, 'Moscow and the Middle East', *Washington Post*, 18 May 1975.

30. *Economist*, 3 November 1973. For an account of American perceptions, see Elmo R. Zumwalt, 'The lessons for NATO of recent military experience', *Atlantic Community Quarterly*, Winter 1974-5.

31. Cited in Sunday Times Insight Team, 'Insight on the Middle East War', p.238.

32. *New Scientist*, 4 June 1970.

33. N.B. General Herzog's view that the destruction of the SAM 2 system in Egypt in 1969 meant that 'weapons systems on which depended the anti-aircraft defence of the Soviet empire had been found wanting'. *New York Times*, 3 February 1971.

34. *International Herald Tribune*, 18 February 1976. The poorest African countries have seen their essential fuel imports rise from 10 per cent to

between 30 per cent and 40 per cent of export earnings. The cost of Indian oil imports rose from £110 million in 1972-3 to £650 million in 1974-5. *Financial Times*, 30 September 1975.

35. *Guardian* and *Daily Telegraph*, 25 February 1977.
36. 'Besides the sentimental and ideological aspects of his defence of non-alignment, Tito calculated that the greatest long-term threat to Yugoslav interests was the possible return of the Middle East to the Cold War arena. This was similar to what had happened after the 1956 Arab-Israeli conflict and was one of the primary stimulants for the initial Yugoslav participation in non-alignment.' Tito was reported to have advised the Egyptians not to give bases to the Soviet Union. Whetten, op.cit., p.380. Hottinger, op.cit., p.143.
37. *New York Times*, 4 March 1971, suggesting that the main Rumanian and Hungarian concern was the effect of such pressure on domestic politics, particularly of the continued relaxation on central control. For Yugoslav and Rumanian precautions during the Yom Kippur War, see Jon D. Glassman, *Arms for the Arabs*, p.146.
38. The non-oil developing countries account for only around 10 per cent of annual world oil consumption. M.J. Williams, 'The aid programmes of the OPEC countries', *Foreign Affairs*, January 1976, p.311.
39. 'The oil crisis in perspective', *Daedalus*, Fall 1975, p.21. But a large proportion of Japan's oil came from Iran. Thus Arab oil as a percentage of energy supply was 12.8 per cent in 1956, 33.4 per cent in 1967 and 33 per cent in 1973. Maull, op.cit., p.3.
40. *Daedalus*, op.cit., p.21.
41. Ibid., p.95. Denmark is the West European country most heavily dependent on oil as a source of energy.
42. Ibid., p.21.
43. *Economist*, 2 October 1976.
44. Memorandum by Secretary of Treasury William Simon, 14 January 1975. N.B. This analysis excludes other economic interests such as trade and investment which tend to fall outside the category of interests to be protected or promoted by military means. The one exception here would be the postwar British military presence which is largely outside the scope of this study.
45. *Washington Post*, 18 November 1974.
46. While much Soviet propaganda in the late 1950s and the early 1960s concentrated on the question of the establishment of Western bases in Iran, the Soviet Union was probably more concerned with the political proximity of Iran's relations with the West. See Shahram Chubin and Sephar Zabih, *The Foreign Relations of Iran*, chap. 1.
47. 'You are worried about Cuba. You say that it worries you because it lies at a distance of ninety miles across the sea from the shores of the United States. However, Turkey lies next to us. Our sentinels are pacing up and down and watching each other . . . You have stationed devastating rocket weapons, which you call offensive, in Turkey, literally right next to us . . .' Elie Abel, *The Missiles of October*, p.165. 27,000 American troops were at the time stationed in Turkey, as well as Jupiter IRBMs.
48. Jeremy Russell, 'Energy considerations in Comecon policies', *World Today*, February 1976, p.47.
49. *Petroleum Economist*, March 1977, p.86.
50. Exports to Eastern Europe have long been regarded as an instrument of Soviet control and in the mid 1970s Comecon depended on the Soviet

Union for more than 80 per cent of its oil supplies. Nevertheless East
European demand is also rising and in 1969 the East Europeans were told
to make their own arrangements for supplies with producers. Oil exports
to Western Europe provide the largest single source of Soviet hard currency;
according to one Western estimate, more than 30 per cent of Soviet hard
currency earnings came from oil and gas exports. The future level of Soviet
oil dependence in the Middle East will depend largely on the performance
of the Soviet economy. Russell, op.cit., pp.40, 42.

51.   Kohler, Goure and Harvey, *The Soviet Union and the October 1973 Middle East War,* p.22.

2 MILITARY AND NON-MILITARY ACTORS

The list of countries which have pursued some form of military policy in the Middle East falls into four categories. There are the sixteen countries which had, as of 1975, contributed contingents to the three United Nations peacekeeping forces established in connection with the Arab-Israeli dispute.[1] Of these, seven were European,[2] two African,[3] three Latin American,[4] and three Asian.[5] Secondly there are the various Communist countries which have supplied military resources, including training, and in some cases also specialist combat forces such as pilots, to the more radical Arab states.[6] With the exception of China, which for a time made limited military aid available to the Popular Front for the Liberation of the Occupied Arab Gulf, in Oman (PFLOAG), and also Yugoslavia, these countries were probably largely motivated by their relationship with Moscow.[7] Thirdly there were the former imperial European powers, whose military role in the region was on a significantly larger scale than those of the two previous groups, and finally, and by far the most important, the two superpowers.

Thus with the exception of those smaller countries which sought to protect their indirect interests in the region by means of limited contributions to the United Nations peacekeeping forces, military involvement in the Middle East remained essentially the prerogative of the Great Powers and their allies. Of the former European Great Powers, Britain as late as the mid 1970s retained a base on Cyprus, while the 21,000-strong French overseas interventionary force was earmarked for operations in areas outside Europe specifically including the Middle East. The mid 1970s in fact witnessed a revival of French military interest in the region. French naval units were deployed in the Indian Ocean and from 1975 a French carrier group began to operate in the Mediterranean.[8]

Yet compared with two decades or even one decade earlier, these forces were not substantial,[9] and it is striking that the list of major military actors excludes some of the world's richest and most heavily industrialised countries, many of which were geographically close to the Middle East and had vital interests in the region. That is not to say that Western Europe had entirely eschewed its military option in the region. In addition to the former imperial powers, two European NATO countries, Denmark and Norway,[10] as well as three European neutrals,

Austria, Finland and Sweden, had participated in the UN peacekeeping forces. There remained also a recognition of the Western moral commitment to the survival of Israel, the destruction of which, declared the British Foreign Secretary during the Yom Kippur War, 'could not be tolerated'.[11] This view received particularly strong support in the Netherlands, which was one of the few countries willing to participate in an international force to maintain free navigation through the Straits of Tiran just prior to the Six Day War, and during the Yom Kippur War offered the use of airfields for the United States airlift to Israel.[12]

Nevertheless the new economic powers which had emerged in the two decades after the Second World War did not pursue a military policy in the Middle East. In West Germany and Japan attitudes to military power were heavily overshadowed by the disasters of the last fifty years.[13] West German forces had been specifically designed as an integral part of NATO, and under provisions of the treaties signed by West Germany and the Western allies authorising and establishing the Bundeswehr, West German soldiers cannot be stationed outside West Germany.[14] A military policy in the Middle East would be particularly sensitive because of the legacy of Nazi persecution of the Jews on West German-Israeli relations.[15] Similarly the Japanese constitution specifically forbids the deployment of Japanese forces outside Japanese territory, and not even the oil shock of 1973 seemed to shake the pacifist strand deeply ingrained in postwar Japanese thinking. In May 1974 the Japanese Foreign Minister was quoted as saying that it was 'fanciful to pretend that small, crowded and vulnerable Japan . . . could send its military forces overseas to secure sources of raw materials'.[16]

In addition to these historical determinants there was evidence of a remarkable complacency about the security of oil supplies, which is again particularly notable in the case of Japan. Prior to the Yom Kippur War the Japanese had done little to develop their relations with individual Arab countries: they provided little economic aid to the Middle East and their contribution to UNRWA was substantially below that of any other industrialised country. The Japanese assumed that because they had no colonial history in the area, were in no way involved in the Arab-Israeli dispute and did not have a major oil company, they would be immune from any oil supply disruptions. Japanese policymakers not only underestimated the instability of the Middle East, and the consequent danger of supply disruptions, but they overlooked the possibility that Japan's close relationship with the United States would make Japan into a useful target through which political pressure might be transmitted against the economically much less vulnerable, but politically much more important superpower. As a result the Japanese were taken completely by surprise not just by the outbreak of the Yom Kippur War, but also by their classification by OAPEC as an 'unfriendly' state.

The new economic powers were however fortunate in that their interests, in particular the security of their oil supplies, were in large degree shielded by the military policies of Britain and the United States. Britain's contribution to the stability of the Gulf in the 1950s and 1960s provided an additional degree of economic security for all Gulf oil consumers. Similarly the American attempts to limit Soviet military and political influence in the Middle East contributed to the military security of NATO, and in particular to the states of the southern flank. As Macmillan privately noted at the time of the 1957 Syrian crisis:

> Unless Russian influence in the Middle East can be stopped, (sic) Britain and Europe 'have had it' (as they say). Only the Americans can bring the power to bear (a) to stop Arabs, etc. from falling, (b) to risk the consequences – i.e. Russian threats to Turkey, Iraq, etc., (c) to stop this degenerating into global war – by the American air threat to Russia.[17]

Yet this was a view which few other Western countries seemed willing to acknowledge, let alone support. NATO concentrated its attention on the central flank, and its European members had quickly proved politically sensitive about extending the strategically rather arbitrary borders which determine the area covered by the North Atlantic Treaty. American support in 1950 for Greek and Turkish membership of the alliance, support based mainly on strategic grounds, met with opposition from those European members who were either unwilling to extend the area of their security commitments as far as the eastern Mediterranean, or who felt that Greek and especially Turkish membership was incompatible with the concept of NATO as a North Atlantic community, with common cultural, religious, social and economic values. For partially similar reasons attempts by Israel to join the alliance in 1957 were totally unsuccessful.[18] Fourteen years later, as a result of Pentagon concern that the movement of Soviet Tu 16 bombers to Egypt constituted a long-range threat to the southern flank of NATO, and that the Soviet presence might be increased in this area in the wake of any United States withdrawals from Europe negotiated under MBFR, the Americans argued for the establishment of a permanent NATO fleet in the Mediterranean.[19] Again they met with European opposition.

In retrospect the arguments advanced against Greek and Turkish membership of NATO have been shown to have had some validity. Greece and Turkey are the only two NATO countries to have come to the brink of war with each other, and Turkey's exposed position as a flank country, as well as its connections with the Moslem world, have on occasions made it a rather difficult member of the alliance. But the problems generated by contrasting American eagerness and European reluctance to secure the defence of the eastern flank of NATO, have been nowhere near as bitter as the quarrels caused by differing European and American policy in the Middle East. The reasons for Anglo-American conflict over Suez are complex, although the very different relative dependence of the United States and Britain on Middle East oil was certainly one factor. But whereas in 1956 it was the United States which feared the consequences of the use of force by Britain and France in the Middle East, by 1970 the situation had reversed itself. The Six Day War passed without serious incident in transatlantic relations. The war was short, and there was no need for the Americans to provide arms to the Israelis. In the summer of 1970 however it became clear that any form of American military response to the growing Soviet presence in Egypt, even the sale of the large numbers of aircraft requested by the Israelis, would meet with opposition in Western Europe, notably from France and Italy.[20] The American Secretary of Defence, Mr Laird, was quoted in June 1970 as criticising the European allies for their lack of support over the Middle East situation.[21] And when in September the Americans sought to mount minatory deployments in support of Jordan, several European countries adopted a restrictive policy towards American overflights and the use of bases on their territory.[22]

This problem became much more serious during the Yom Kippur War, when the Europeans were, for the first time, actually faced with the threat of an oil embargo. Most alarming from the American point of view was an incident after the end of the war. The Americans had been indiscreet in allowing Israeli ships publicly to load American supplies at a German port, and the German Foreign Ministry issued a statement declaring West German neutrality in the Arab-Israeli conflict, and demanding that the Americans should stop sending military equipment from West Germany to Israel.[23] West Germany provided the main American base complex in Europe, hence, in part, the sharpness of the American response. The Secretary of Defence, Dr Schlesinger, declared that the United States maintained forces in Germany 'because it provides us with enhanced readiness. The reactions of the Foreign Ministry of Germany raised some questions about whether they view readiness in the same way that we view readiness and consequently we will have to reflect on that matter'.[24]

The ensuing crisis was bitter. It was exacerbated by the strain already placed earlier in 1973 on transatlantic relations by disagreements over Dr Kissinger's 'Year of Europe' initiative, by the strains on American foreign policymakers caused by Watergate, and by the fact that in 1973, as in 1956, the Americans had a Secretary of State who found inter-allied consultations difficult, if not irksome. Nevertheless the issues raised by the crisis were very real ones, and they illustrate many of the factors underlying the long-term tensions in European-American relations over the Middle East.[25] The problem was less a conflict of interests between the United States and its European allies than the difference in priorities afforded to those interests. Security and oil were at stake for both Western Europe and the United States. But Western Europe gave a much higher priority to the security of its Middle Eastern oil supplies, which it perceived as directly threatened, than to its military security which was perceived as only indirectly threatened. This in spite of the fact that the war involved two countries neighbouring NATO territory — Turkey, it is not always remembered in discussions of NATO strategy, borders Syria and Iraq — and that Soviet divisions in eastern Europe were put on alert.[26] The United States on the other hand placed strategic considerations well above the security of oil supplies and once Soviet arms supplies began to reach significant proportions, Washington saw the conflict primarily in terms of the balance of power between the superpowers.[27] The survival of an American client was in jeopardy at the hands of a Soviet client. There was the threat of renewed Soviet penetration of the Middle East.

The United States, in other words, to use the implied distinction made by Dr Kissinger in his 'Year of Europe' speech, saw the conflict from the perspective of a superpower, not of a regional power. And to a superpower the scope of the possible was much greater than for regional powers. This is both a matter of resources and a state of mind. Thus the American Secretary of the Treasury, Mr Simon, on the sub-sequent issue of oil prices, said, 'We don't just sit here and quake in our boots, we're a great nation, we're a powerful nation.' Less flamboyantly, this attitude underlay the American attempt to get a peace settlement in the Middle East and the United States deterrent role against Soviet military intervention in the region, roles beyond European capabilities.

But whatever the underlying causes of the conflict, the point was that the United States needed European support, and this support had, at least in part, been denied. For the American armslift to Israel, far from helping to secure Western Europe's immediate interests, was actually putting these interests at greater risk. There was a blunt contradiction between the requirements of Western European strategic security, which necessitated support for the United States over the long term, and those of Western European economic security, which meant that Western Europe must distance itself from the United States in the short term. This contradiction was understood, if not necessarily appreciated, in the United States, which subsequently took steps to minimise its dependence on Western European bases in the event of another war. A couple of years later few obvious traces of the crisis remained,[28] although the problem of how to react in a similar situation was known to have caused deep divisions in the West German cabinet.[29]

It is therefore ironical to recall that American military involvement in the Middle East was primarily a response to the withdrawal of European, largely British, power from the region, and that the Americans recognised the essentially indirect nature of their interests there, conceiving them in broadly Western, rather than specifically continental American terms. If the Europeans were unwilling to see the Americans as their de facto military proxies in the Middle East, this is nevertheless how the Americans effectively saw themselves. The basic objective of American policy was the containment of Soviet military power and influence, the Middle East being but one more regional theatre of the Cold War or arena for superpower rivalry. American Middle East policy was defined by a series of Cold War doctrines. The Truman Doctrine of 1947 was promulgated in response to events in the eastern Mediterranean, although it was of much more than purely regional significance. In 1957, as a result of what Washington perceived as a power vacuum in the Middle East, created in the wake of the abortive Anglo-French Suez operation, Congress passed the Joint Resolution to Promote Peace and Stability in the Middle East – known as the Eisenhower Doctrine – authorising the President to undertake 'in the general area of the Middle East, military assistance programmes with any nation or group of nations desiring such assistance'. Furthermore the resolution declared that

the United States regards as vital to the national interest and world peace the preservation of the independence and integrity of the nations of the Middle East. To this end, if the President determines the necessity thereof, the United States is determined to use armed force to assist any such nation or group of nations requesting assistance against armed aggression from any country controlled by international Communism.[30]

Twelve years later the Nixon Doctrine marked a more cautious approach to the role of force in American policy. The United States, declared President Nixon,

> will keep all its treaty commitments. We shall provide a shield if a nuclear power threatens . . . In cases involving other types of aggression we shall furnish military and economic assistance when requested and as appropriate. But we shall look to the nation directly threatened to assume the primary responsibility of provid-ing the manpower for its defence.

United States policy in the Middle East had a second, and originally totally separate, objective. American support for Israel, which predated the foundation of the Jewish state in 1948, had its roots in domestic American politics. Americans, and not only the 'Jewish lobby', wanted Israel to survive and prosper, even though the survival of Israel was *per se* of limited advantage to the United States. Israel was after all a small state which was an irritant rather than a force for stability in Middle Eastern politics. But it quickly became an extremely strong state, the only Middle Eastern state with a democratic and stable government, and a formidable military power. These military qualifications facilitated Israeli co-operation with the French in the 1950s and with the United States after the mid 1960s. The Pentagon regarded the Israeli air force as a 'unique cost effective deterrent'[31] against Soviet moves in the Mediterranean, and Israel came to be variously described as a military 'bulwark' against Soviet expansion and an anti-Communist 'bastion' in the Middle East. And indeed Israel did play an important role in the system of checks and balances operating in the region, at various times tacitly defending Syria, Jordan and Lebanon against Egyptian territor-ial ambitions and supporting Jordan against Iraq and Syria. It was also a factor in the Saudi-Egyptian conflict of the early and mid 1960s, forcing Egypt to maintain troops on its own territory, thus limiting their use in support of revolutionary purposes in the Arabian Peninsula.[32] In addition the de facto American commitment to Israel created derivatory interest in that the credibility of American commitments came to be involved.[33]

Truman's policy of support for the creation of Israel had been opposed in 1948 by the Departments of State, the Navy and Defence, and by the Joint Chiefs of Staff, who at a time of rapid depletion of

American oil reserves feared the impact of American policy on future oil supplies, and believed that the Arabs might consequently turn to the Soviet Union.[34] These fears proved prescient. The Arabs did indeed begin to turn to the Soviet Union seven years later, and the Israeli connection was largely responsible for providing them with military access to the area. Yet the basic contradiction between two American objectives of containing Soviet influence and supporting Israel only became acute in the late 1960s, when they were disguised by Israel's emerging role as an American proxy in the Middle East. For after 1967 the Americans became the virtual prisoners of their client's victory, just as the Russians became the effective prisoners of their clients' defeat. American support for an Israel unwilling to surrender the territorial security it had so unexpectedly gained after years of in-security, pushed the Arab confrontation states into a seemingly ever-deepening dependence on the Soviet Union. The Americans thus faced the prospect of a polarisation of the Arab-Israel conflict, in which the Russians championed the Arabs, while the Americans grad-ually became isolated in their support of Israel, losing in the long run even the friendship of such conservative regimes as Jordan and Saudi Arabia. Such a development would have increased Soviet penetration of the region, removed the possibility of America capitalising on its influence with both Arabs and Israelis in order to achieve a settlement, and it would have meant, in Dr Kissinger's words, that every Middle East conflict would have 'the insoluble quality of a superpower confrontation'.[35]

Hence from 1969 onwards there were repeated, but unsuccessful, American attempts to bring about some form of settlement of the Arab-Israeli conflict. The Nixon Administration reaffirmed the traditional American policy of 'even-handedness' in the Arab-Israeli dispute, making it also clear that while it would guarantee the security of Israel, it would not underwrite Israel's territorial conquests.[36] Prior to the 1973 war, the Administration formulated four separate initiatives – the proposed package settlement between Israel and Egypt and Jordan of October 1969; the ceasefire agreement along the Suez Canal of August 1970; the partial accord to reopen the Suez Canal of March and April 1971; and proposals for proximity talks, accepted only by Israel, in February 1972. But the underlying political conditions for achieving a political settlement remained unfavourable until the Yom Kippur War, by which time the urgency of a political solution had been underscored by a growing realisation in Washington that American support for Israel, and projected American requirements for heavily increased

Middle Eastern oil imports, were in the long term incompatible. Indeed in July 1973 the American Assistant Secretary of State, Mr Sisco, stated on Israeli television that while American and Israeli interests ran parallel on most issues, there were exceptions, and he specifically instanced oil as one of these.[37] Some indications of the problems of reconciling American newfound direct Middle Eastern oil interests with the existing framework of American Middle East policy were reflected in the remarkable juxtaposition of American threats to invade Saudi Arabia in January 1975, followed six weeks later by the announcement that United States civilians were to train the Saudi National Guard to defend Saudi oil installations. But whatever the problems of reconciling American policy objectives in the Middle East, the fact remains that they have all involved some American defence of the status quo, a defence which relied heavily on the availability of American military power and influence, even though the Americans were careful to avoid formal commitments in the region.

The framework of American policy is much easier to outline than that of Soviet military policy. There are obvious shortages of factual information, and the high level of opportunism characterising Soviet policy makes it extremely difficult to determine any clear priority of objectives. In the 1940s the Soviet Union attempted to exploit the fluid conditions created by the Second World War in order to extend its influence vis-à-vis the countries lying on its southern periphery. Thus the much-quoted episode of the Molotov-Ribbentrop talks of 1940[38], Soviet demands in 1945 for a base on the Bosphorus and the cession of the Turkish province of Kars and Ardahan, plus an outlet on the Mediterranean. In 1946 the Russians refused to evacuate Iranian Azerbaijan. But, meeting in all these instances with determined Turkish and Iranian opposition, opposition supported by the United States, the Russians backed down. After a significant interval, the Russians managed for the first time to gain limited military access to the Arab world in the mid 1950s. Their actions were determined in large degree by considerations of security, being immediately motivated by the formation in 1955 of the Baghdad Pact which threatened to complete the ring of pro-Western military alliances encircling the Soviet Union, joining NATO in Europe with SEATO in south-east Asia. As a result the Russians were to some degree drawn into the ongoing struggle between conservatism and revolution, a struggle in which they appear however not to have been militarily prepared, or indeed capable, of playing a major role.

Only in the mid 1960s is there evidence of Soviet attempts to consolidate their political role in the Middle East.[39] By then the

Russians were already looking for Middle Eastern facilities for the Mediterranean squadron,[40] and the need for such facilities grew with the expansion of Soviet mobile conventional forces in the late 1960s and early 1970s. The success of this search, a success which proved shortlived, owed much to the Six Day War. But the war, although it came at a time when the Russians were now able to provide substantial military aid and to mount significant minatory deployments in the region, deeply implicated them in support of clients involved in an ongoing conflict in which they were quite manifestly outmatched, and whom the Russians could only imperfectly control. The essential problem for the Soviet Union therefore became the need to consolidate its position in the Middle East. This meant not only the need to regain initiative over events in which its prestige and the security of its military facilities were now involved, but to achieve recognition of the Soviet role as a Middle Eastern power, a power which had to be consulted on major regional issues, most notably an Arab-Israeli settlement. The Russians appeared to recognise that, as American influence in the Middle East could not be removed, some kind of accommodation had to be reached with Washington. The notion of condominium has deep roots in the Soviet view of the world and the international class struggle, and has been advanced by the Russians in relation to the Middle East on a number of occasions since 1948.[41] But whereas the United States appeared willing to negotiate with Moscow over the Middle East in 1969, after the Yom Kippur War the Russians were deliberately excluded from Dr Kissinger's peacemaking efforts.

While the Soviet Union was therefore quite clearly a revisionist power in the Middle East, twenty years of political involvement had deprived it of real freedom of action. In large degree its original postwar involvement in the Middle East was determined by considerations of security. But it was one thing to seek to eliminate British military influence; it was quite another to prevent British military influence from being replaced by the United States and, in an area still highly sensitive to foreign encroachments, to seek to establish military facilities and political positions of its own. The level of Soviet military involvement in the late 1960s and early 1970s therefore came to be determined largely by the need to defend derivatory interests established for other purposes over the last fifteen years. That the Soviet Union had aspirations in the area, few doubted. That it had priority objectives, or that it had any long-term strategy for achieving those objectives, was far more dubious.

Notes

.1.   The two United Nations Emergency Forces in Sinai, UNEF 1, established in
      1956, and UNEF 2, established in 1973, and the United Nations Disengage-
      ment Observer Force on the Golan Heights, established in 1974.
2.   Austria, Denmark, Finland, Norway, Poland, Sweden and Yugoslavia.
3.   Ghana and Senegal.
4.   Brazil, Panama and Peru.
5.   Indonesia, Nepal and India. Both India and Pakistan also provided
      military training, especially pilots, to a number of Middle Eastern states.
6.   These include Cuba, Czechoslovakia, East Germany, North Korea and
      North Vietnam. In addition, Bulgarian warships exercised with the
      Mediterranean squadron, and as of the early 1970s Bulgarian ships were
      the only non-Soviet Warsaw Pact vessels to have visited an Arab port.
      George S. Dragnich, 'The Soviet Union's quest for access to naval
      facilities in Egypt prior to the June War of 1967' in McGwire, Booth and
      McDonnell, *Soviet Naval Policy: Objectives and Constrains*, p.264.
7.   Cuban motives are particularly obscure. Articles in the *International
      Herald Tribune* of 3 February and 2 March 1976 referred to a mixture of
      ideology, opportunism and willingness to further Soviet aims abroad.
      N.B. also the Cuban presence in Africa, in particular their operational role
      in Angola in late 1975.
8.   Continued French interest in the Lebanon was evident from French offers
      to send a peacekeeping force made by President Giscard D'Estaing in the
      spring of 1976.
9.   See the debate in Britain in the mid and late 1960s on the future of the
      British presence 'east of Suez'. A useful summary is to be found in chap. 8
      of Patrick Gordon-Walker's *The Cabinet*.
10.   Another NATO contributor to the UN peacekeeping forces was Canada.
11.   Sir Alec Douglas-Home continued, 'This was a commitment of the whole
      Western world.' Subsequently Britain offered to participate in an inter-
      national peacekeeping force. But British policy during the war, which
      had included an arms embargo on both sides, an embargo which had been
      much more damaging for Israel than for the Arabs, was strongly criticised
      at the time, both in Britain and Israel.
12.   President Nixon in a newspaper interview, cited in *Jewish Chronicle*, 12
      December 1975.
13.   For similar reasons Japan and West Germany also adopted a very
      restrictive line on arms sales to areas of conflict, including the Middle East,
      although West Germany had provided arms to Israel in the early 1960s as
      part of a policy of reparations for Nazi persecutions of the Jews.
14.   *Guardian*, 31 March 1976.
15.   According to one report at the time of President Sadat's visit to West
      Germany in March 1976, West German governmental circles were also very
      reluctant to contemplate what might be seen as a rebirth of the Afrika
      Corps. Ibid.
16.   *International Herald Tribune*, 23 May 1974.
17.   Harold Macmillan, *Riding the Storm*, p.281.
18.   According to Shimon Peres' account of this incident, it was the Norwegian
      attitude which proved decisive in persuading the Israelis not to pursue their
      attempts to join NATO. The arguments against Israeli membership advanced
      by the Norwegian Foreign Minister, Dr Lange, were very similar to the
      grounds on which the Norwegians had opposed Greek and Turkish member-
      ship of the alliance. *David's Sling*, pp. 146, 147.

19. *International Herald Tribune*, 14 January 1972. However in response to the Soviet naval build-up after the Six Day War, NATO did establish an air surveillance unit, Maritime Air Forces Mediterranean. An Allied Naval On-Call Force for the Mediterranean (NAVOCFORMED) was also established. After the Six Day War the American representative to NATO was quoted as saying that 'while the Middle East is generally outside the "NATO area", the whole of the Mediterranean sea is part of the defence area within which the (NATO) Treaty says an attack on one ally is an attack on all'.

20. *Washington Post*, 8 June 1970. These countries were concerned that such sales might endanger their oil supplies. There was particular concern over Libyan reaction, 28 per cent of Italian oil imports coming from Libya.

21. *Washington Post*, 18 June 1970.

22. See chap. 3.

23. N.B. that the West German move came after the imposition of Arab oil sanctions.

24. *Washington Post*, 27 October 1973. It was in reaction to the sentiment underlying this statement, if not the statement itself, that a European source was quoted as saying that the alliance 'is not just an instrument of American foreign policy'. *New York Times*, 13 November 1973.

25. There was however also, in the case of both France and Britain, an element of rivalry in relations with the United States over the Middle East. As late as 1975 it was reported that British sources in Oman felt that the Americans were trying to get them out of the country, while the Americans argued that the British were dragging their feet over the war in Dhofar and the Omanisation of the local armed forces to prolong their own commanding position in the area and to gain trade and other advantages. *Times*, 7 February 1975.

26. See chap. 7.

27. N.B. however, that in the first week of the war both the United States and its Western European allies adopted a policy of maintaining a low profile. The divergence in United States-Alliance relations only began with the Soviet airlift.

28. In December 1975 Dr Kissinger told a meeting of American ambassadors that 'we are now closer to the Atlantic partnership than we envisaged with the Year of Europe in 1973'. *Times*, 8 April 1976.

29. *Washington Post*, 7 January 1975.

30. The Resolution was reaffirmed in 1961. In 1970 the senatorial sponsors of a proposal to cancel or reduce America's worldwide commitments decided not to recommend repeal of the Joint Resolution.

31. Edward Said, 'United States policy and the conflict of powers in the Middle East', *Journal of Palestine Studies*, Spring 1973, p.38.

32. Yair Evron, *The Middle East: Nations, Super Powers and Wars*, p.201. By extension the Israelis argued that their presence alone prevented the oil sheikhdoms being overrun by Egypt and Syria. Sunday Times Insight Team, *The Yom Kippur War*, p.27.

33. Cf. in slightly different form, former Senator Fulbright's view that 'Israel is largely a creation of the conscience of the West, particularly that of the United States; for that reason alone her survival qualifies as an American national interest'. *Washington Post*, 7 July 1975.

34. William Quandt, 'United States policy in the Middle East: constraints and choices', in Hammond and Alexander, *Political Dynamics in the Middle East*, p.497.

35. Press Conference, 18 June 1974.

36. See Stewart Alsop's article, *Newsweek,* 3 August 1970.
37. Robert Freedman, *Soviet Policy towards the Middle East since 1970,* p.116.
38. For an account which places this much-quoted incident in historical perspective, see Hannes Adomeit, 'Soviet policy in the Middle East: problems of analysis', *Soviet Studies,* April 1975, pp.296,297. It was on this occasion that the Soviet Union declared that its aspirations lay 'in the area south of Batum and Baku in the general direction of the Persian Gulf'. Adomeit argues that the Russian declaration was made for tactical reasons in response to German pressure.
39. Freedman, op.cit., pp.19-21.
40. The original establishment of the Mediterranean squadron was probably largely a response to the presence of American strategic weapon systems in the Mediterranean.
41. Coral Bell, 'Middle East: crisis management during detente', *International Affairs,* October 1974, p.535. In 1948 the Soviet Union advocated a joint United States-Soviet force to impose partition in Palestine. During the Suez crisis the Russians again advocated joint United States-Soviet intervention, and in late May 1967 they proposed a bilateral United States-Soviet conference to agree a joint plan to enforce a settlement. According to Brezhnev's account of his visit to the United States in the summer of 1973,'I kept Nixon up almost all night on the Middle East, trying to convince him of the need to act together. Otherwise there would be an explosion.' *International Herald Tribune,* 15 November 1974.

3 THE REQUISITES OF MILITARY POLICY

The requisites for the pursuit of military policy in the Middle East, other than for limited transfers of military resources, are as much political as they are military. They include not only the availability of specialist interventionary forces and the necessary base infrastructure to allow their deployment in the region, but also military access in the Middle East, the consent of those intermediary countries providing support facilities or from whom overflying rights are needed, and a domestic political environment willing to support, or at least accept, a military policy. The experience of both the former European and the superpowers shows that none of these requirements can be taken for granted.

The pursuit of military policy is only in the long term possible, if it is acceptable domestically. A study of the last two decades of the British military presence in the Middle East shows that decision-makers became increasingly sensitive to the reaction of public opinion to any military response to regional crises, and that the generally hostile attitude within the Labour Party towards the continuation of a British military presence 'east of Suez' was a significant factor in the final decision to withdraw from the Gulf.[1] While Soviet policymakers do not appear to be subject to similar constraints,[2] in the United States the general mood towards the pursuit of military policy has become more restrictive as a result of Vietnam and the growth of Congressional power over foreign policy. The Legislature has shown itself much more sceptical about the military instrument than has the Executive. It has taken a more relaxed view of superpower rivalry in the Third World and has been more concerned to judge military policy according to the viability of military access rather than by the criteria of an American-Soviet zero-sum game in which prestige is all.

These developments coincided with a growing American military interest in the Middle East as a result of the worsening of tensions following the Six Day War and increasing Soviet penetration of the region. After the mid 1960s therefore, a whole range of issues connected with American military policy in the Middle East became the subject of controversy. The Mansfield Resolution of 1969 which called for substantial reductions of United States forces permanently stationed in Europe specifically alluded to naval units, although the Sixth Fleet came

42

under less intensive scrutiny than did United States ground forces in West Germany. The decision to continue the small United States presence in Bahrain after the British withdrawal from the Gulf, and the extension of American naval facilities on the Indian Ocean island of Diego Garcia, both met with Congressional opposition.[3] So too, in spite of the pro-Israeli lobby, did American support for Israel. American opinion, while overwhelmingly pro-Israeli, has proved highly sensitive to any development in military relations with Israel which might possibly escalate into a larger American military involvement. Hence there was opposition to the grant of $2.2 billion after the Yom Kippur War,[4] and to the stationing of 200 American civilians to man early warning stations in Sinai under the second Egyptian-Israeli Disengagement Agreement. In these and other cases, parallels have been drawn with American involvement in Vietnam, on the grounds that the latter had evolved out of what was originally a low-level military resource transfer relationship.[5]

Indeed the whole question of military resource transfer to the Middle East came under scrutiny following the sudden and massive rise in American arms sales in the early 1970s. Critics argued that Administration policy lacked co-ordination and that by fuelling the several Middle Eastern arms races, the United States was not only contributing to regional instability but risking American involvement in future conflicts as a result of the presence of large-scale American training teams. Legislation was introduced in Congress to control major arms sales,[6] and in 1975 Senator Edward Kennedy suggested a six months' moratorium on American arms sales to the Gulf.[7] Although this proposal was not adopted, Congressional pressure in 1976 led to the scaling down of missile supplies to Saudi Arabia. An additional constraint on arms transfers came from the activities of the ethnic lobbies. The pro-Greek lobby was largely responsible for the suspension of arms shipments to Turkey after the Turkish invasion of Cyprus in the summer of 1974, while the pro-Israeli lobby opposed various arms sales to the Arab countries, including a Hawk SAM system to Jordan in 1975 and the sale of six C130 Hercules transport aircraft to Egypt in 1976, the first American military resource transfer to Egypt for many years.

This opposition did not however amount to a veto, and the Executive in fact eventually got its way in most of the issues already cited. Nevertheless public opinion has constrained military policy. That is evident from the promulgation of the Nixon Doctrine with its emphasis on military resource transfer rather than direct American intervention, and also from a number of specific instances in which the Administration showed itself reluctant to react militarily to Middle Eastern developments. President Johnson's insistence on collective rather than unilateral action to ensure free navigation through the Straits of Tiran in May 1967 and his unwillingness to take any action without the passage of a new Congressional resolution authorising the use of force by the President, even though the Joint Resolution of 1957 was still legally valid, were dictated by the controversy aroused by Vietnam, and deprived the Administration of freedom of action in a fast-moving situation.[8] Three years later similar considerations contributed to the Administration's unwillingness to respond demonstrably to the build-up of the Soviet air-defence presence in Egypt and later to intervene in the Jordanian crisis of September.[9] However domestic constraints did not prevent minatory developments, nor it appears would they have stopped some form of more direct intervention if the situation in Jordan had deteriorated further.[10] The latitude of action allowed to the Administration in Middle Eastern military matters would seem to depend very much on such variables as the immediacy of the crisis, the leadership given by the Executive and the quality of the policies the Executive pursues.

Military access in the Middle East has presented a more serious constraint on superpower policy, being limited in terms of the countries and circumstances in which it was available, and frequently being of uncertain long-term reliability. The United States enjoyed military access via Israel to the Arab-Israeli conflict, via Jordan, Saudi Arabia and on occasion Lebanon to the conflict between nationalism and conservatism, and via the non-Arab Moslem states of Turkey and Iran to the 'Northern Tier' and in the latter case, also to the Gulf. These relationships generated relatively little friction since the circumstances in which the United States sought military access were restricted to ensuring the security of the states and the regimes involved. The weakness of the American military access position however was the uncertain long-term viability of the conservative regimes and the relatively heavy reliance on non-Arab states, notably Iran and Israel.

Soviet military access centred on the Arab-Israeli conflict and on the fringes of the Arabian Peninsula-Gulf region. It was almost exclusively dependent on the revolutionary states – Syria and, until at least the mid 1970s, Egypt, in the case of the Arab-Israeli conflict; Iraq, the Yemen Arab Republic and the People's Democratic Republic of the Yemen (PDRY) in the case of the Arabian Peninsula-Gulf region. But the Soviet Union suffered from the disadvantage that the purposes for which it sought military access were not always acceptable to its clients. They were frequently willing to act as Soviet proxies to undermine Western influence or strategically to offset Western clients, and for such purposes the Soviet Union had ample military access for the transfer of military resources. But military access for minatory or operational deployments was largely confined to conflicts in which the Soviet Union has little or no intrinsic interest. Moreover virtually no Soviet client was willing to afford its patron real influence over its decision-making in either domestic or foreign policy, nor were clients readily willing to provide the Soviet Union with military facilities.

This latter consideration appears to have caused the Soviet Union considerable problems. While Soviet declaratory policy opposed foreign bases, operational requirements determined a rather different policy. The expansion of the Soviet navy initially into the Mediterranean and then into the Indian Ocean created the need for local port facilities,[11] as well as bases or staging posts from which air reconnaissance and ideally also air cover could be provided.[12] The value of the former can be gauged from the fact that Soviet shipdays in the Mediterranean increased nearly threefold once naval facilities had become available in Egypt, and the number of submarines was increased from 2-4 to 6-9 after support ships began to use sheltered berths at Alexandria.[13]

From a relatively very early stage in relations with its Middle Eastern clients, the Soviet Union began to expand and develop existing local military infrastructures. After the 1958 coup the Soviet Union started to improve the Iraqi inland waterways system, as well as the port of Basra.[14] In the Yemen Soviet engineers had developed the port of Hodeida and airfields by the mid 1960s.[15] In the late 1960s Soviet technicians were reported to be supervising the building of docks, stores and maintenance facilities at Latakia and Tartus while Russian specialists worked on the modernisation of Syrian airfields which were subsequently visited by Soviet bombers.[16] A related development appears to have been the encouragement given to the Egyptian navy to develop beyond the size necessary for strictly Egyptian purposes, thus obliging the Egyptians to create the necessary infrastructure of berths and port installations which could subsequently be used by Soviet vessels.[17]

The Soviet Union however experienced considerable difficulty when it came to trying to gain permission to use these facilities, for the revolutionary states remained extremely sensitive about the presence of any foreign military installations on their territory. It took the Soviet Union six years to gain military facilities in Egypt. In December 1961, shortly after the loss of the Soviet naval base in Albania, Admiral Gorchkov paid the first of four visits to Egypt made before the Six Day War. A Soviet request for naval facilities is known to have been made by the end of 1963,[18] but was refused. Only after the Six Day War did the Egyptians finally give way: the Soviet bargaining position had then been greatly strengthened as a result of the Arab defeat and the subsequent Soviet resupply effort, and Nasser was anxious to facilitate the development of a Soviet force to offset the power of the Sixth Fleet.[19] On his visit to Cairo on 21 June 1967 Podgorny demanded a command post and repair shop at Alexandria, to be controlled and guarded by Russians. Although these latter demands infuriated Nasser[20] the Russians were given a large dry dock, two floating docks and a repair yard for their exclusive use in Alexandria. A formal agreement allowing the Soviet Union access to 'facilities on the Mediterranean'[21] was signed in March 1968. The same year Soviet-piloted aircraft with Egyptian markings began to operate from Cairo West. By June 1970, as a result of their assumption of control over the Egyptian air defence system, the Russians had gained exclusive control over a total of six airfields — Inchas, El-Mansura, Jiyanklis, Beni Suef, Cairo West and Aswan, of which the latter two were of particular importance.[22] The following year Egypt was described as being in many respects a Soviet forward base area.[23] The naval presence had also been extended to include use of a modern deep-water port at Mersa Matruh, where the Russians had facilities for stores and shore leave.[24]

These however reflected only a part of Soviet demands. Both before and after Nasser's death the Russians had asked for quarters for naval families to be guarded by Soviet marines at Mersa Matruh and Bernis on the Red Sea.[25] Prior to September 1970 they had also asked for the right for Soviet warships to enter any Egyptian port without prior notice, for permanent staging and overflying rights across Egypt for the Soviet air force and for the right to use Egyptian airfields at only a few hours' notice.[26] It was even reported that in May 1972 the Russians had sought permission to send an airborne division of 7,000 men to Egypt to participate in joint manoeuvres with the Mediterranean squadron.[27] All these requests had been refused, and by 1972 the Egyptians had come to feel both frightened and humiliated by the growing Soviet demands, especially as access to some Soviet facilities was denied to Egyptian officers. General Sadeq was reported to have told Egyptian officers that as long as he was Minister of War 'the Russians will never get one base in Egypt ... If the Russians enter

Matruh and establish a base there, we will never be able to get them out'.[28] Such sentiments were a significant factor in the decision to expel the Soviet presence, and the transfer to Egyptian control of Soviet installations set up since 1967 was one of the specific demands made by Sadat in July 1972.

The Russians thus lost control of the six Egyptian airfields, including Cairo West, which meant the withdrawal of the Tu 16 squadron flying reconnaissance missions against the Sixth Fleet.[29] Soviet bunkering privileges were severely curtailed,[30] but they were allowed to maintain some repair facilities in Alexandria. The Egyptians were not ready for a complete break and they appear to have appreciated that the threat to withdraw this last privilege was a useful means of exerting pressure on their Soviet patron.[31] The 1968 agreement for Soviet 'facilities on the Mediterranean' expired in 1973, and in December 1972 the Egyptians indicated their willingness to renew it, although their demarche was phrased in a manner to suggest that the final decision would be dependent on the quantity and quality of Soviet arms deliveries.[32] These were apparently satisfactory,[33] but the new agreement proved an insecure one.'In April 1974 Sadat told an interviewer that the future of the facilities was under study and that the Egyptians might decide on an arrangement similar to that in Yugoslavia. This would mean giving repair facilities to ships of all nations, on condition that such repairs were carried out by Egyptian workers and experts.[34] In 1975 the Russians stopped using Mersa Matruh and an anchorage off Sollum and in July, apparently in an attempt to bring pressure on the Soviet Union to reschedule Egyptian debts, restrictions were placed on Soviet access to Alexandria.[35] Facilities at Alexandria were finally withdrawn in April 1976, following the abrogation of the Treaty of Friendship and Co-operation.[36]

The Soviet Union therefore only managed to maintain its military facilities in Egypt for eight years and it is very doubtful whether it would even have been as successful as this had it not been for the Arab-Israeli conflict. The only other country to allow access to naval facilities for such a lengthy period was Syria. Like the Egyptians, the Syrians were probably motivated by the need for Soviet arms and by the added sense of protection gained from such a Soviet military presence. But Latakia and Tartus had the disadvantage of being relatively small and the Syrians appear to have denied repeated Soviet requests to gain exclusive facilities similar to those enjoyed in Alexandria, restricting the Mediterranean squadron to refuelling and making small scale repairs.[37]

Those countries less dependent on Soviet military support also

proved less accommodating regarding military facilities. Both Libya
and Algeria were very stinting with regard to the facilities they were
willing to make available.[38] East of Suez the main Soviet facilities were
established in Somalia. Although a squadron of Tu 22 bombers was
stationed in Iraq in 1973 and the Soviet Union was reported to have
the right to use several Iraqi airfields, access to the port of Um Qasr
was apparently restricted.[39] At the mouth of the Red Sea, the PDRY
was reported to have turned down Soviet requests for naval facilities;[40]
as of 1975 the permanent Soviet shore party was limited to a few dozen
men, with all naval visits having to be prearranged.[41] Only support
ships, and on occasion also small warships, refuelled at Aden[42] although
Soviet transport aircraft periodically landed at the ex-RAF base of
Khormakhsar.[43] Some very limited Soviet military activity has been
reported on the island of Socotra but the airstrip there is small and,
while there are Soviet fleet anchorages off the island, as of early 1975
there were no fuel storage or port facilities.[44] Thus more than ten
years after the Soviet vessels first entered Middle Eastern waters, they
had no secure or permanent repair or storage facilities,[45] nor any base
from which air reconnaissance or air cover could be provided. Only in
emergency, and in particular in the case of a Middle Eastern crisis in
which its clients were involved, would facilities for the deployment
of Soviet forces probably be available. As of 1972, sixty-seven such
airfields could reportedly be used in Egypt, Syria and Iraq.[46]

In contrast to the Soviet Union, the American base structure in the
Middle East was largely built up in the first decade of the Cold War,
though it was never anywhere near as extensive as that in Europe or
Asia and, with the exception of Turkey, did not include land forces.
It was moreover significantly reduced after the mid 1960s. According
to one estimate the United States had some sixty support facilities and
airfields in the Arab world at the beginning of that decade, compared
with less than ten in the early 1970s.[47] Certain bases became redundant
as a result of technological changes, including several Strategic Air
Command and IRBM bases. Others succumbed to political pressure. The
large American airfield at Wheelus was lost following the Libyan coup
of 1969, while US forces in Turkey had been reduced from some
23,000 in the early 1960s to around 7,000 in 1972.[48]

The scaling down of the American presence in Turkey was largely
the result of the strains in American-Turkish relations which had developed over the previous decade, including left-wing pressure against the
American base presence, and the problem of Cyprus. In July 1975
Turkey abrogated the joint American-Turkish Defence Agreement of

30 July 1969, in retaliation against the Congressionally-imposed arms embargo on Turkey which followed the Turkish invasion of Cyprus. While NATO facilities remained unaffected and the American Sixth Allied Tactical Airforce, equipped with tactical nuclear weapons, also continued to operate, United States intelligence facilities, the most important of which were Pirinclik, Karamursel, Sinop and Belbasi, stopped operating. The result, according to Dr Schlesinger, was that a 'major portion' of United States intelligence coverage of the Soviet Union was affected, some 30 per cent according to one estimate.[49] Apart from their role in monitoring Soviet strategic weapons developments,[50] Turkish facilities were of importance in monitoring developments in Black Sea shipyards, most notably Nikolayev,[51] as well as military movements and communications in the southern half of the Soviet Union, the Black Sea and the Mediterranean. Thus Turkish facilities played a role both in NATO defence and in support of United States military policy in the Middle East, since from Turkey it was possible to monitor Soviet arms shipments to the Middle East, as well as any possible Soviet military movements connected with the region.[52] Turkish facilities also provided information about Arab communications.[53]

Another facility which came under political pressure in the mid 1970s was the small port of Bahrain. In the wake of the 1973 war the Bahrain government gave notice that it would terminate its basing agreement with the United States. Over the following year however the government experienced a change of heart. It was reluctant to see the departure of its powerful friend, and was probably very willing to listen to Iranian and Saudi advice that the United States should stay.[54] Following the Iranian-Iraqi agreement of March 1975 and the joint Iranian-Iraqi declarations against any external military presence in the Gulf, the Bahrainis again asked the United States to leave, this time by 30 June 1977, a decision the government subsequently showed signs of regretting, but did not rescind.[55]

In emergency, the United States, like the Soviet Union, can probably count on the use of a much larger number of facilities.[56] Even under normal conditions, the United States uses other military facilities on an ad hoc basis. British bases in Cyprus have been used on occasion, in support of the 1958 landings in the Lebanon, for U2 reconnaissance flights following the 1970 and 1973 Egyptian-Israeli ceasefire agreements, and in support of the American operation to clear the Suez Canal.[57] It was reported in 1975 that the United States still had men and equipment at the Israeli base of Hartserim, used by the United States aircraft during the 1973 resupply operation.[58] In the Gulf region the United

States has intelligence gathering facilities in Iran; United States ships have refuelled at the naval base of Bandar Abbas, while United States aircraft have sometimes used the nearby airfield.[59] Dharan was still being used as an important transit base by Military Air Command ten years after United States control over the Saudi base had ceased in 1962. Further signs of United States interest in the expansion of military facilities in the general Gulf area were evident in early 1975, against the background of increasing Soviet naval activity in the region and uncertainty over the future of American bases in Greece, Turkey and the Azores. These centred on Oman and in particular the island of Masirah, strategically situated near the mouth of the Gulf, where the British had built a large airfield. In 1976, the year before the British finally withdrew, American reconnaissance aircraft began using Masirah for refuelling during patrols of oil transit routes,[60] and the Omanis publicly indicated that America would be allowed to use logistic and transit facilities in Oman during peacetime.[61] United States planners were also reported to assume that they would be able to make use of the Iranian base of Chah Bahar if a carrier task force were committed to the Indian Ocean.[62]

The forces supported by these limited American and Soviet base structures were commensurately modest. The superpowers did not have the combined land, sea and air bases maintained by the British in Aden as late as the 1960s. With the exception of the American presence in Turkey, which was largely connected with NATO, and the more temporary Soviet presence in Egypt, the standing forces they assigned to the Middle East were almost exclusively naval, and, in the nature of the flexibility of seapower, the missions of these fleets were only partially Middle East-orientated. They were concentrated in the Mediterranean, where American naval forces had operated since the Second World War. Until the 1960s, the Sixth Fleet was by far the strongest force in the Near East, but the emergence of the Soviet Mediterranean squadron broke the Sixth Fleet's naval monopoly in the region, and the increasing size and sophistication of local air forces meant that the Fleet's air wing became a relatively small air force by local standards, although it continued to enjoy superiority in such qualitative factors as crew-skills, electronic support and ground-control.[63] The fleet was also reduced in size, and regional political problems developed. Arab politicians denouncing 'United States imperialism', as well as the Left in Turkey, regarded the Sixth Fleet as a prime target and this served to reduce its military access, most notably its ability to visit ports in the eastern Mediterranean. For a year after the Six Day War, Sixth Fleet ships were banned from visiting any Arab port, and visits to Turkey were also curtailed.[64] But these restrictions did not prove to be permanent and the improvement in United States-Egyptian relations after the 1973 War was symbolised by United States naval participation in the clearing of the Suez Canal and the presence of the flagship of the Sixth Fleet in the opening ceremony of June 1975. The Sixth Fleet remained a formidable force, grouped around two large attack carriers each carrying between seventy and ninety aircraft. In addition, as of 1976, it had sixteen surface combatants and a reinforced marine battalion, 1,800-strong, aboard an amphibious warfare ship unit of between five and seven ships.[65] Apart from its role as a symbol of United States military power in the eastern Mediterranean, the Sixth Fleet can perform a critical interpositionary and tripwire function to deter Soviet naval intervention in the region, while its airwing gives the United States a local capability to establish onshore air superiority and to conduct air strikes against onshore targets. The amphibious unit would usually constitute the spearhead of any local interventionary force, although it would require substantial external reinforcement.[66]

Soviet naval activity in the Mediterranean dates from the late 1950s, although it was only in 1964 that a special Mediterranean unit was formed as a part of the Black Sea fleet. This development was connected with an upsurge in Soviet-Turkish relations resulting from a resurgence of the Cyprus conflict. Operations were initially seasonal, the squadron withdrawing into the Black Sea in winter. After the Six Day War and the acquisition of naval facilities in Egypt, the Soviet Mediterranean presence became continuous. The build-up was rapid. By 1968 the squadron was some forty-five ships strong, compared with twenty-five at the end of 1966.[67] Average strength during slack periods in the mid 1970s was around fifty to sixty ships.[68] Only between 1968 and 1972, however, were aircraft available in Egypt to provide tracking and positional information on NATO vessels,[69] and the presence of a Tu 16 squadron armed with Kelt standoff missiles, which could be launched against Sixth Fleet vessels from a range of 180 kilometres, necessitated a permanent state of alert just short of war-footing on American carriers.[70] During the same period a small number of Ilyushin 38 and Be 12 aircraft, also based in Egypt, provided the Soviet Union with a modest anti-submarine capability.[71]

This absence of an integral air component not only deprived the squadron of air cover but also meant that the squadron lacked the local onshore interventionary capability enjoyed by the Sixth Fleet, a limitation reinforced by the small size of its amphibious unit. Nevertheless the very existence of a standing naval force increased Soviet influence in the region. In crises the presence of an interpositionary or tripwire force greatly enhanced Soviet capability to deter American intervention and allowed the Soviet Union to lend greater credibility to their minatory diplomacy. Moreover during crises the Mediterranean squadron could expect reinforcement. The concern of the American navy at the local balance of power under these circumstances was already evident at the time of the 1970 Jordan crisis, and again more dramatically, during the Yom Kippur War. The 1977 Defence Posture Statement declared that the ability of the United States navy to operate in the eastern Mediterranean in wartime 'would be, at best, hazardous'.[72]

To the east, in the Red Sea, the Gulf and the Indian Ocean, the permanent naval presence is on a much smaller scale. A largely symbolic United States presence, consisting normally of two destroyers and a flagship, was established in 1949. Known as MIDEASTFOR, the flagship was home-ported in Bahrain in 1966, but the destroyers were rotated from the Atlantic fleet, spending only six weeks of the year actually at Bahrain. After the 1973 war United States naval task forces, including carriers, began regularly to visit the Indian Ocean.[73] The Soviet presence dating back to 1968 was concentrated in the Arabian Sea-Red Sea area. In 1973 a typical Soviet force consisted of five surface ships, one diesel submarine and six auxiliaries.[74] The main support facilities were located not in the Middle East, where they had proved difficult to obtain,[75] but in Somalia on the Horn of Africa, close to the mouth of the Red Sea.

Given the small size of their permanent Middle East military presences, both superpowers have relied heavily for arms and forces from outside the region in order to mount substantial minatory deployments, interventionary operations, and major arms supply operations. This strategy however has been complicated by several factors. While both superpowers have succeeded in drawing on their prestige and their ability to manipulate the nuclear risk factor in order to mount effective minatory deployments, no external power since the early 1950s has possessed the mobile military forces necessary to mount major land operations in the Middle East. In 1956 the British had to ally themselves not only with the French, but also with a local regional power in order to obtain the resources necessary to mount the Suez operation. It was nevertheless a failure, in part at least because the three allies did not have the capability to deploy force sufficiently quickly so as to be able to present the world with a fait accompli. The smaller American operation in the Lebanon two years later was more effective, but even this put strains on the American logistics system.[76] Each subsequent major American minatory deployment, in particular the Six Day War, the 1970 Jordanian crisis and the Yom Kippur War, all of which coincided with the American involvement in south-east Asia, presented American planners with serious problems over the availability of mobile interventionary forces, including ships.[77] The Soviet Union on the other hand simply did not have, prior to the late 1960s, the necessary capability to mount interventionary operations in the region, and even during the Yom Kippur War there were serious questions about the Soviet capability to intervene on the ground.[78]

A further logistic and political complication arises from the distance between the respective Soviet and American home bases from the Middle East. In simple geographical terms the problems have obviously been more serious for the United States than for the Soviet Union. During the 1973 resupply operation American aircraft flew an average distance of 6,450 nautical miles, compared with some 1,700 nautical miles flown by Soviet aircraft.[79] Seaborne supplies sent from the east coast of the United States took thirty days to reach Israel, compared with four days taken by Soviet supplies sent from Black Sea ports to Egypt and Syria. But given the size of the American Military Air Command and the availability by the early 1970s of giant long-range airfreighters such as the C5 Galaxy, these difficulties have not proved critical, although distance does present more serious problems for naval forces. It increases the number of ships required to maintain forces permanently on station in the Middle East area[80] and since its worldwide base structure was not designed for the support of the Middle Eastern operations, the United States has only limited capability to mount speedy large-scale operations especially east of the Suez Canal. An amphibious task force sent from the west coast of the United States to the Gulf would take a month to reach the area[81] and the redeployment of vessels from the east coast of the United States to the Mediterranean may take between ten and fourteen days. The Soviet Mediterranean squadron thus enjoys an important advantage over the Sixth Fleet as a result of the proximity of its reinforcements in the Black Sea.[82]

In theory, and to some extent also in practice, these problems are offset by the availability of American bases and staging posts in Western Europe. Some American equipment stored in West Germany is painted in desert camouflage for use in the Middle East.[83] In the

Mediterranean, the Americans used naval bases in Greece during both the Six Day and Yom Kippur Wars.[84] Further west, bases in Spain were used for tanker aircraft involved in the 1973 airlift,[85] for which the Portuguese base of Lajes in the Azores was of critical importance. But as already indicated, experience in 1970 and 1973 has shown that bases in NATO countries are not necessarily available for unilateral American operations in the Middle East.[86] Official Greek attitudes have been affected by the presence of a large Greek ethnic population in the Arab world. As early as 1957 there were signs of Greek displeasure over the use of Greek bases for American operations in the Middle East and, although naval bases were used in 1973, the Greeks refused to allow the use of air bases, thus upsetting American air force contingency plans which had assumed at least tacit Greek co-operation.[87] Turkey, as an Islamic country, tends to be sympathetic towards the Arab cause in any Arab-Israeli conflict and is in any case uneasy about the long-term credibility of the American guarantee.

Most other West European countries however are concerned about interference with their oil supplies and this consideration has overridden even the closest of relations with Washington. Hence the American-German difficulties at the end of the Yom Kippur War and the fact that Britain discouraged United States requests for the use of United States bases in the United Kingdom as staging posts for the American airlift to Israel and insisted on strict secrecy over a proposal to use British bases for American SR 71 reconnaissance aircraft.[88] The Portuguese on the other hand were willing to accept the use of Lajes because much of their oil came not from the Middle East but from the Portuguese colony of Angola, and because they hoped in return for a more sympathetic American attitude towards their policy in Africa. But following the overthrow of the Caetano government, Angola gained independence and on 8 April 1975 Prime Minister Goncalves announced that in the event of another Middle East war, Portugal would not allow American aircraft bound for Israel to refuel on her territory.[89] An appendix to the American-Spanish Treaty of Friendship and Co-operation of January 1976 however included Spanish acquiescence in American use of air and naval bases 'for flights by aircraft of the land, sea or air forces of the United States . . . in transit through Spain en route to other destinations'. To cope with a repetition of this contingency, the Americans prestocked equipment in Israel, reportedly sufficient to fight a 21-day war at the intensity of warfare in 1973[90] and trained crews to undertake the refuelling of C5 Galaxies in the air, thus allowing the United States to stage transport flights direct from the United States to the Middle East.[91]

The United States has also experienced difficulties in gaining overflight permission across Western Europe during Middle East crises. During the Lebanese crisis of July 1958, Greece refused overflight rights for fighter aircraft being flown from the United States to bases in Turkey,[92] and Greece, Spain, Italy and France were reportedly among the countries which refused the United States overflight rights during the 1973 war. Once again alternative arrangements were available, although they involved penalties. Provisional plans drawn up in September 1970 for the airlift of troops to Jordan from Germany and elsewhere meant long detours over water around central Europe because of anticipated overflight problems.[93] In 1973, the main air supply routes direct from the United States via Lajes had to continue through the Mediterranean parallel to several thousand miles of potentially hostile Arab airspace, the route being monitored by specially deployed ships from the Sixth Fleet, which could also have provided air defence in the event of any interference.[94]

As the Soviet Union exercises a much closer degree of control over the Warsaw Pact than does the United States over NATO, the use of forward bases has been much less of a problem for Soviet defence planners than it has been for their American opposite numbers. Hungary was the principal staging post for flights to Egypt and Syria during the Yom Kippur War. Flights from Kiev staged through Budapest, while part of the large quantities of equipment drawn from the reserves of Soviet forces in eastern Europe, as well as from the reserves of other Warsaw Pact countries, was flown direct from Budapest.[95] It was also reported that a land link was established between Hungary and the Yugoslav port of Rijeka from where heavy supplies were shipped to Egypt, Syria and Algeria, while cargo flown from Turkere, the Soviet airbase in Hungary, was broken down in Titograd or held there for further shipment.[96]

Transit however presents more serious political problems. At least one Communist country, Rumania, might create and indeed may already have created, difficulties in the event of a Soviet request to overfly the country en route to the Middle East.[97] Yugoslavia, however, while frequently at odds with Moscow, has strong pro-Arab sympathies, and has been the main air transit route to the Middle East. The Yugoslav position appears to be that Soviet overflight rights will only be granted if a third party friendly to Yugoslavia requests them, and a Soviet request for automatic overflight rights reportedly made in November 1976 was refused.[98]

All other routes lie across NATO territory. During the Yom Kippur War Soviet overflights were reported across Greece and, more important, Turkey. Here the Soviet Union had the advantage of a number of transit agreements. Article 23 of the Montreux Convention requires Turkey to make available air routes 'in order to assure the passage of civil aircraft between the Mediterranean and the Black Sea'. A Soviet-Turkish air traffic agreement of 1969 lays down certain air corridors across Turkey, which can be used by Soviet civil aircraft at 24 hours' notice. This agreement specifically excludes military aircraft with fixed weapons or reconnaissance devices, although the freight carried of course remains uncontrolled. There is also a Soviet-Turkish highway agreement, which allows Soviet trucks to pass through Turkey en route to Arab countries. These agreements appear to have been both used and abused. Among larger Soviet operations mounted across Turkey were the Soviet exodus from Egypt in July 1972, an airbridge to Syria in November of the same year, and the 1973 resupply operation in which an airbridge beginning at Erivan, and following the Iranian border to Aleppo, was used, mainly for the supply of Syria.[99] But it was believed that the Russians were also sending combat planes, which they had previously notified as civil aircraft.[100] On earlier occasions Soviet Migs en route to Arab air forces had been sent across Turkey, some even staging through Turkish airports, a practice the Turks discouraged but did not always oppose.[101]

More important from the Soviet point of view was Turkish control over the Straits and hence over the only line of communication between the Mediterranean squadron and its Black Sea base. Passage through the Straits is governed by the Montreux Convention, which imposes restrictions on the freedom of Soviet naval movement. No aircraft carrier is allowed to pass through the Straits; ships of more than 15,000 tons must pass singly and can be escorted by only two destroyers, and there are restrictions on the passage of submarines. Turkey is entitled if at war or under the threat of war to deny passage through the Straits to all warships. In the unlikely event of an American-Soviet conflict in which Turkey remained a non-belligerent, she would be obliged to close the Straits to all warships of the belligerent powers, although the Soviet Union would be permitted to withdraw warships from the Mediterranean into the Black Sea.

The Turks have been scrupulous in their application of the convention and the restrictions imposed by a document drawn up to meet the naval and political circumstances of the mid 1930s have not proved excessively onerous.[102] The limitation on the passage of submarines does mean that the Mediterranean squadron has had to draw its sub-marine component from the Arctic and Baltic fleets, rather than from the Black Sea, a requirement which is costly in terms of efficiency. The restriction on the movement of capital ships may also slow down re-deployment in crisis.[103] Most controversial however is the restriction on the passage of aircraft carriers. No protests were made by the Western Powers in 1976 when the first Soviet carrier, the Kiev, transited the Straits, and shortly afterwards an authoritative article in the Soviet navy's monthly magazine *Morskoi Sbormik* claimed that 'passage through the Straits by any ships of states on the Black Sea does not contradict the letter and the spirit of the convention'.[104]

The real question for the Soviet Union then would appear to be what would happen in the event of war, or a major East-West crisis. In war the Straits could be blocked,[105] but in the event of a major East-West crisis the letter of the convention is probably less important than such political factors as the recent state of Soviet-Turkish relations and the credibility of the American guarantee. Turkish willingness to stand up to Soviet pressure would not unnaturally depend heavily on the extent to which Turkey believed she could depend on the United States.

Superpower military policy has thus been hampered by a variety of difficulties: interventionary capabilities have been limited; military access has proved uncertain, and there have been problems over both base and transit rights. In addition the United States faced the complications arising from a domestic political environment which since the time of Vietnam has become critical of the pursuit of military policy in the Middle East, or indeed anywhere else. Nevertheless the basic requisites for military policy were there.

Notes

1. See Peter Mangold, *The Role of Force in British Policy Towards the Middle East, 1957-66,* chap.10.
2. See chap. 10.
3. In the case of Bahrain part of the difficulty arose because the American-Bahrain Agreement was an executive agreement and did not require Congressional approval. It was therefore seen by some members of the Senate Foreign Relations Committee as an example of the Administration undertaking new foreign commitments without gaining the prior advice and consent of the Senate.
4. Sunday Times Insight Team, *The Yom Kippur War,* p.437.
5. In August 1970, when the possibility of American participation in a Middle East peacekeeping force was briefly under public discussion, Senator Mansfield was quoted as saying, 'I'm not keen on United States forces

being stationed anywhere outside the United States. Once we get in, it is awfully hard to get out.' *Washington Post*, 20 August 1970.

6.   Under a 1974 amendment of the Foreign Assistance Act, Congress has twenty days to disallow any arms deal worth more than $25 million by concurrent vote of both Houses.

7.   *Washington Post*, 23 February 1975.

8.   According to Nadav Safran, Johnson was initially inclined to take forceful action in support of past American assurances to Israel. But no sooner had he revealed this in a statement of 23 May 1967, than 'a groundswell of opposition began to build up in Congress and outside of it against unilateral American action. The President promptly taking account of this mood, switched to the idea of collective initiative . . . '. Johnson in fact records that he told the Israeli Foreign Minister, Abba Eban, on 26 May, 'I am fully aware of what three past Presidents have said, but that isn't worth five cents if the people and the Congress do not support the President.' Nadav Safran, *From War to War*, p.297, and Lyndon Baines Johnson, *The Vantage Point*, p.293. See chap. 8.

9.   At the time President Nixon was quoted as saying that the American people 'do not have the heart to get into another war'. *New York Times*, 27 September 1970.

10.   See chap. 6.

11.   'Given the greater mobility of modern navies and their increasing self-sufficiency both in terms of supply and communications, the importance of highly complex bases has decreased. Therefore, it is more appropriate to talk about technical facilities.' Curt Gasteyger, 'Moscow and the Mediterranean', *Foreign Affairs*, July 1968, p. 680.

12.   The first Soviet carrier only left the Black Sea in 1976.

13.   Michael McGwire, *Soviet Naval Developments: Capabilities and Contexts*, pp.354, 494, 518.

14.   *Neue Züricher Zeitung*, 4 February 1968.

15.   The latter were regarded as useful in the development of air connections to East Africa. Mordechai Abir, 'Red Sea politics' in *Conflict in Africa*, p.26.

16.   Areyeh Yodfat, 'The USSR, Jordan and Syria', *Mizan*, March-April 1969, p.84.

17.   Areyeh Yodfat, 'Arms and Influence in Egypt: the record of Soviet military assistance since June 1967', *New Middle East*, July 1969, p.29.

18.   George S. Dragnich, 'The Soviet Union's quest for naval facilities in Egypt prior to the June War of 1967' in McGwire, Booth and McDonnell, *Soviet Naval Policy: Objectives and Constraints*, p.252. Dragnich provides a detailed account of Soviet policy during this period.

19.   Mohamed Heikal, *The Road to Ramadan*, p.47.

20.   Heikal quotes Nasser as saying, 'This is just Imperialism. It means we shall be giving you a base'. Ibid., p.48.

21.   *Washington Post*, 21 July 1972. The Russians also had access to facilities at Port Said.

22.   *Strategic Survey 1970*, p.49.

23.   *Strategic Survey 1971*, p.31.

24.   Heikal, op.cit., p.166.

25.   The Russians reportedly offered to provide the Egyptians with sea-based intelligence as an inducement to agree to these port facilities. Ibid., p.166. Galia Golan, *Yom Kippur and After*, p.283.

26.   Heikal, op.cit., p.166.

27.   *Washington Post*, 20 August 1972.

28.   Cited by Arnold Hottinger, 'The Great Powers and the Middle East' in William Griffith (ed.), *The World and the Great Power Triangles*, p.142.

29. This forced the Russians to use Kotlin class destroyers to trail the Sixth Fleet, a much more expensive method than air reconnaissance. Lawrence Whetten, *The Canal War*, p.397. Mig 25 reconnaissance aircraft operated from Egypt between 1971 and 1972, and again between late 1973 and 1975. Soviet-controlled Mig 25s are also reported to have operated from Syria after the Yom Kippur War. Golan, op.cit., p.213; *Daily Telegraph*, 21 March 1977.

30. Whetten, op.cit., p.396.

31. Yaacov Ro'i, *The USSR and Egypt in the Wake of Sadat's July Decisions*, p.27.

32. Dragnich, op.cit., p.270.

33. See chap. 7.

34. *New York Times*, 22 April 1974.

35. *International Herald Tribune*, 28 July 1975, *Washington Post*, 18 April 1976.

36. Alexandria was reportedly the only Mediterranean port where the Soviet Union could service diesel submarines. According to Admiral Zumwalt the Soviet navy would now be forced to do more refitting and repairing in Black Sea ports and to place greater emphasis on anchored tenders out at sea for ships servicing. This of course assumed that a replacement port could not be found in the Mediterranean. *Daily Telegraph*, 27 March 1976.

37. Such requests are believed to have been made in 1972, following the curtailment of Soviet facilities in Egypt, in 1975 or 1976 and again in 1977. *Observer*, 22 August 1976 and *Neue Züricher Zeitung*, 6 May 1977.

38. *International Herald Tribune*, 26 May 1976. The Algerians have taken a lead in calling for the withdrawal of both American and Soviet fleets from the Mediterranean, although as of January 1976 Soviet aircraft did make use of an airfield near Algiers. *Daily Telegraph*, 30 January 1976.

39. In 1975 there were reports that a new military protocol had been appended to the Soviet-Iraqi Treaty of Friendship and Co-operation of 1972, permitting Soviet forces unlimited facilities in specified Iraqi ports and airfields. These however were to remain under Iraqi military control. *Africa-Asian Affairs*, 15 January 1975, and *Neue Züricher Zeitung*, 17 January and 6 April 1975.

40. J. Bowyer Bell, 'Bab el Mandeb, strategic troublespot', *Orbis*, Winter 1973, p.987.

41. *Washington Post*, 9 July 1975.

42. William Colby, Congressional Record, 22 March 1975.

43. Ibid. During a worldwide naval exercise during the spring of 1975 Soviet aircraft operated from PDRY. *Times*, 10 December 1975.

44. William Colby, op.cit.

45. In early 1977 there were doubts about Soviet facilities in Syria.

46. *Journal of the Royal United Service Institute*, September 1972, p.53.

47. *Journal of Palestine Studies*, Winter 1974, p.121.

48. *SIPRI Yearbook*, 1972, p.269.

49. *Financial Times*, 31 July 1975 and 16 December 1976. Some of the work normally done in Turkey was reportedly transferred to other countries, including Iran. *Guardian*, 20 April 1976.

50. In the 1950s the United States kept track of Soviet ICBM progress from radar stations in Turkey, as well as by the use of U2 reconnaissance aircraft based on Incirlik. U2s were subsequently supplanted by satellites. By the use of monitoring facilities in Turkey the United States obtained a sharper picture and better reception. The main target was the Tyuratam missile base in Soviet Kazakhstan, from where long-range missiles were test-fired

into the Pacific. *Washington Post*, 26 July 1975; *Financial Times*, 31 July 1975; *Guardian*, 20 April 1976.

51. Nikolayev, along with neighbouring Odessa, is one of the two main Russian naval shipyards,where the first two Soviet aircraft carriers were built. Information on these shipyards, and on the Black Sea fleet, was complemented by the United States radar at Sinop. *Financial Times*, 31 July 1975.

52. According to one report, Turkish facilities were of special importance in providing evidence of Soviet military movements during the Yom Kippur War. They were also important, if not essential, in proving to Turkey that Moscow was violating Turkish air space in flying equipment to Syria. *Washington Post*, 25 August 1975.

53. *Financial Times*, 31 July 1975.

54. In May 1975 the Iran government announced its support for the withdrawal in 1977 of American base rights in Bahrain. This decision was at least partly motivated by an attempt to improve Iranian credentials as a rallying point for regional autonomy, which had been damaged by the Shah's close ties with the United States, including his support for the establishment of an American base at Diego Garcia. *Strategic Survey 1975*, p.89.

55. It was subsequently reported that although the United States was to leave Bahrain, US ships would be able to continue to take on supplies. Thus Bahrain would avoid the embarrassment of being accused of harbouring an American base, while the United States would still be able to use essential facilities there. *International Herald Tribune*, 16 May 1977.

56. According to one report the USAF has identified 125 airstrips in the Middle East for possible use in an emergency. *Observer*, 16 December 1973.

57. There are also important intelligence facilities in Cyprus in the Eastern Sovereign Base area, including 'over-the-horizon radar'. *Guardian*, 25 November 1975.

58. *Financial Times*, 20 February 1975.

59. *Washington Post*, 26 January 1974.

60. *International Herald Tribune*, 3 May 1977.

61. *Le Monde*, 19 November 1976, Survey of World Broadcasts, Second Series, ME/5373, 25 November 1976. There had been earlier reports that the United States was also interested in landing rights on the Mossendam peninsula on the Straits of Hormuz. *International Herald Tribune*, 10 March 1975.

62. *Far East Economic Review*, 27 May 1974; *Washington Post*, 28 February 1976. Pakistan had offered to allow the United States naval and air bases on the Arabian Sea. *New York Times*, 22 January 1975.

63. Edward Luttwak, *The Political Uses of Seapower*, p.51.

64. Hammond and Alexander, *Political Dynamics in the Middle East*, pp.81, 82. There were no visits to Turkish ports between 1971 and 1975. *International Herald Tribune*, 15 January 1975.

65. *The Military Balance 1976-7*, p.7.

66. Another function of the Sixth Fleet was the evacuation of American citizens in the Middle East in the event of conflict. Immediately after the Yom Kippur War the commander of the Sixth Fleet was quoted as saying that there were 60,000 American citizens in the Middle East, 45,000 of whom were in Israel, and in many cases might not wish to leave. The Sixth Fleet had the capacity to evacuate 25,000. *New York Times*, 9 November 1973.

67. Harry N. Howard, *Turkey, the Straits and US Policy*, p.270.

68. Michael T. Klare, 'Super power rivalry at sea', *Foreign Policy*, Winter

1975-6, p.161. In 1972 the typical strength of the Soviet squadron was given as 0-2 helicopter carriers, 10-12 major surface combatants and 8-10 submarines. *SIPRI Yearbook*, 1972, p.271.

69. Robert F. Pajak, 'Soviet arms and Egypt', *Survival*, July-August 1975, p.168.
70. *Guardian*, 9 October 1972.
71. 'Soviet involvement in the Middle East and the Western response', Hearings, House of Representatives, Committee on Foreign Affairs, Subcommittees on Europe and the Near East, 1971, p.47.
72. *International Herald Tribune*, 31 January-1 February 1976. However Soviet contingency planning would have to take into account the possibility that other fleets, including those of Italy, Spain, Yugoslavia, Greece and France, might become involved in hostilities connected with the Middle East. R.D. McLaurin, *The Middle East in Soviet Policy*, p.63.
73. In June 1970 Secretary of Defence Laird was quoted as saying that the Seventh Fleet would act to offset the Soviet navy in the Red Sea once sufficient American ships were relieved from duty in Indo-China. *Washington Post*, 18 June 1970.
74. William Colby, Congressional Record, 22 March 1975.
75. It was reported in 1970 that four reconnaissance Tu 16s had been deployed at Aswan in Upper Egypt, from where the aircraft could operate over the Red Sea and the Arabian littoral of the Indian Ocean. *Aviation Week*, 18 May 1970.
76. Dwight Eisenhower, *Waging Peace*, p.290.
77. For an account of the extent of the problems encountered by American planners during the 1970 Jordan operation, see David Schoenbaum, 'Jordan: The Forgotten Crisis', *Foreign Policy*, Spring 1973, pp.171-7.
78. The Soviet Union has seven airborne divisions of some 49,000 men. As of 1970 the Soviet air transport fleet was estimated to have the capability to transport two divisions and supporting elements simultaneously over short to medium ranges. In October 1973 some American military planners believed that it would take at least a week to move one division to the Middle East. *The Military Balance, 1970-1*, and *Washington Post*, 1 November 1973.
79. *Armed Forces Journal*, August 1974.
80. It required six destroyers to maintain two permanently in the Gulf: two in the Gulf, two in Norfolk, Virginia, and two in transit. A.J. Cottrell, *The Indian Ocean: Political and Strategic Future*.
81. SIPRI, *Oil and Security*, p.163. This was before the establishment of naval facilities at Diego Garcia.
82. According to the Commander of the Sixth Fleet, during the September 1970 Jordan crisis, the Soviet Mediterranean squadron had around fifty additional ships and submarines available 'within less than one day steaming time', Admiral Kidd, 'View from the bridge of the Sixth Fleet', United States Naval Institute Proceedings, February 1972, p.27. This estimate however would appear not to take fully into account the limitations imposed on Soviet naval deployment into the Mediterranean by the Montreux Convention discussed below.
83. *Guardian*, 6 January 1975.
84. *International Herald Tribune*, 3-4 August 1974.
85. According to one report the 1970 Spanish-American base agreement had been accompanied by a secret understanding that American bases in Spain would not be used during an Arab-Israeli conflict. In 1973 the Americans used the bases for tanker aircraft without notifying the Spanish authorities. In general the operation of tanker aircraft is less obtrusive, and therefore

easier for the host government to ignore, than that of transports staging through intermediary bases.

86. In September 1970, at the time of the Jordan crisis, Italy had announced that bases on Italian territory could only be used for NATO purposes. After the Yom Kippur War American officials admitted that there was no real commitment on the part of NATO members to allow American aircraft to use bases for the shipment of arms to Israel and defence planners were clearly not surprised by the difficulties they experienced in 1973. Lt. Commander Dur, 'The United States Sixth Fleet: the search for consensus', United States Naval Institute Proceedings, June 1974, p. 22, and *New York Times*, 13 November 1973.

87. The Greek situation is very complicated. On the one hand there is the ethnic Greek community in the Arab world and the Greek government is concerned to gain Arab support over Cyprus. The Cyprus question has also put serious strains on Greek-American relations during both the late 1950s and the early and mid 1970s. On the other hand the Greek Junta was very concerned to obtain American arms and support. According to one report secret arrangements were made in September 1970 for Greece to provide staging areas and base support in the event of American forces being moved into Jordan. *New York Times*, 25 October 1973; *Newsweek*, 10 July 1972.

88. *Guardian*, 5 February 1974.

89. *Strategic Survey 1975*, p.72. Similar statements were made by the Italian Foreign Minister and the Greek Prime Minister. *Times*, 24 January 1975, and *Le Monde*, 26 December 1974.

90. *Strategic Survey 1974*, p.16.

91. According to the USAF Chief of Staff speaking in February 1975, the United States has the capability to deliver more material to Israel nonstop with the use of air-refuelling, than was sent during the Yom Kippur War. This would be 'fairly expensive, a little bit more difficult, but we can do it'. Hearings before the Senate Armed Services Committee, 94th Congress, First Session, Fiscal Year 1976, part 2, p.843.

92. Neville Brown, *Strategic Mobility*, p.74.

93. *International Herald Tribune*, 14 June 1971.

94. *Aviation Week*, 10 December 1973.

95. 'The seeming efficiency with which the concentration of supplies and the airlift were handled suggested that, if the operation had not been specifically organised well in advance, it at least was a contigency which had been well planned for.' Jon D. Glassman, *Arms for the Arabs*, p.145. Cf. however Golan, op.cit., p.87.

96. *Aviation Week*, 19 November 1973. According to Glassman, reports in the same journal that Soviet airborne and air transport units had been deployed in Yugoslavia during the war were false. Ibid., p.229.

97. Ibid., p.146.

98. According to one report Tito flew to Kiev to remonstrate with Brezhnev in November 1973 for misusing Yugoslav overflight rights. *New York Times*, 19 October 1973, *Guardian*, 13 December 1976, and *International Herald Tribune*, 15 December 1976.

99. *Frankfurter Allgemeine Zeitung*, 18 October 1973.

100. Ibid. According to other reports some aircraft were sent across Turkey without prior notification. *Washington Post*, 28 August 1975, and Zeev Schiff, *October Earthquake: Yom Kippur 1973*, p.151.

101. Areyeh Yodfat, 'The USSR and Turkey', *International Problems*, February 1975, p.37.

102. The first twenty-year term of the Convention expired in 1956. No moves

however were made to call a review conference and the convention remains in force under its provision for automatic self-renewal. Barry Buzan, 'The status and future of the Montreux Convention', *Survival,* November-December 1976, p.244.
103. During the Yom Kippur War Soviet naval reinforcements were sent both through Gibraltar and the Dardanelles. The Montreux Convention requires that ships transiting the Straits should give eight days' notice. In practice the Soviet Union has got round this requirement by flooding the Turks with transit applications, some of which may not in the event be used. Captain John Moore, *The Soviet Navy Today,* p.31. Ferenc A. Váli, *The Turkish Straits and NATO,* p.108.
104. Buzan, op.cit., pp.233-4.
105. It was reported that a series of military devices including artillery, surface-to-surface missiles and seabed mines which can be made 'live' at the turn of a switch, have been emplaced at the Black Sea end of the Bosphorus. *International Herald Tribune,* 5-6 June 1976.

4 OIL AND FORCE

The agenda of interventionary politics in the Middle East is most conveniently defined in terms of a series of regional conflicts and security problems. The Arab-Israeli conflict, the conflict between conservatism and nationalism, the problems of stability in the Gulf, are familiar and useful headings. But before proceeding to consider them in detail, it is worth examining a more general problem which is of virtually exclusive importance to the West, the security of oil supplies. Nearly all members of the Western alliance depend directly or indirectly on Middle Eastern oil and consequently are vulnerable to domestic economic disruption as a result of interruption to supplies. Indeed it can be argued that economic security is a more immediate problem for many countries than military security. The threats to Middle Eastern oil supplies are numerous, and there is no comprehensive system for containing them similar to the politico-military balance established by the West to contain Soviet power. Not only are some threats entirely dependent on regional political developments in the Middle East, and particularly in the Gulf, but experience in the early 1970s suggests that there are relatively fewer constraints on the deployment of the oil weapon by OAPEC than there are on any Soviet attempt to exploit a military advantage vis-à-vis Western Europe.

In addition the impact of changes in the strategic balance is of a much more contingent and hypothetical nature than that of any interference with oil supplies. The deployment of Soviet aircraft in Egypt in 1970 had ominous strategic implications. But it had no immediate, nor indeed necessary, effect on Europe, whereas the deployment of the oil weapon in 1973 caused widespread governmental panic, and was felt in homes throughout Western Europe, Japan and America. In Elizabeth Monroe's words, 'Strategically all-important, oil is also a cardinal commodity from the standpoint of society. Shortage leads to more fuss, bad temper, exaggeration and publicity than shortage of any other industrial raw material because it so quickly causes discomfort as well as fear.'[1]

Nevertheless the role of force in the defence of oil interests is a surprisingly obscure subject. As already indicated, few Middle Eastern oil consumers have attempted to use military policy in defence of supplies although concern over the security of transit routes did prompt

64

France to maintain naval forces in the Indian Ocean. The majority have either lacked the necessary resources, doubted the viability of a military policy, or regarded the security of their supplies as satisfactory. Even following the economic unpheavals caused by the Yom Kippur War, suggestions that, in extremis, force might be used to prevent the strangulation of Western economies by Arab oil producers met with scepticism, if not fear. And there was virtually no question at all that the shift in the economic, and ultimately also in the political, balance of power between oil producers and consumers, a development of potentially much greater long-term significance than the fall of the much-discussed Indo-Chinese dominoes, should be forcibly prevented or forcibly redressed.

Such an approach was however at marked variance with that adopted by an earlier generation of British policymakers. For some sixty years after the conversion of the Royal Navy to oil in 1911, the protection of oil interests had played a key role in British policy in the Middle East,[2] and British experience in the twenty-five years following the end of the Second World War provides an excellent illustration of the scope and limitations of force as an instrument of policy in the defence of oil interests.[3] In 1946 troops were sent from India to Basra during serious disturbances at the Abadan refinery, though in the event they did not intervene. Military action was considered at the time of the Iranian nationalisation of the Anglo-Iranian Oil Company in 1951. The object would have been the seizure of the Abadan refinery, then providing one-third of Britain's petrol, not the oilfields. But the operation was regarded as prohibitive in terms of the prospective political costs, both domestic and international, as well as militarily difficult to mount given the forces and bases available. The validity of these arguments was confirmed five years later by the Suez operation, although in the aftermath of the Iraqi coup of July 1958 precautionary military movements were undertaken in the Arabian Peninsula area, and pre-emptive landings in the Gulf sheikhdoms were anxiously considered.[4] Lord Home bluntly warned that

> should a third party, whether it is Russia or Nasser, seek, by calculated, deliberate policy, to deprive us of our oil supplies, and to deprive Western Europe of its oil supplies, and thereby to put a veto on the industrial expansion in the Western world, then it is as well to make plain and unmistakable that that situation could not be tolerated by the United Kingdom.[5]

But by the late 1950s the main British rationale for the role of force in defence of oil interests had changed. Force was no longer to be used to try to seize or hold oil facilities against local governments, but rather to create and maintain political conditions in which oil prospecting could be safely undertaken, production would continue unhindered by regional conflict, and local governments would not interfere unduly with the operating companies or the oil price. In official parlance the British sought to uphold the 'stability' of the Gulf. The classic example of this strategy was the minatory deployment mounted in order to deter a threatened Iraqi invasion of Kuwait in 1961, but for the most part a symbolic, and rarely very visible, presence proved effective. Prestige, the reputation of British power, remained high, the sheikhdoms were small in size and their enemies for the most part ill-equipped. Altogether 5,700 men had been landed in Kuwait but other minatory and operational deployments were much smaller, and in some areas, such as the Trucial States, were mainly mounted by a force of British-officered local levies, the Trucial Oman Scouts, who operated in co-ordination with the police and the Royal Navy.[6] In addition the British enjoyed ready military access to the sheikhdoms based on connections, many of which dated back to the nineteenth century, and the British military presence was exclusive. Hence for some two decades after the nationalisation of the Anglo-Iranian Oil Company, force continued to play a significant role in the defence of consumer oil interests. It was not very visible – large-scale forces were only permanently stationed in the Gulf after the British withdrawal from Aden in 1967. It was not omnicompetent – it did not prevent minor oil production stoppages during and after the Six Day War, although officials have argued that without the British presence oil interests would have suffered more seriously. Nevertheless the British military presence did contribute significantly to the stability of the main oil-producing area of the Middle East during two decades of rapid change and serious political instability.

With the British withdrawal in 1971 the security of the Gulf region and of the oil installations became primarily a local responsibility. This was not entirely a new development. The National Guard in Saudi Arabia, one of whose major roles was the defence of oil installations, had protected Americans working in the oilfields during the riots there sparked by the Six Day War,[7] and this force was now expanded. Three specific threats were identified for the local producers to counter. The first was sabotage. Oil production, loading and transit facilities are very vulnerable to manportable weapons, and could pose a tempting target to revolutionary organisations, including some of the Palestine liberation groups.[8] But while the effects of sabotage could be dramatic from the point of view of propaganda effect, its disruptive impact on oil supplies would be unlikely to be very great in the absence of any systematic campaign throughout the Gulf. A second scenario envisages the closure of crucial waterways to tanker traffic. Considerable attention has been paid to the possibility that the Straits of Hormuz at the mouth of the Gulf, and also the less important Straits of Bab el Mandeb at the mouth of the Red Sea, might come under the control of governments hostile to the interests of oil consumers. Such fears were lent credibility by the activities of PFLOAG in Oman,[9] including the discovery of plans for PFLOAG operations in the Mossendam peninsula by the Trucial Oman Scouts in 1970, and by the Marxist orientation of the PDRY. But the actual vulnerability of these waterways to military action from the shore has been disputed[10] and it can be assumed that any attempt to close the Straits of Hormuz would result in military action being taken by Iran.

The third and more serious threat derives from the possibility of fighting in or between the main Gulf oil producers, fighting which would certainly disrupt oil shipments, and might well damage oil installation. The avoidance of this possibility depends largely on the ability of the Gulf states to work out an effective regional security system, and the military influence of the consumers is largely restricted to the transfer of military resources to the Gulf and possibly also to minatory diplomacy in crisis situations.[11]

Given the imbalance in power between the small and often very rich sheikhdoms and their three large neighbours, as well as the latent conflict between conservatism and revolution, the Gulf system remains in the mid 1970s basically unstable. The pessimist can make an impressive case. Between 1965 and 1975 there were coups in Oman, Abu Dhabi, Sharjah and Qatar; King Feisal of Saudi Arabia was assassinated and attempts were made on the life of the Shah. Fighting has taken place in two oil-producing states – Oman and Iraq: indeed control over the Kirkuk oil region was a major factor behind the 1974 fighting against the Kurds. Relations between Kuwait and Iraq remained strained. In 1969 the Iraqis began encroaching on the north-east of the sheikhdom, culminating with the occupation of two Kuwaiti police posts in March 1973.[12] More serious were the tensions in Iranian-Iraqi relations which developed after the Qasim coup of 1958, and became acute in the late 1960s. At issue was not only the underlying hostility between Arabs and Persians and between conservatives and revolution-

aries, but a dispute over the navigation rights over the Shatt el Arab, a
border dispute, and Iraqi claims to the oil-rich Iranian province of
Khuzistan. In April 1969 the Iranians unilaterally abrogated the 1937
Treaty of Navigation over the Shatt, and tension remained such that a
year later the Iranian air force was still on a state of full alert.[13] Between
October 1972 and May 1974 there were at least ten major exchanges
of fire across the border[14] and by the end of 1974 Iranian artillery and
SAMs had been moved into Iraqi Kurdistan in support of the Kurdish
revolt.[15]

On the other hand, there is much evidence to suggest that the Gulf
was a more stable region in 1975 than it had been ten or even five
years earlier. A number of long-standing disputes had been solved. The
Iranian claim to Bahrain had been abandoned and the border between
Saudi Arabia and Abu Dhabi and Oman settled. The Trucial States had
merged into a federation whose cohesion and stability confounded its
critics while the assassination of King Feisal exposed the underlying
strength of the Saudi political system.[16] Elsewhere in the Gulf the
prevalence of wealth created conditions, if not always of stability,
then at least of widespread affluence. On the positive side of the balance
sheet there was also the ending of the Dhofar insurgency in December
1975, and more important, the Iranian-Iraqi agreement of the previous
March which involved the settlement of the Shatt navigation dispute in
Iran's favour, and the cessation of Iranian support for the Kurds. The
agreement initated a detente in Iranian-Iraqi relations and apparently
reflected an Iraqi decision to concentrate on internal economic development, a decision which necessitated the ending of the Kurdish war and
Iraqi support for revolutionary movements in the Gulf. The result was
to defuse the most dangerous conflict in the area.

This detente may not prove of indefinite duration. But it is a particularly notable example of the ability of the Gulf states to recognise
that, following the British withdrawal, their overriding interest lies in
the development of a modus vivendi.[17] The March 1975 agreement
served common Iraqi-Iranian interests in making the former less
dependent on the Soviet Union, and in reducing the risk of a war in
which both countries might suffer serious economic damage. The
Iranians were concerned over the vulnerability of their oil refineries,
and in 1972 were reported to have warned Iraq that bombardment of
Abadan, which was in range of artillery fire from the Iraqi border,
would be met by massive Iranian air attacks on the Iraqi oilfields of
Kirkuk, Mosul and Jambur.[18] There would seem then to be a fair chance
that peace will prevail in the Gulf, and that oil supplies will not be

disrupted as a result of purely regional conflicts. But, as the next chapter underlines, this assumption cannot be taken for granted, and if it is disproved, then, depending on the area and the nature of the conflict, the disruption to oil supplies could be substantial. Even a period of very high tension might deter tankers from entering the Gulf.[19]

It is in fact arguable that the threat from conflicts in the Gulf, precisely because of the scale of the possible damage to oil installations, poses a more serious danger to oil consumers than does the 'oil weapon'. The use of oil as a political weapon has been a recurrent theme in Arab political thought since the early 1940s[20] but until 1973 actual disruptions in oil transit and production appeared haphazard and with the exception of Suez relatively ineffective. In 1948, a year after Arab spokesmen warned the United States that support for the creation of Israel could jeopardise American oil stakes in the Middle East,[21] Iraq cut the IPC pipeline from Iraq to Haifa. In the aftermath of Suez another IPC pipeline was cut, this time by Syrians acting without consultations with the Iraqis, and in 1969 the ARAMCO pipeline from Saudi Arabia was sabotaged. During both the Suez and the Six Day Wars the Suez Canal was blocked, a development which in 1967 contributed to the devaluation of sterling five months later, and in 1956 had led to oil shortages in Europe.

Production stoppages during the Six Day War were insignificant in terms of effect. They resulted from government decisions in Kuwait and Iraq, and strikes by oil workers in Libya and Saudi Arabia. The stoppages were later replaced by relatively shortlived selective embargoes against Britain, the United States and West Germany. The position however had altered drastically by the time of the Yom Kippur War in 1973. The Syrian and Egyptian attack took place against a background of growing imbalance in the structure of the international oil trade. The development of a seller's market in oil in the early 1970s and the growth of producer cash reserves meant that the producers could much more easily afford the costs of limited disruption in oil supplies than could the consumers. Moreover the controls over producer behaviour exercised through the oil companies and, to some extent also through Western political influence, had been eroded over the previous years.[22] Already in April 1973 the Saudis had begun to warn Washington that unless there were changes in American policy towards Israel, Saudi oil production would not be raised to meet the large projected increases in American oil requirements, requirements which only they could fulfil. This development represented a significant change in Saudi policy, since the Saudis had previously always tried to keep oil and politics as separate issues.[23]

In fact the oil weapon was not deployed until the second week of the war, when the tide had already turned against the Arab armies. What then emerged was an overall cutback in production by nearly all the main Arab oil producers,[24] plus a total embargo on exports to the United States and Netherlands[25] and threats of selective embargoes against other non-friendly consumers. The main weapon was intended to be the embargo, the general cutback being necessary to prevent the circumvention of the embargo through the diversion of oil from the non-embargoed to the embargoed states.

At their meeting on 17 October, the Arab oil ministers agreed to cut production

> by a minimum of 5 per cent forthwith, using the September 1973 level as a base, and thereafter by a similar percentage each month, using the previous month's reduced output as a new base, until such time as a total evacuation of Israeli forces from all Arab territory occupied during the June 1967 war is completed and the legitimate rights of the Palestinian people are restored, or until the production of every individual country reaches the point where its economy does not permit of any further reduction without detriment to its national or Arab obligations.

The latter proviso proved important. It was soon evident that Arab production cuts could not be maintained until the total evacuation of Israeli-occupied territory without catastrophic effects on the economies of the consumers and ultimately also therefore of the producers. Moreover the United States almost immediately sought to utilise the opportunities created by the war to seek a settlement, an approach which found a ready response in Egypt, and this even though the United States was far less vulnerable to the effects of the oil weapon than many of its allies who had not been embargoed. The embargo on the United States was therefore lifted five months later on 18 March 1974, on the basis of promises rather than performance.[26]

By then however the Arab states had managed to establish oil as one of the most effective weapons in their armoury, and as a factor of long-term importance in international politics.[27] The economic damage inflicted on the consumers had not been irreparable, but the capability to inflict such damage and the sensitivity of the consumers to that capability, when, that is to say, the threat of its imposition suddenly appeared imminent, had been clearly registered.[28] Within both NATO and the EEC member states had adopted 'sauve qui peut' policies at the expense of their allies, an approach encouraged by the system of classifying some consumers as friendly, thus partially or totally exempting them, at least in theory, from the oil measures.

There are however significant constraints on the use of the oil weapon. In 1973 the international oil companies succeeded in spreading the damage fairly evenly around all consumers, and hence the embargo which had been the core of the discriminatory strategy failed, leaving the general cutback as the only effective sanction.[29] Thus so long as the international distribution system remains outside the control of the producers, the oil weapon remains dangerously inflexible in so far as non-target states are likely to be affected, and thereby politically alienated.[30] A more serious general problem is underlined by Hanns Maull:

> The economic consequences of a serious supply interruption stretch over years and are hardly controllable by the producers. Oil supply shortages cause fertiliser shortages, which in turn affect the grain harvest months after the oil weapon has been sheathed. Higher oil prices speed up inflation and trigger off a wage-price spiral. In so far as the oil weapon aims at the basic functions of a society, the decision to apply it resembles the decision to go to war: once it is made, the exact course of events and consequences might get out of control.[31]

The political repercussions of such developments could hardly fail to feed back into the Middle East. It is not in the interests of the conservative producers, nor indeed of most of the confrontation states, that United States power be seriously eroded, nor, as happened in the aftermath of the Yom Kippur War, that the economic balance of power between the United States and its main West European and Japanese allies be tipped still further in the former's favour. Nor can it be in the interests of most of the producer states and in particular Saudi Arabia to exacerbate instability in either Western Europe or the Third World.[32]

While therefore the consumers are likely to remain sensitive to threats to reimpose the oil embargo, threats which were indeed made on a number of occasions after March 1974 in order to ensure continued American involvement in the process of peacemaking,[33] it is not inevitable that this would actually be done. The growing economic interdependence between oil producers and Western consumers, the heavy dependence of Saudi Arabia on the United States, not only for arms but also for large military training missions, as well as Riyadh's intense concern over the economic and political health of the West, all make it unlikely that the oil producers would lightly reimpose an embargo. The Saudis, while obviously anxious not to rule out this possibility, nevertheless preferred in 1976 to use their leverage within OPEC to hold down oil prices on the clear understanding that some political quid pro quo was expected both with regard to progress towards a settlement of the Arab-Israeli conflict and to a more forthcoming Western approach to the 'North-South' dialogue between industrialised and developing countries. Even in the case of a renewed round of Arab-Israeli fighting, immediate reimposition might not be automatic.[34] Much would depend on the course of the war, a serious Arab setback or very visible American support for Israel being the conditions most likely to lead to a renewed deployment of the oil weapon. Over the longer term, radical political change within the main producer states or local conflicts in the Gulf might occasion producer states to use, or to threaten to use, the oil weapon, in order to gain support from certain consumers or to discourage consumers from intervention on the part of local adversaries.[35]

One response to the emergence of the oil weapon, and a response limited to the United States, has been the debate on the possible use of force to break an oil embargo. Before the 1970s American policy had resolutely refused to contemplate the use of force in direct relationship to oil interests,[36] but the sudden 'energy crisis' of the early 1970s appears to have caused some reappraisal even before the Yom Kippur War. In May 1973 the then Chairman of the Senate Foreign Relations Committee, Senator Fulbright, made a speech notable for its emotive imagery. He argued that military action might be necessary to 'secure our exposed jugular', and described the oil producers as 'gazelles in a world of lions'.[37] Around the same time the American military also began to show some interest in the possibility of action against oil states, and these contingency plans were reflected in exercises held before October 1973.[38] After the war and the embargo a great deal of planning was done by the Pentagon and this became evident in early 1975 when detailed scenarios for American seizure of Middle Eastern oil states began to appear in public.

Two possible target areas were discussed:[39] the oilfields in Libya and Algeria, and those in the Gulf, primarily Saudi Arabia. Interest concentrated on the latter. The Libyan fields were well inland, and sabotage was thus more likely before any occupation could be completed. Logistically the United States enjoyed the advantage of substantial forces in the vicinity in the form of the Sixth Fleet and bases in southern Europe. However the political availability of the latter was very uncertain and any operation involving naval forces would have to take into account the presence of the Soviet Mediterranean squadron. Operations in the Gulf also presented problems. There too, the Americans would have no military access. No local party in the Gulf could be expected to support or in any way facilitate their operation. The Americans had no major base facilities in the vicinity, and no demonstrated capacity to mount a quick surgical strike. Nevertheless the area presented an obvious target. A stretch of coast some 400 miles long and forty miles wide stretching between Kuwait and Qatar held thirty one oilfields, nine refineries and ten ports. Much of American military thinking was reflected in an article published in *Harper's Magazine,* the intention of which may have been partly to lend credibility to American minatory diplomacy. The author, who signed himself 'The Unknown Soldier', suggested the initial seizure of the Saudi base of Dharan by American paratroops, some of whom would stage through Israel and who would then go on to take the Ras Tanara jetties and storage tanks, some installations of the great Ghawar oil field, and the nearby Abqaiq field. Marines would be landed twenty-two hours later to consolidate the base and expand the area held. A total force of some 40,000 men was envisaged.[40] Some sabotage would be inevitable, and between D + 7 and D + 60 (D + 90 at the latest) Saudi production would probably be cut off, as would production in Iraq, Libya and Algeria. The maximum production shortfall would be around 7 million barrels per day.

Once seized, the main military problem would be control of the area against guerilla attack. This might be achieved by the establishment of a 500-mile long perimeter running at least twenty miles outside the major installations, guarded by a combination of automatic sensors, minefields and helicopter patrols.[41] Offshore rigs would however be more vulnerable to terrorist attack than those onshore, tankers transiting the Straits of Hormuz would have to be protected from attack by mines or small ships, and there would be a shortage of airfield space for the aircraft and several hundred helicopters. And once in it would be very difficult to withdraw without the risk of sabotage to the fields; the United States might therefore be faced with the prospect of an indefinite occupation.

The political costs and repercussions would also be far-reaching. British experience in the two decades after the Second World War had indicated that the use of force to seize and hold economic assets against local populations or governments was prohibitively expensive. Writing to Eden in the month before Suez, Eisenhower had warned that

> the use of force would ... vastly increase the area of jeopardy. I do not see how the economies of Western Europe can long survive ... the denial of Near East oil. Also, the peoples of the Near East and North Africa and, to some extent, of all Asia and of all Africa, would be consolidated against the West to a degree which, I fear, could not be overcome in a generation and, perhaps, not even in a century, particularly having in mind the capacity of the Russians to make mischief. Before such action were undertaken all our peoples should unitedly understand that there were no other means available to protect our vital rights and interests.[42]

The warning remained prescient nearly two decades later. American military action against the oil producers would substantially change the political map of the Middle East. It would probably radicalise the remaining conservative states in the area and polarise the Arab-Israeli conflict, especially if Israel had been in any way involved in the operation, thus making any Arab-Israeli settlement virtually impossible in the foreseeable future. Further, by inducing a wave of anti-Americanism and creating fears about a spread of a new American colonialism, it would open the region as well as other parts of the Third World to Soviet penetration. Thus the Soviet Union would be an important beneficiary, a beneficiary who would not have to take any very substantial or dangerous action in immediate response to the American intervention. There would be inevitable Soviet concern about American military operations in the general vicinity of the Soviet borders, and just to the south of a Soviet client, Iraq.[43] But the Soviet Union has no commitments to the main target states and, unless the Iraqis attempted to pre-empt American action by taking Kuwait, there would be no need for any military clash between American and Iraqi forces. United States interests would be much more heavily involved than Soviet, and this argues further for Soviet restraint.

In extremis it is probable that America's main allies, Western Europe and Japan, would have to support, or at least to accept, United States intervention. Indeed, since these are the countries most vulnerable to strangulation, it is possible that demands for such actions might in fact originate with them. The real problem, the one emphasised in Eisenhower's warning of 1956, would be a situation in which the judgements of the United States and her principal allies on the desirability of the use of force diverged. This was clearly evident in December 1974 and January 1975 when minatory diplomacy was still at a relatively low level. While some Western officials, including the Secretary-General of NATO, were prepared to endorse Dr Kissinger's warnings, much of the reaction in Western Europe, particularly in Western Germany, was highly unfavourable.[44] A more serious crisis might thus be expected in the event of a limited embargo during which the United States reiterated its warnings about possible intervention, mounted some minatory deployments as part of a war of nerves, or suddenly resorted to pre-emptive attack. Strangulation is a long drawn-out process. At what stage does it become intolerable? The dangers of sabotage and the gradual depletion of consumer oil reserves might encourage earlier rather than later action. So long however as the Western consumers believed in the possibility of a political settlement of the immediate crisis, such American intervention would be deeply resented. Nevertheless the secret of alliance leadership is sometimes seen to reside in the fait accompli.

But if American military intervention would be both difficult and dangerous, it would not necessarily be impossible and, like the oil weapon, the threat of such intervention has become an element in consumer-producer relations. It was first used, although with little apparent effect, during the oil embargo. In January 1974 the American Secretary of Defence, Dr Schlesinger, warned that the Arab states would run the risk of violence if they used their control over oil supplies to 'cripple the larger mass of the industrial world'.[45] A much more sustained campaign of minatory diplomacy was undertaken at the end of the year, at a time when the Administration was seriously concerned about a renewed Arab-Israeli war.[46] It was reported from Washington that top-level policymakers, in conversations with newsmen, were 'not holding back from candid discussions' about the possibility of military intervention.[47] In late November 1974 a United States carrier suddenly broke off from a CENTO exercise and entered the Gulf, the first visit by an American carrier for twenty-five years. This was apparently intended as a warning to the Gulf states that the United States would not tolerate interruptions in oil supply.[48] The message was made much more explicit when Dr Kissinger was asked a month later in an interview with the magazine *Business Week* about the possibility of military intervention. In a reply which quickly reverberated around the Middle East and Europe, he described it as a very dangerous course .. I am not saying that there's no circumstance where we would not use force, – but it's one thing to use it in the case of a dispute over price, it's another where there is some actual strangulation of the industrialised world.[49]

The warning was carefully worded. The United States was, after all, threatening its own clients with possible invasion, and Dr Kissinger was therefore concerned to make it absolutely clear that such action would only be taken as a last resort. Nevertheless the purpose of this minatory diplomacy was to put OAPEC on notice that the consumers would not be impotent in the face of a major embargo, and that they should not be pressed to the stage at which the irrational became rational. There was a blunt psychological logic in Dr Kissinger's warning, a logic which had been more clearly spelled out a few months earlier by the West German Finance Minister, Herr Apel. 'When nations are hopeless, when they don't see any further way out, when they have to fear the destruction of their social wealth or democratic structure, then everything might happen.'[50] The producers moreover were clearly vulnerable. Orders for sophisticated military equipment had yet to be transformed into effective military power, and the survival of indefensible sheikhdoms, as well as of conservative regimes generally, would be at risk were the United States to resort to military action. And in spite of threats by some oil producers that oil installations would be sabotaged, there was evidence to suggest that Gulf producers had taken the American warnings seriously. The Kuwaiti oil minister was quoted as saying publicly that any excessive reduction of oil production was likely to accelerate the outbreak of a possible war launched against the Arab producers by the advanced industrial countries.[51] The warning was repeated by Dr Schlesinger in May 1975 and the Saudis, who had been assured two months earlier that they had nothing to fear from the United States, moved troop reinforcements to the oilfields.[52] Mr Carter however appeared to eschew the military option during his election campaign by describing an oil embargo as an economic declaration of war and threatening to retaliate by severing all economic relations, including the sale of arms.

The final threat to oil supplies which has concerned Western defence planners is the possibility of Soviet interference with, or even control over, Middle East oil production or transit. This fear dates back to the early days of the Cold War and was a major preoccupation in London during the mid 1950s,[53] but the nature of the Soviet threat has never been very clear. Western concern with the possibility of Soviet interference with a vital source of raw materials located close to the Soviet Union reflected a mixture of fear and 'worst possible case' thinking. Some scenarios, in particular those elaborated in the 1950s, envisaged Soviet seizure of the Middle Eastern oilfields, an operation inconceivable outside the context of an East-West war. More important, since it underpinned much of American crisis thinking, was a Middle Eastern domino theory, according to which the overthrow of any one conservative regime in the Middle East, including those in the eastern Mediterranean, risked a chain reaction in the Gulf and the establishment of a series of radical regimes in the oil-producing areas which would be subject to Soviet influence, if not control.[54] The evidence of the period between the mid 1950s and the mid 1970s however suggests that, while revolutionary states are likely to develop political and military relations with the Soviet Union, this is certainly not synonymous with Soviet control over their policies. Moreoever the establishment of the revolutionary regime in Iraq did not lead to a chain reaction throughout the Gulf, although Iraq did encourage subversion there and in 1961 threatened neighbouring Kuwait. In some part at least its lack of success in changing the status quo in the Gulf was due to Western military counteractions.

A third and later scenario envisaged Soviet naval interference with Western oil routes near the Straits of Hormuz or in the Indian Ocean. This followed the appearance of a Soviet naval presence in the Indian Ocean in 1968 and was the subject of a lengthy debate in 1970 in Britain in connection with the discussion of arms sales to South Africa under the Simonstown agreement. Subsequently it provided an important rationale for the growing American naval presence in the Indian Ocean and the build-up of a new American base facility on the island of Diego Garcia. In a demonstration of naval strength in November 1974 the largest maritime exercise in CENTO's history was held in the approaches to the Gulf, where Soviet naval and air activity had recently shown signs of increase.[55] The following May Dr Schlesinger outlined details of these developments, warning, 'that kind of expansion suggests that they are more than mildly interested in their military power astride the lifeline of the industrialised world to the Persian Gulf'.[56] At least one government colleague was less sure. The Director of the CIA told a Congressional committee that the normal composition of the Soviet Navy in the Indian Ocean, in particular the lack of submarine forces, suggested that the interdiction of western oil supplies was not a major Soviet objective in the area.[57] In military terms, any Soviet threat is confined to conditions of near or actual war.[58] But a political threat does exist in so far as the general knowledge that the Soviet Union has the capability to control traffic into and out of the Indian Ocean may give the Soviet Union some influence over those countries which would be most affected in the event of action actually being taken. It is also conceivable that, emboldened by a Soviet military presence, small states such as PDRY and Somalia might blockade the Straits of Bab el Mandeb, if for example there were to be another Arab-Israeli war.[59]

Capabilities apart, Soviet intentions vis-à-vis Western oil supplies are difficult to assess. Few in the West would quarrel with Pravda's view that 'to stop pumping Arabian Gulf oil . . . will be like an economic earthquake in the entire capitalist world'.[60] At the same time however the United States has made it abundantly clear that it will tolerate neither the strangulation of the Western economies, nor Soviet domination of the Middle East: indeed the Americans have risked nuclear war to prevent the latter development. In addition, Soviet policymakers must take into account the fact that the Eastern bloc is not entirely immune from the impact of a Middle Eastern-induced 'earthquake in the entire capitalist world'. Eastern Europe is politically sensitive to economic disruptions, while on historical evidence a crisis in capitalism in Western Europe is as likely to result in a swing to the right as to the left.[61]

That is not to say that the Soviet Union has ignored the difficulties experienced by the Western consumers, or avoided seeking to exacerbate them. For a complex of reasons, economic as well as political, the unity of producers, the increase in oil prices, the use of oil revenues for the support of national liberation fronts in the Middle East, as well as the deployment of Arab capital as an 'effective weapon' against the West, have all been either supported or encouraged by Soviet propoganda. Soviet propaganda also supported nationalisation of Western oil companies and the use of the oil weapon in 1967 and 1973. On the latter occasion the Soviet Union sought to dissuade OAPEC from lifting the oil embargo the following spring. There is also some evidence of limited Soviet military influence being brought to bear vis-à-vis Soviet oil interests in Iraq. Soviet naval visits in 1969 coincided with Soviet-Iraqi negotiations over Soviet involvement in Iraqi oil exploitation, and one of the reported Iraqi motives for seeking the Soviet-Iraqi Treaty of 1972 was an Iraqi fear that nationalisation of IPC would lead to Western intervention.[62]

Inevitably the possibility of some Soviet threat to Middle Eastern oil supplies will remain of concern, at least to defence planners, as long as there are serious tensions in East-West relations. But the evidence of some three decades of Soviet-American rivalry suggests that the risk-reward calculus would have to alter dramatically in Soviet eyes for the threat to take serious military form. That is not of course impossible, but it assumes a substantial shift in the East-West balance of power and probably also in the political geography of the Gulf region. Even then Soviet policymakers would have to bear in mind that 'when nations are hopeless, when they don't see any further way out, when they have to fear the destruction of their social wealth or democratic structure, then everything might happen'.

The role of force in defence of oil interests has diminished since the Second World War. With the British withdrawal from the Gulf, much of the responsibility for the defence of oil installations there, as well as for the general stability of the region, has shifted from the consumers to the producers, although the necessary military resources have come largely from the United States and Western Europe. Experience suggests that military influence can be effective in helping to contain the threats posed to Western oil supplies by the Soviet Union as well as by the oil weapon as wielded by the producers. But military power could only be deployed by consumers against producers with the greatest of difficulty; hence economic security can only partly be a function of military policy. Much must depend also on the development of close economic and political relations between consumers and producers, on the build-up of consumer oil stockpiles, and on the establishment of sharing arrangements for emergencies on the lines of those drawn up by the International Energy Agency.

Notes

1. Elizabeth Monroe, *Britain's Moment in the Middle East, 1914-1956,* p.97.
2. Hugh Thomas, *The Suez Affair,* p.39 (revised edition).
3. For a more detailed account of British policy during this period, see Peter Mangold, 'Force and Middle East oil', *Round Table,* January 1976.
4. See Macmillan's account of the incident, *Riding the Storm,* p.523.
5. House of Lords Debates, vol. 211, col. 290, 28 July 1958.
6. For an account of the operation of the 1,000-strong Trucial Oman Scouts in what subsequently became the United Arab Emirates, see *New York Times,* 26 February 1961, *Financial Times,* 23 February 1968 and 5 November 1968, and *Guardian,* 16 April 1970.
7. *Washington Post,* 22 May 1975.
8. For a discussion of the threat of sabotage to oil facilities, see 'The Security of the Cape route' in Patrick Wall (ed.), *The Indian Ocean and the Threat to the West.*

9.   Mordechai Abir, *Oil, Power and Politics*, p.117. PFLOAG cells were later discovered in the UAE, Bahrain and Kuwait. *Economist*, 9 June 1973.

10. According to a public CIA report of 1973, the Straits of Hormuz are too deep and wide to be blocked by sunken ships and too wide to be controlled by coastal artillery. Naval and air power would also be required to close them. *Defence Monitor*, April 1974.

11. See chap. 5.

12. The Iraqi objective was apparently to gain control over the islands of Warba and Bubiyan which commanded the approaches to the new Iraqi port of Um Qasr. *Financial Times*, 5 April 1972.

13. *Guardian*, 20 April 1970.

14. R.M. Burrell and A.J. Cottrell, *Iran, Afghanistan and Pakistan: Tensions and Dilemmas*, p.5.

15. Iraq supported subversion in Iranian Baluchistan, as well as the Iranian Tudeh party.

16. *Guardian*, 7 March 1975.

17. Both the Royalists in the Yemen and Sultan Qaboos in Oman received military aid from a large number of conservative states in the Middle East.

18. J. Meister, 'Iran's naval build-up', *Swiss Review of World Affairs*, July 1973.

19. For a week after the Yom Kippur War, oil was in fact available at eastern Mediterranean terminals, but tankers were unwilling to take the risk of entering the area. 'Proposed expansion of United States military facilities in the Indian Ocean', Hearings, House of Representatives Committee on Foreign Affairs, Subcommittee on the Near East and South Asia, p.53.

20. Fuad Itayim, 'Strengths and weaknesses of the oil weapon' in *The Middle East and the International System*, pt. 2, p.1. One of the most notable references to Arab oil power, and one which received much prominence in Britain, was in Nasser's *Philosophy of the Revolution* published in 1955.

21. Charles Issawi, 'Checking on the consequences of the oil squeeze by Arab states', *International Perspectives*, March-April 1974, p.9.

22. Hanns Maull, *Oil and Influence*, p.4

23. Itayim, op.cit., p.2.

24. While Iraq refrained from any overall cutback, apparently for fear of loss of oil revenues, it did embargo the United States and the Netherlands as well as nationalising their oil interests.

25. The embargo against the Netherlands appears to have been a response to a number of pro-Israeli actions including a Dutch offer before the war to replace Austria as a relay centre for Soviet Jews emigrating from the Soviet Union to Israel; pro-Israeli statements by various Dutch leaders; recruitment, with official permission, of volunteers for service in Israel; and the use of the official Dutch airline, KLM, for charter flights to Israel in connection with the war effort. George Lenczowski, 'The oil producing countries', *Daedalus*, Fall, 1975, p.65.

26. A specific price for the lifting of the embargo was Dr Kissinger's 'shuttle' between Tel Aviv and Damascus which culminated in the Israeli-Syrian Disengagement Agreement. Edward Sheehan, 'Step-by-step Diplomacy in the Middle East', *Foreign Policy*, Spring 1976, p.36.

27. Maull, op.cit., pp.35,36.

28. N.B. also the pro-Arab statement issued by the EEC countries on 6 November 1973.

29. Deficits during the last quarter of 1973 ranged from 9 per cent in the case of the Netherlands to 25 per cent in the case of Denmark, with the United States, Germany, France and Italy in the 11-14 per cent range. Maull, op. cit., p.7.

30. For a discussion of the likelihood of producer control over the international distribution system, see Maull, op.cit., pp.12-14.

31. Ibid., pp.15-16.

32. In an interivew with the West German magazine, *Der Spiegel,* in December 1976, at the time of Saudi opposition to OPEC oil price rises, the Saudi Oil Minister, Sheikh Yamani, said, 'We are extremely worried about the economic situation of the West, worried about the possibility of a new recession, worried about the situation in Britain, Italy, even in France and some other nations. And we do not want another regime coming to power in France or Italy.'

33. *International Herald Tribune,* 16 December 1976, and *Times,* 21 February 1977.

34. See the views expressed early in 1975 by Heikal and Sheikh Zaid of Abu Dhabi, *Newsweek,* 27 January and 10 March 1975.

35. Maull, op.cit., p.32.

36. The United States had resolutely refused to use other than very mild diplomatic persuasion on Saudi Arabia before the early 1970s, while not however objecting to the rather more rugged methods used by the British in the Gulf Sheikhdoms.

37. The term 'jugular' has been used with reference to the Gulf both by British leaders in the 1950s (who also applied it to the Suez Canal) and by the Shah in the 1970s. Reference was made by Senator Fulbright to the possibility that Iran might seize some of the Gulf oil sheikhdoms.

38. Eqbal Ahmad and David Caploe, 'The logic of military intervention', *Race and Class,* Winter 1976, p.323.

39. See the article by Robert Tucker, 'Oil: the issue of American intervention', in *Commentary,* January 1975.

40. Two Army divisions, two Marine divisions with an 'organic' air wing consisting of eight squadrons of F4s, two reconnaissance squadrons and eight 'attack' squadrons.

41. 'Out of the fire', *Economist* Supplement, May 1975, p.36.

42. Dwight Eisenhower, *Waging Peace,* p.667.

43. In his interview with *Business Week,* Dr Kissinger had commented that 'any president who would resort to military action in the Middle East without worrying what the Soviets would do would have to be reckless. The question is to what extent he would let himself be deterred by it'.

44. In a radio interview the French Foreign Secretary, M. Sauvagnaurges, commented that he would not have 'said it that way, but I'm not criticising the American Secretary of State'. In contrast a West German government spokesman was quoted as saying, 'We are not interested in any kind of confrontation with the oil countries but rather in co-operation, and we would probably be overestimating our powers and betraying our political aims if we resorted to force, even if we just thought of it. We do not have the use of force in mind, and do not share such thoughts.' *Financial Times,* 13 January 1975, *New York Times,* 20 January 1975 and 6 January 1975.

45. Klaus Knorr, 'The limits of economic and military power', *Daedalus,* Fall 1975, p.237.

46. In December 1974 President Ford told the columnist Joseph Alsop that he put the chances of an Arab-Israeli war breaking out in the near future at above 70 per cent. *Washington Post,* 27 January 1975.

47. *United States News and World Report,* 2 December 1974. See also *Financial Times,* 14 January 1975, *Sunday Times,* 9 February 1975.

48. *Christian Science Monitor,* 26 November 1974, cited in Ahmad and Caploe,

op.cit., p.323. Two weeks later, 2,000 Sixth Fleet marines landed in Sardinia in a mock invasion of an Arab oil state, and the commander of the Sixth Fleet was quoted as saying that 'we don't want to invade (the Middle East) but we are prepared'. Ibid.

49.   Cited in *Strategic Survey* 1974, p.30.

50.   *International Herald Tribune*, 24 October 1974.

51.   *Guardian*, 6 January 1975. An article in the *Washington Post* quoted officials officials in several Arab countries speaking of America's irrationality and its propensity to resort to force in order to resolve international problems. This could be taken as a vindication of the view, attributed to aides of Dr Kissinger, that the American warning had been intended to strengthen moderate forces against Arab radicals over the oil question. *Washington Post*, 7 February, 1975 and *New York Times*, 20 January 1975.

52.   *Washington Post*, 22 May 1975, and *Financial Times*, 12 January 1976.

53.   While on a visit to Britain in 1955, Khrushchev and Bulganin had been warned that the British would fight for their oil. Macmillan subsequently commented in his memoirs, 'Whether this was wise or not, it seems to have made a deep impression on our visitors.' Op.cit., p.96.

54.   Kalb and Kalb, *Kissinger*, p.192.

55.   *New York Times*, 21 November 1974.

56.   *Daily Telegraph*, 19 May 1975. Reports at the beginning of 1975 spoke of the build-up of Soviet bases within fighter-bomber range of the Gulf. According to one scenario, the Russians might attempt to blockade the Gulf during an oil embargo in order to prevent Iranian oil being sent to Israel. During worldwide naval exercises in 1975 the Soviet navy rehearsed tactics for cutting sea-lanes. Admiral Stansfield Turner, 'The naval balance: not just a numbers game', *Foreign Affairs*, January 1977, p.342; *International Herald Tribune*, 23 January 1975, and *New York Times*, 7 April 1975.

57.   Congressional Record, 22 March 1975. It was also argued that the Soviet navy was ill prepared to engage the West in long-range conventional warfare and that there were areas outside the Indian Ocean much closer to Soviet home bases which would be more suitable for the interdiction of tankers.

58.   Limited disruption of oil routes in peace time could be caused by the Russians declaring an exercise or a missile test zone there. The Russians have closed areas to shipping in this way in the past, particularly in the Norweigan Sea, *Financial Times*, 20 January 1976.

59.   Arthur Jay Klinghoffer, 'Soviet oil politics and the Suez Canal', *World Today*, October 1975, p.404.

60.   Cited in Kohler, Goure and Harvey, *The Soviet Union and the October 1973 War*, p.23.

61.   In addition such a development would threaten Soviet imports of Western technology. According to one report, even before the end of the Yom Kippur War, Soviet envoys in the Middle East were active in discussing ways of reducing the pressure of high oil prices on those states to whom the Soviet Union provided economic aid. Jon Kimche, 'Soviet oil diplomacy', *Midstream*, December 1974, pp.11, 12.

62.   A.J. Cottrell and R.M. Burrell, 'Soviet naval competition in the Indian Ocean', *Orbis*, Winter 1975, pp.1113-14.

5 THE GULF AND THE ARABIAN PENINSULA

The Arabian Peninsula and the Gulf are not only the centre of Middle Eastern oil production, but also of political conservatism. In consequence the West has been able to maintain something of a monopoly of effective military influence in the area. Oil and the relative proximity of the Soviet Union, bordering on Iran to the north, have determined attention. Insecurity, ideology and historical connections have allowed military access. For the Soviet Union on the other hand, the Iraqi coup of 1958, and the complex of rivalries in and between the Yemens, have provided little more than rather uncertain footholds in an area where anti-communism is strong and where 'revolutionary' states have suffered political isolation.

For much of the three decades after the Second World War, until the early 1970s in fact, the political geography of the Arabian Peninsula and the Gulf underwent relatively little change. The political impact of expanding oil production was slow in making itself felt and, in the sheikhdoms, its initial effect was probably destabilising. Continuing political and military weakness forced most of the countries in the area to look outside the Middle East for military support. Many of them looked to Britain. Britain was a member of CENTO and, until 1975, maintained nuclear forces on Cyprus 'declared' to the alliance. Reinforcements were based at Aden, and later also Bahrain and Sharjah, for operations in support of the sheikhdoms, with whom treaty connections dated back to the nineteenth century. This network of relationships allowed the British to underwrite the most vulnerable part of the Gulf system. By helping to protect the sheikhdoms against internal threats, Britain ensured that they did not become revolutionary bridgeheads into the system; and by protecting them against attack from their large neighbours, Britain helped offset the considerable imbalance of power existing in the Gulf. For with an external power holding the ring, Iraq, Iran and Saudi Arabia were either deterred from pressing their territorial claims against the small states, or persuaded to shelve them. The sheikhdoms were thus able to survive without becoming a bone of local contention.

The Pax Britannica did however enjoy some more or less visible American bolstering. American interests in the Gulf were symbolised by MIDEASTFOR at Bahrain, but on occasion more substantial support

83

was needed. In the immediate aftermath of the Iraqi coup, plans were made for possible American operations in support of Kuwait. The Joint Chiefs of Staff were instructed to employ, subject to Eisenhower's personal approval, 'whatever means might be necessary' to prevent an Iraqi attack on the sheikhdom. And Eisenhower approved a JCS recommendation for the movement by sea of a Marine Regiment combat team at Okinawa to take stations in the Gulf.[1] The immediate danger was soon over but the Iraqi threat lingered on. In 1959 the British were asked for a definite assurance of help in the case of Iraqi aggression. And it is interesting to note from Macmillan's account that the willingness to give the assurance was influenced by the fact that the British government was now 'reasonably certain that we would receive full moral support and perhaps some practical help from our American friends in protecting Western interests in the Gulf if serious trouble were to break out'.[2]

Another American response to the coup was the stepping up of their attempts to offset subversion in one of the most important Gulf states.[3] While American military policy vis-à-vis Teheran was primarily a function of the military and political threat from the north,[4] its main objective for much of the 1950s and early 1960s was to keep the Shah in power.[5] Relatively little of American resource transfer policy was aimed at attempting to give the Iranian forces an effective capability to resist Soviet attack, a task which probably appeared impossible at the time and which the Americans regarded as being best catered for through the contingency planning carried out by CENTO.[6] Additional attempts to reassure the Shah and reinforce the deterrent power of the de facto American guarantee were contained in the Iranian-United States bilateral agreement of 1959. Thereby the United States agreed to take in accordance with its constitutional procedures, 'such appropriate action, including the use of armed force, as may be mutually agreed upon' in the case of Soviet aggression.[7]

On the southern shore of the Gulf the United States maintained military relations with Saudi Arabia, with whom Britain had clashed in the mid 1950s during the Buraimi oasis dispute.[8] The American military mission in Saudi Arabia dated back to 1943. In 1950 President Truman had assured Ibn Sa'ud of American interest in the territorial integrity of the kingdom. Later in the decade the Americans came to see the main threat as coming from internal subversion,[9] and the two threats appeared to coalesce in late 1962 following the outbreak of the Yemeni civil war and the introduction of Egyptian troops on the side of the Republican forces. These developments were widely regarded as the preliminary to the destruction of the monarchy,[10] and necessitated a more active American involvement than the limited military resource transfer programme pursued until then.[11] On 25 October 1962 therefore Kennedy sent a letter to Crown Prince Feisal giving an assurance of 'full United States support for the maintenance of Saudi Arabian integrity',[12] and in November American military aircraft twice staged demonstrations over Jeddah and Riyadh.

American diplomacy over the next few months was aimed not simply at providing immediate protection for the Saudis but also at ensuring the longer-term stability of the Middle East by bringing about an end to the civil war. In early 1963 therefore the Administration devised a project, known as 'Hardtop'. This sought to trade an American commitment to defend Saudi Arabia for Saudi agreement to end their support for the Royalists in the Yemen, which in turn was intended as a bargaining counter to persuade the Egyptians to withdraw their forces. But the symbolic deterrent force of a single American fighter squadron for the defence of Saudi airspace appealed neither to the Pentagon, who objected that lacking proper ground environment and radar, the aircraft would be sitting targets, nor to Feisal who had little confidence in this implied commitment to defend Saudi Arabia and resented the accompanying diplomatic pressure for internal reforms.[13] In the event, a fighter squadron, plus 500 servicemen, did go to Saudi Arabia for joint manoeuvres, but they were not sent to defend Saudi airspace and were kept away from areas in which Egyptian air activity had been reported. The squadron was withdrawn in January 1964 following a disagreement over the extension of a disengagement agreement in the Yemen. The Saudis subsequently acquired their own air defence system, operated by civilian British pilots under contract.[14]

In contrast to the West, Soviet military policy in the region during the 1950s and the 1960s was much more limited and also less successful. With the exception of post-1958 Iraq, military access to the Gulf and the Arabian Peninsula was confined to the southwestern quarter of Arabia. The Soviet relationship with the Yemen affords an interesting example of the immediate benefits and long-term dangers of Soviet revisionist military policy in the Middle East. The Soviet Union gained military access to the fiercely conservative state of the Yemen in the mid 1950s, when the Imamic regime was attempting to pursue its claims against the neighbouring Aden Protectorates. The first Soviet arms began to arrive in October 1956, followed the next year by military instructors and mechanics, and this very minor transfer of military resources forced the British to step up their defences in Aden.[15]

The Republican coup of 1962, in which the Egyptians quickly became involved, promised more dramatic repercussions. Although the poorest country in the Arabian Peninsula, the Yemen enjoyed an important strategic position near the mouth of the Red Sea, and the civil war offered a useful base from which to exert pressure on the newly formed and fragile South Arabian Federation, established to provide a political framework within which the British could maintain the Aden base.

The Egyptian intervention had however been ill-judged. The Egyptians soon found themselves fighting a guerilla war with forces trained only to deal with conventional warfare, and for nearly five years up to 60,000 Egyptians were involved in the fighting. During this period some $200 million of Soviet military aid was channelled via the Egyptians to the Republicans.[16] Logistic support was also provided in the form of sea transport for Egyptian troops transiting between Egypt and the Yemen, and an arms agreement of June 1963, significantly the most important so far concluded between the Soviet Union and Egypt, included twenty-four Antonov transport aircraft for the Cairo-Luxor-Yemen route. These were flown by Soviet pilots with Egyptian co-pilots.[17]

With the enforced Egyptian withdrawal from the Yemen in the wake of the Six Day War, the capital of Sana came under siege by Royalist forces, and the Soviet Union took on a more active involvement. A policy of military resource transfer escalated into a minor operational deployment. In November and December 1967, 10,000 tons of equipment was sent in by emergency airlift.[18] A squadron of Mig 19s plus other aircraft was made available to the Republicans, complete with ground crews and instructors, and for a short while Soviet pilots flew aircover for the Republican forces. The operation did not last long; a Russian-piloted aircraft was soon shot down and the pilot identified. Thereafter Soviet pilots were replaced by Syrians. The Royalists did not in the event take Sana, but in August 1968 when a new round of fighting was expected, Soviet arms were again airlifted to the Republicans.[19]

The Soviet military investment in the Yemen did provide some long-term returns. In Northern Yemen, the Soviet Union eventually gained little and relations with Sana deteriorated in the early 1970s and the country was kept short of military spares and ammunition. Military links were finally broken off by North Yemen, under Saudi prompting in 1976.[20] Nor had the Yemeni civil war led to the overthrow of the Saudi monarchy, a development the United States had intervened to prevent; on the contrary it had rather strengthened the regional position of King Feisal at the expense of President Nasser. But the civil war did spill across the South Arabian border, where it contributed to the development of the insurgency campaign which quickly made the Aden base untenable. With the withdrawal of the British in November 1967 the South Arabian Federation collapsed, to be replaced by what soon became the first Marxist regime in the Arab world.

The British withdrawal from the Gulf proved a much less destabilising operation than the final evacuation of Aden. When withdrawal was announced in January 1968, it was made clear that the troops would leave only four years later. This allowed both London and the Gulf capitals to review the situation and to settle at least some of the local disputes. The British role in the Dhofar war was in fact stepped up in 1970.[21] Elsewhere in the Gulf, before and after the military withdrawal of 1971, Britain helped various countries to develop their own forces. In this context arms were perhaps less important than training and personnel. Britain enjoyed a close relationship with the Iranian navy, advising on the establishment of Iranian naval bases in the Gulf, and training an amphibious commando battalion,[22] an important unit for Iran's strategy of maintaining stability in the area. British companies were closely involved in training and maintenance for the Saudi air force. British personnel and liaison teams remained in a number of the sheikhdoms, including Bahrain, Abu Dhabi and Ras el Khaimah where the commanding officers of the security forces were British.[23] A liaison team in Kuwait provided technical skills, and a certain sense of reassurance to a generally rather isolated and insecure state.

Not only therefore was the British withdrawal orderly,[24] but the timing proved less unfortunate than some had feared it might be. Certainly the decision was unwelcome in the Gulf, and it owed more to domestic British political considerations than to any appraisal of the immediate outlook for stability in the area.[25] But the hostile Iranian reaction to subsequent suggestions that the British decision might be reconsidered quickly showed that the days of the Pax Britannica would in any case have been numbered. Oil wealth was beginning to create a new self-confidence, a self-confidence which was in the long term incompatible with the maintenance of a foreign military presence. And the build-up of oil revenues, which gained momentum with the price rises of the early 1970s, provided the Gulf states with the resources to build up their own armed forces. The level of armaments quickly reached the point at which the British presence of a decade earlier began to appear insignificant.

Thus the announcement of the British withdrawal, instead of opening up a power vacuum, rather precipitated developments which allowed the emergence of an essentially indigenous security system. Although local rivalries did not allow the development of any formal security structure, self-interest did make for a modus vivendi between the various states, a modus vivendi in which the independence of the sheikhdoms was respected, and in which exclusion of the forces of the Great Powers came to be emphasised. But underlying these developments was the rapid expansion of local armed forces. The creation of effective military capabilities, as opposed simply to the stockpiling of arms, was very much a long-term development. Much of the burgeoning military budgets of the Gulf states went on the construction of basic infrastructure projects, and there was a heavy demand for the transfer of foreign military skills in order to provide training for the use of highly sophisticated military equipment in an area where the level of technical education was still low, and where skilled manpower was in short supply. For some considerable period to come therefore, the Gulf states continued to remain militarily dependent on external powers.[26]

In effect this meant the United States. The British decision to withdraw had been unwelcome in Washington, where it forced a reappraisal of the American role in the Gulf. It was no longer possible to continue the traditional American policy of trying to stay out of trouble and let the British get on with the job, but the Americans quickly made it clear that they would not replace the British presence. MIDEASTFOR was modernised, but not enlarged. Its role was primarily psychological, in that it was a local symbol of American power and support, and its port visits had for many years provided the only official contact between the United States Government and some of the smaller sheikhdoms. It was officially felt that the withdrawal of MIDEASTFOR would be interpreted, particularly by the sheikhdoms, as a diminution of the United States interest in the area.[27]

Otherwise United States policy was in accord with the Nixon Doctrine. The Americans sought to encourage the development of an indigenous security system, to create what an American official described as a 'self-sufficient, self-reliant, self-confident community of countries in the Gulf'.[28] This meant support for local co-operation, but also a large-scale transfer of military resources, so as to provide Iran and Saudi Arabia with the eventual capability to defend not only themselves, but also the sheikhdoms.[29] Of the latter, only Kuwait had been quick to try to develop a defence relationship with the United States. This followed the abrogation of the 1961 Anglo-Kuwaiti Exchange of Letters which had provided Kuwait with a British defence guarantee which might be called upon as a last resort. In 1972 an American team conducted an in-depth analysis of Kuwaiti defence requirements,[30] and orders for American aircraft and other equipment were placed subsequently.

Iran and Saudi Arabia had much more to offer the United States than the rich but sometimes almost indefensible sheikhdoms. Neither country was any longer the weak client of one or two decades earlier. Saudi Arabia was emerging in the mid 1970s, after the oil crisis and the death of King Feisal, as a major force in both international and Middle Eastern politics. What it lacked was a large population or armed forces, and the Americans were at pains to try to dissuade the Saudis from buying some of the more sophisticated equipment ordered by Iran, which the Saudi forces could not be expected to operate effectively.[31] The Americans were building up some branches of the Saudi armed forces almost from scratch. This also meant that the supply of military services, including training, servicing and infrastructure projects, constituted the major part of the American resource transfer programme, and of the $3.8 billion spent in the United States during 1975 and 1976, only some 10 per cent was spent on actual military hardware.[32] In 1971 an American programme, scheduled to run until 1983, was agreed for the development of the navy. This involved the supply of nineteen small ships, training, and the construction of shore facilities.[33] In the air force, Operation Peacehawk, which provided for the construction of airfields, training and maintenance in connection with the relatively simple F5 aircraft, was valued at some $3 billion.[34] Four mechanised infantry battalions and one artillery battalion of the Saudi National Guard, politically the most sensitive and the fastest growing branch of the Saudi forces, were trained by a private American company.[35]

These developments were one reflection of what amounted to an informal economic and military alliance between Saudi Arabia and the United States, a relationship based on the Saudi side on the view that the United States constituted a potential guarantor of the regime and a natural ally in a world threatened by Communism. Here the Saudis could make their own contribution. At the international level this was reflected in Saudi pressure within OPEC to keep down oil prices and its anxiety to ensure the stabilisation of key Western economies. In the Middle East Saudi Arabia was regarded as an important force for moderation in Arab politics. The Saudis had played a key role in the ending of the Lebanese civil war in autumn 1976. In the Arabian Peninsula they began to try to exert a moderating influence on the policy of the two Yemens. Substantial economic aid was promised in return for the ending of PDRY aid for PFLOAG. In 1974 the Saudis turned a North Yemeni arms shopping list over to the Americans, and a Pentagon team was sent to study North Yemeni defence needs. North Yemeni purchases were to be financed by Saudi Arabia, and both the Americans and the Saudis hoped thereby to terminate the North Yemeni-Soviet military resource transfer relationship.[36] The Americans were however reported to have turned down a Saudi offer to finance a military and economic aid programme to Somalia, aimed at eliminating the much more substantial Soviet presence there, although the Saudis subsequently offered direct financial aid to Somalia.[37]

Between 1972 and 1976 the United States sold some $10.4 billion worth of arms to Iran in what was the largest American military resource transfer programme, judged in terms of size and cost, and one which included a quite unprecedented range of highly sophisticated military equipment.[38] The initial decision to make large-scale transfers of military resources to Iran was taken after the visit by President Nixon to Teheran in July 1972. It was reportedly hotly debated within the Administration, and reflected the degree of American concern at the possibility of Soviet penetration of the area of the Middle East of most direct economic importance to the Western alliance.[39] Iran had substantial advantages as a local proxy. Judged in terms of factors such as size, population, GNP, political leadership and military capability, Iran was by far the strongest country in the Gulf,[40] and indeed in the Middle East. In 1975 Iranian defence expenditure outran that of Egypt and Israel combined.[41] The country's military build-up fulfilled a number of purposes useful to Washington. In the Gulf Iran established a capability based on a large helicopter and hovercraft fleet for operations on the southern shore to maintain, in the tradition of the Pax Britannica, the territorial and political integrity of the sheikhdoms.[42] Further afield, the Iranian navy was under development to assume an eventual Indian Ocean capability in defence of oil transit routes,[43] while the Iranian military build-up was also valuable vis-à-vis the Soviet Union, both because it offset Soviet arms supplies to Iraq, and because it involved the establishment of a potential new centre of military power directly on the Soviet periphery.[44] Iran, in the words of one senior American official, provided the United States with a Middle East ally 'without the umbilical cord showing'.[45]

The effectiveness of these proxy roles was already evident by the early 1970s. The Iranians appeared to be 'warehousing' American military equipment for use by third parties. Iranian F5 aircraft were sent to Jordan and Morocco and also in 1972 to Vietnam to help the

United States beat the Vietnam ceasefire resupply deadline.[46] Nearer home, Iran, the United States and possibly also Israel[47] had co-operated in providing covert support for the Kurds, whom the American Administration saw as a 'uniquely useful tool' for weakening Iraqi 'adventurism'. According to published reports, American aid which was channelled via the Iranians, began in 1972 at the urgent request of the Shah and totalled some $16 million.[48] The direct Iranian involvement was on a larger scale and included operational units. Similarly the Iranians began in 1973, reportedly with American encouragement, to provide operational support for the Sultan of Oman against PFLOAG.[49] The 3,000-strong Iranian contingent provided an important numerical contribution to the Sultan's forces. Additionally Iran guaranteed Omani airspace against incursion from aircraft from the PDRY, while a joint Iranian-Omani patrol, involving the operation of Iranian aircraft and ships on the Omani side of the Straits of Hormuz, was instituted at the beginning of 1975 with the primary objective of stopping 'any form of subversion'.[50] This complemented previous Iranian arrangements for ensuring free navigation through the Straits of Hormuz, including the fortification of the islands of Abu Masu and the Tumbs, occupied by the Iranians in December 1971, just prior to the British withdrawal.

While military resource transfer policy was obviously designed to reduce the likelihood of any more direct American military intervention in the area, it did nevertheless involve risks. The transfer of military resources placed several tens of thousands of American technicians in key posts in the Saudi and Iranian forces, notably communications, logistics, intelligence and aircraft maintenance, and in consequence the effectiveness of these forces was for some considerable period dependent on the United States.[51] This gave the Americans some control over the actions of their proxies in case of crisis or conflict. But it also meant that the United States was more likely to become directly involved if conflict were to break out. And it was arguable that this likelihood might in fact have been increased as a result of the scale of resource transfer to the area.

That was partly the Administrations' own fault. No major National Security Council study had been carried out on the implications of Gulf arms sales, which under the Nixon and Ford Administrations were considered individually on a case by case basis and used as tactical foreign plicy tools.[52] Iranian demands were particularly heavy and the scale of arms sales to Iran quickly reached proportions which had not been anticipated in official circles. Not only did such a large armaments programme deepen Iraqi dependence on the Soviet Union, but by creating uncertainties throughout the Gulf about Iranian long-term intentions, it helped to spark off an arms race. This threatened to undermine the very regional security Iran wanted to safeguard: it complicated the process of political co-operation between the Gulf states which the United States sought to encourage, and created military conditions liable to destabilise the area in time of crisis. The destructive power of many of the highly sophisticated weapons systems being acquired, and the relatively short distances between the Gulf countries, meant that major advantage would accrue to the party launching the first strike in any conflict.[53] The general rise in arms levels in the Gulf could also affect developments in south-west and south Asia and north-east Africa.[54]

The United States thus quickly found that the scale of its military resource transfer policy was being determined by the wishes of its clients, rather than by its own assessments of the optimal conditions of stability in the Gulf.[55] In addition it was faced with the longer-term question of whether or not it would retain a community of interests with its proxies. The Arab-Israeli conflict remained an element of latent tension in relations between the United States and Saudi Arabia and during 1974 and 1975 there were differences between the United States and Iran over the question of oil prices. It was interesting therefore to note that when in 1975 the United States agreed to provide Iran with a highly advanced intelligence system capable of monitoring political and military communications throughout the Gulf and possibly beyond, a system to be operated by former American intelligence personnel, some officials at least voiced doubts over the long-term implications of the sale. They admitted that the system could theoretically be used to monitor United States military groups in Iran or elsewhere in the Gulf, and that the Iranians might some time in the future develop counterintelligence measures to prevent the United States intercepting and decoding Iranian signals. It was also admitted that the system might at some time in the future be used against Israel.[56]

Some of these problems had long-term implications for Soviet military access to the area. As of the mid 1970s this remained limited. The Soviet Union was still something of an outsider, its political footholds restricted to the political periphery of the Arabian Peninsula and the Gulf. Military access was confined to the two radical states, PDRY and Iraq, and the revolutionary movements they supported. The most important of these was PFLOAG, which at one stage was believed to have considerable destabilising potential in the Lower Gulf. Direct

Soviet aid to the movement was not extensive, and captured documents suggested that Soviet training had been found unsuitable to the conditions of guerilla warfare in the Dhofar.[57] Other aid for PFLOAG had come from China and Cuba,[58] and had been offered by East Germany.[59] In PDRY itself Cuban pilots were reported to be training and flying defensive missions for the air force, and at the end of 1975 during the final stage of the Dhofar war Soviet advisers were reportedly directing fire across the PDRY border into Oman.[60] But although Aden possessed valuable base facilities left behind by the British, and the country controlled the Straits of Bab el Mandeb, Soviet military and economic aid had initially been limited and was only stepped up after 1970.[61]

Relations between the Soviet Union and Iraq reached a high point in 1972, with the signature in April of a Treaty of Friendship and Co-operation. Politically isolated and feeling themselves encircled by American clients, the Iraqis looked to the Soviet Union for a counter-weight. To the latter the Treaty offered a framework for continuity in bilateral relations with a country which for the last fourteen years had experienced acute political instability. But such military commitments as the Treaty contained were very cautiously worded. The Treaty stated only that each side would co-ordinate its positions with the other in the case of any threat to peace.

Soviet-Iraqi relations had had a chequered history since the overthrow of the monarchy and this pattern quickly reasserted itself. The Iraqis were uneasy about becoming over-dependent on the Soviet Union and the nationalisation of the Iraqi Petroleum Company created a new sense of self-confidence which had been lacking in 1972. Among new issues of contention to emerge were Iraqi anger at the Soviet failure to consult Baghdad over the Yom Kippur War, as the Soviet Union had been bound to do by the 1972 Treaty, and the Iranian-Iraqi conflict. The Iraqis naturally looked for more wholehearted Soviet support than Moscow, anxious not to endanger its relations with Teheran, was prepared to provide, with the result that Soviet credibility and prestige in Baghdad suffered.[62] By 1975 Iraq was again turning towards the West. A potentially ominous development for Soviet military access to the Gulf was the declaration in the Iranian-Iraqi communiqué of March that the Gulf 'should remain immune from external interference'. By July Soviet displeasure at the development of Iraqi policy was demonstrated by the suspension of all arms shipments,[63] but another large arms deal was concluded in 1976.

Military resource transfer has been the main element of Soviet military policy towards Iraq. Soviet arms began arriving in Iraq shortly after the 1958 coup and after 1969 Iraq was virtually dependent on the Soviet Union for its arms supplies.[64] By 1971 some 500 Soviet military personnel were stationed in the country, servicing Soviet-built equipment and training Iraqi personnel.[65] The Treaty of Friendship and Co-operation was followed by a marked increase in the level of Soviet arms deliveries,[66] and the Kurdish campaign of 1974-5, which at one stage involved between and 70 and 80 per cent of the Iraqi army, was supported by Soviet money and arms.

The other element of Soviet military policy towards Iraq was naval visits. The first of these took place in 1968, after the announcement that British forces would be withdrawn from the Gulf. Eleven visits were recorded in 1971, fourteen in 1972 and sixteen in 1973.[67] The timing of visits was sometimes significant. Two visits in 1969, in February and June, coincided with Soviet-Iraqi negotiations over oil concessions. Soviet ships arrived at Iraqi ports three days after the signature of the Treaty of Friendship and Co-operation, in what some observers saw as a demonstration of support and reassurance for Iraq and a warning vis-à-vis the Iranians.[68] More intriguing was a visit paid by Admiral Gorchkov aboard a Soviet cruiser between 3 and 11 April 1973. This followed shortly on the Iraqi occupation of two Kuwaiti border posts and inevitably excited concern and speculation throughout the Gulf. The immediate motive for the visit remained obscure, but the Russians may have been attempting to demonstrate solidarity with their difficult ally, as well as manifesting support for border adjustments which would provide Iraq with greater economic and physical security vis-à-vis its more 'reactionary' neighbour.[69] In late 1976 a Soviet naval visit to both Iraq and Iran coincided with a conference of Gulf foreign ministers in Muscat on the subject of Gulf security.

There were other relatively minor examples of Soviet military activity in the early and mid 1970s. According to reports in 1975 Soviet intelligence-gathering vessels were maintaining a constant surveillance of the Straits of Hormuz.[70] Soviet Mig 25 reconnaissance aircraft made a number of flights over Iran,[71] and there have on several occasions in the 1970s been troop movements along the Soviet-Iranian border.[72] But there is little evidence to show what impact these minatory deployments, if such indeed they were, had on Iranian policy. In general it would seem that the desire not to offend Iran acted as an important constraint on Soviet military policy in the Gulf, and that this was a constraint second only in importance to the lack of military access in the area. Neither Iraq nor PDRY had proved very effective as local revisionist proxies.

Until the 1970s therefore, the Gulf and the Arabian Peninsula were heavily dependent on Western military support. This was a direct result of local weakness, ideological affinity and historical connections. And against a variety of threats – Soviet pressure in the case of Iran, military invasion in the case of Kuwait and several other states, and subversion throughout the area – Britain and the United States made an important, if for the most part relatively undramatic, contribution to local stability. As a result most of the local states succeeded in surviving a period of high political instability, in which there had been unprecedented pressure on conservatism throughout the Middle East, as well as various local difficulties caused by the development of oil production. Eventually however the impact of oil revenues, combined with the decline of British power, brought about important changes. The Gulf states sought, some willingly, some less so, to develop their own arrangements for the security of themselves and the area as a whole. In so doing they continued to rely on support from the outside. But what they looked for were military resources rather than military guarantees, and while it would take time for these resources, which involved military skills as much as arms, to be translated into real capabilities, over the long term it seemed as though external military access to the area would continue to decline.[73]

Notes

1. Dwight D. Eisenhower, *Waging Peace,* p.278.
2. Harold Macmillan, *Riding the Storm,* p.536. The 1961 operation was mounted without American support, although there were some naval deployments at the time.
3. Trevor Taylor, *The Supply of Arms to the Middle East and United States Policy 1950-68,* p.62.
4. For an account of Soviet pressure on Iran, see Shahram Chubin and Sepehr Zabih, *The Foreign Relations of Iran,* pp.49,57. The Americans were also concerned about the possibility of Soviet diversionary action against Iran during East-West crises both in and outside the Middle East.
5. Taylor, op.cit., p.50.
6. But the Iranians were not happy with CENTO. The alliance never developed a central command structure, nor were any forces formally allocated to it. CENTO confined itself to joint planning and exercises, co-operation on countersubversion, the development of a regional communications infrastructure and various economic development projects. While the alliance made a useful but undramatic contribution to the security of its local members, the low level of its activities and its exclusive relevance to the Soviet threat, as opposed to what proved more pressing issues for some members – Nasserist subversion in the Gulf in the case of Iran – proved an evident disappointment in the Northern

Tier. But CENTO survived, if only because it was there, and there was no obvious reason for dismantling it, and the local members came to accept, if grudgingly, the limitations of the aid they could hope to get from it. Security was a problem all along the Soviet periphery, and CENTO provided an added link with the West.

7. The Shah later described this commitment as 'not very explicit – and rather evasive'. E.A. Bayne, *Persian Kingship in Transition*, p.210.

8. The Buraimi affair involved a dispute between Saudi Arabia and Muscat and Oman. The expulsion of Saudi troops from the oasis in 1955 severely strained Anglo-Saudi relations until after the beginning of the Yemen civil war.

9. Taylor, op.cit., p.35.

10. Joseph S. Malone, *The Arab Lands of Western Asia*, p.161.

11. Whereas between fiscal years 1950 and 1972 Iran had received $833.122 million under the American Military Assistance Programme, Saudi Arabia had received only $36.111 million.

12. Dana Adams Schmidt, *Yemen – The Unknown War*, p.192.

13. Ibid., pp.193,194. The rules of engagement for the forces initially stated that the Americans would intercept aircraft violating Saudi airspace, and, if they failed to withdraw, destroy them. Weintal and Bartlett, *Facing the Brink*, pp.43, 45.

14. What however these pilots would have done if they had encountered hostile opposition was not clearly spelled out.

15. In the view of a former senior British official in South Arabia, Soviet aid to the Yemen in 1956 was of 'far greater' significance than that to Egypt. Sir Kennedy Trevaskis, 'The Arabian Peninsula and the adjacent islands' in A.J. Cottrell and R.M. Burrell (ed.), *The Indian Ocean: Its Political, Economic and Military Importance*, p.114.

16. *Middle East Record*, 1967. p.29.

17. George Lenczowski, *Soviet Advances in the Middle East*, p.148.

18. Walter Laqueur, *The Struggle for the Middle East*, p.108.

19. SIPRI, *The Arms Trade with the Third World*, p.568.

20. *Washington Post*, 4 August 1975, and *Strategic Survey*, 1976, pp.90, 129.

21. While the number of British forces involved was very small, they included a squadron of the elite Special Air Service. See *Observer*, 11 January 1976.

22. Richard Burt, 'Power and the Peacock Throne', *Round Table*, October 1975, p. 354.

23. *Financial Times*, 22 May 1975.

24. Whereas the British withdrawal from Aden was followed by the collapse of the South Arabian Federation, in the Gulf the announcement of the British withdrawal was followed by the establishment of a federation between the Trucial States.

25. The decision was part of the package of public expenditure cuts which followed the devaluation of sterling in November 1967. It had however no immediate impact on the level of public spending, and may well have been the political price paid by the Labour government to make cuts in social services acceptable to its left wing.

26. According to one estimate it would take at least seven years until the Saudis could operate their equipment effectively. *International Herald Tribune*, 19-20 July 1975.

27. In many ways, though, this was a decision taken on negative grounds. The issue was less the impact of a force which, United States officials were anxious to reassure sceptical Congressmen, in no way represented an American commitment to the countries of the area, but the fear that its

withdrawal would lead some Gulf states to believe that the United States was becoming less interested in the area.

28. 'The Persian Gulf, 1974: money, politics, arms and power', Hearings, House of Representatives, Committee on Foreign Affairs, Subcommittee on the Near East and South Asia, 1974, p.91.

29. The United States encouraged the Kuwaitis to work closely with Iran and Saudi Arabia and to acquire United States military equipment compatible to that used by these two countries, whom the Americans evidently envisaged providing military aid in case of attack. 'New perspectives on the Persian Gulf', Hearings, House of Representatives'Committee on Foreign Affairs, Subcommittee on the Near East and South Asia, 1973, p.4.

30. Ibid., pp.4, 40.

31. United States officials discouraged the Saudi Arabians from buying such sophisticated aircraft as the F4 and F14, both of which had been ordered by Iran.

32. As of the end of 1976, the United States had between 80 and 90 per cent of the Saudi market for military goods and services. The rest was largely shared by Britain and France. *Financial Times*, 21 March 1977.

33. After the Yom Kippur War, Saudi Arabia placed orders for additional naval craft. As of 1976 the US corps of engineers was designing and supervising the construction of two naval bases and a headquarters, while some 200 Saudi officers and men were being trained at a special school at the San Diego Naval Training Centre. *Financial Times*, 5 March 1976, and *International Herald Tribune*, 16 December 1976.

34. *Financial Times*, 11 December 1975. The final phase of this programme runs from 1976 to 1979.

35. *Washington Post*, 22 May 1975. In addition a Pentagon survey was reported to have recommended the build-up of the Saudi armed forces including four mechanised brigades, a tank battalion and other 'combat and service support elements', one airborne brigade, an aviation group headquarters with two assault helicopter battalions, one attack helicopter battalion, two air cavalry battalions and two assault support helicopter companies. This programme would be scheduled to last over a ten-year period. *Washington Post*, 7 November 1974.

36. *Washington Post*, 4 August 1975, and *International Herald Tribune*, 29 April 1976.

37. *International Herald Tribune*, 6 May 1976; *Financial Times*, 16 March 1977.

38. According to a Senate Foreign Relations committee report of August 1976, the Spruance class destroyers on order for the Iranian navy were more sophisticated than those being acquired for the United States, while the F14 Tomcat fighter of which the Iranians had already begun to take delivery was so complex that even the Americans were finding difficulty in keeping their own aircraft operational. *International Herald Tribune*, 6 August 1976.

39. This was reportedly a reversal of a 1968 decision by President Johnson that Iranian arms purchases should be limited to $600 million per year. A particular cause of concern in 1972 was the belief that the Shah had territorial claims in the Gulf. The decision was reportedly taken personally by Nixon and the normal process for reviewing and analysing it was consequently abrogated. *Washington Post*, 11 August 1974; *International Herald Tribune*, 6 August 1976.

40. This becomes clearly evident from a brief glance at the figures for the mid 1970s.

	Iran	Iraq	Saudi Arabia
GNP	$35.6 billion	$5.6 billion	$12 billion
Population	33.18 million	11.09 million	8.9 million
Total Armed Forces	250,000	135,000	47,000

Source, *The Military Balance, 1975-6.*

41. Richard Burt, op.cit., p.349.
42. For a more detailed description of this force see Shahram Chubin, 'Naval competition and security in south-west Asia' in *Power at Sea*, Adelphi Paper no. 124, p.24.
43. But Iran is not expected to become a major Indian Ocean power until the mid 1980s. Ibid., p.25.
44. In the early and mid 1970s Iran was the only Western-aligned state, directly on the Soviet periphery, or neighbouring a Soviet ally, significantly to increase its military budget. Soviet concern was reportedly connected with the size of the American advisory corps, the possibility that the United States might use Iran as a military proxy, and the development of the Ibex intelligence system. *Financial Times*, 23 November 1976.
45. For an account of this relationship see Jack Anderson's article, 'Whatever the Shah wants, the Shah gets' in *Washington Post*, 19 January 1975.
46. *Washington Post*, 30 January 1975.
47. According to M.G. Weinbaum the main elements of Iranian-Israeli military co-operation were exchanges in military personnel and information. Much of this interchange came under the auspices and cover of the United States military aid programmes and the Americans identified and financed programmes of mutual interest to Iran and Israel. 'Iran and Israel: the discreet enter *Orbis*, Winter 1975, p. 1076.
48. Extracts from a House of Representatives Intelligence Committee report, reported in *Sunday Times*, 15 February 1976.
49. *Washington Post*, 19 January 1975. According to another report in the edition of 21 January 1975, the Pentagon had sent a team to observe the Dhofar war several years earlier. 'The advice they brought back was that since this was a Vietnam-type of situation the United States should not get involved. Until now the United States has avoided direct involvement in the Oman fighting, preferring to encourage Iran and Jordan to help the sultan.'
50. Oman Foreign Minister, quoted in *International Herald Tribune*, 3 January 1975.
51. The 1976 Senate Foreign Relations committee report gave a figure of 24,000 Americans involved in the Iranian defence programme. Figures for Saudi Arabia are uncertain. One estimate of early 1977 put the number as high as 30,000. In June 1976 it was reported that ten Hawk SAM battalions in Saudi Arabia were being manned by American civilians, who were also expected to man another sixteen battalions on order. Charles Holley, 'US arms salesmanship to the Gulf can be costly', *Middle East*, February 1977, p.41. *International Herald Tribune*, 16 June 1976.
52. *Washington Post*, 30 January 1975.
53. Edward Kennedy, 'The Persian Gulf: arms race or arms control', *Foreign Affairs*, October 1975, p.25. Kennedy argued, following a visit to the area, that there appeared to be little local realisation of these risks.
54. N.B. the view of a Pentagon expert that the Shah's defence perimeter expands with each new generation of weaponry. *Time*, 5 November 1974.
55. Hence the title of Anderson's article. *Washington Post*, 19 January 1975.
56. *International Herald Tribune*, 2 June 1975. The United States Ambassador to Iran, Richard Helms, a former director of the CIA who had played a role in the development of Iran's basic communication-intelligence needs,

was reportedly involved in determining the requirements of the 'Ibex' system.

57. *Spectator*, 7 February 1976. In 1973 however the Soviet Union reportedly provided sea transport for PDRY forces in order to allow the PDRY to escalate its support for the rebellion in Dhofar and to enhance Soviet status in Aden. Anne M. Kelly, 'Port visits and the "internationalist mission" of the Soviet navy.'

58. *Times*, 5 April 1976.

59. *Frankfurter Allgemeine Zeitung*, 15 July 1975.

60. *Times*, 9 December 1975.

61. Mordechai Abir, *Oil, Power and Politics*, p.88.

62. Anne M. Kelly, 'The Soviet naval presence during the Iraqi-Kuwait border dispute', in McGwire, Booth and McDonnell (ed.), *Soviet Naval Policy: Objectives and Constraints*, p.297.

63. *Strategic Survey 1975*, p.86. There had been previous occasions on which arms supplies had been halted. In June 1963 *Pravda* warned that the Soviet Union would not remain indifferent if Soviet arms were used against the Kurds, and arms aid was curtailed, although the persecution of the Iraqi Communist Party by the Ba'ath may also have been a factor. Arms supplies were again reported to have been temporarily halted in early 1967 following the defection of an Iraqi-piloted Mig 21 to Israel. At the time there was also increasing tension over the Kurds. Robert Pajak, 'Soviet military aid to Iraq and Syria', *Strategic Review*, Winter 1976, p.52, and SIPRI, op.cit., p.557.

64. Robin Edmonds, *Soviet Foreign Policy 1962-73*, p.135.

65. R.D. McLaurin, *The Middle East in Soviet Policy*, p.114. In 1975 the figure was 600. *The Military Balance 1975-6*, p.9.

66. According to one report the Soviet Union had provided Iraq with more than $2 billion of arms between the beginning of 1974 and the Iranian-Iraqi agreement of March 1975. *Washington Post*, 25 April 1975.

67. 'Proposed expansion of United States military facilities in the Indian Ocean', Hearings, House of Representatives Committee on Foreign Affairs, Subcommittee on the Near East and South Asia, 1974, p.159.

68. A.J. Cottrell and R.M. Burrell, 'Soviet naval competition in the Indian Ocean', *Orbis*, Winter 1975, pp.1113, 1114.

69. For a detailed discussion of this incident, see Kelly, op.cit.

70. *International Herald Tribune*, 19-20 July 1975.

71. Mig 25s had also overflown Israeli-occupied territory from Egypt. The overflights of Iran which coincided with indications of Soviet concern over the Iranian arms build-up may well have been made by the photo-reconnaissance version of the aircraft.

72. See Chubin and Zabih on Soviet willingness to resort to minatory diplomacy vis-à-vis Iran during the 1971 Indo-Pakistani war in order to deter Iranian aid to Pakistan. Op.cit., p.84. Again in spring 1974 when Iran began to lend more support to the Kurds, the Soviet Union was reported to have made a significant display of force on the Iranian border, under the guise of regular military exercises. R.M. Burrell and A.J. Cottrell, *Iran, Afghanistan and Pakistan: Tensions and Dilemmas*, p.12.

73. N.B. The view of Sharhram Chubin that the eventual possibility of the littoral states unanimously declaring the Gulf a 'closed sea' and banning the transit of warships of non-coastal states, should not be dismissed. *Power at Sea*, op.cit., p.24.

6 THE CRISES OF CONSERVATISM IN THE EASTERN MEDITERRANEAN

The most active area of superpower military involvement in the Middle East lay not along the Soviet periphery or in the main oil-producing area of the Gulf, but in the eastern Mediterranean. It was here that the incidence of major crisis and warfare was highest and the role of the superpowers in seeking to regulate political change by military means was most dramatically and visibly evident. Egypt was by far the largest recipient of Soviet military resources and, together with Syria, the only country in the region in support of which the Soviet Union had mounted major minatory deployments. The United States also concentrated its military activity on the area, although not exclusively on the Arab-Israeli conflict. It was also deeply concerned with the maintenance of the local conservative order primarily in Jordan and the Lebanon. These were countries in which the United States had relatively little intrinsic interest, but whose survival was regarded as essential to the maintenance of regional stability.

The rationale for this American policy can be found in the spirit, if not always in the letter, of the 1957 Eisenhower Doctrine. It owed rather more to Washington's sometimes exaggerated fears about Soviet purposes in the Middle East than to any more detailed assessment of the complexities of Levantine politics or of the essentially local origins of political crises. In consequence American policy was largely reactive, being characterised by dramatic attempts to control crises rather than by any more sustained attempt to achieve the much more difficult task of working for long-term conditions of political stability. American military policy in other words consisted in large measure of crisis diplomacy, and is as much a chapter of the Cold War as of the history of the eastern Mediterranean.

This emerges clearly from the rather curious story of the Syrian crisis of 1957. Soviet-Syrian relations had begun to develop in 1955, in response to Western attempts to bring Syria into the Baghdad Pact. Two years later the Americans were beginning to betray some of the same kind of alarmist thinking about this relationship as had characterised British fears about Soviet involvement in Egypt the previous year. In Macmillan's words, they were 'talking about the most dramatic action — Suez in reverse'.[1] Indeed this is the only significant occasion where

American military influence was used to aid and abet counter-revolution, rather than to support existing governments or states. Unlike the Anglo-French Suez expedition, the Americans envisaged this as being primarily a proxy-mounted operation, in which the initiative for action lay with Syria's immediate neighbours, while the United States provided military resources and deterred others from intervening. But like Suez, the Syrian operation was envisaged as a military invasion, rather than as a coup d'état.[2]

Concern over Soviet penetration came to a head in mid-August 1957. Washington was informed that Turkey, Lebanon, Jordan and Iraq believed that military action against Syria was imperative before that country was either officially recognised as a Communist satellite or a Soviet-Syrian mutual defence treaty could be signed.[3] The plan apparently then under consideration was for an Iraqi attack, while the other three countries concentrated troops on Syria's border, and may well have involved a pre-emptive operation. Washington was asked what aid it would give. The answer, contained in a letter to the Turkish Prime Minister, Menderes, was that the United States would provide military resources. Arms shipments already committed would be expedited, and the United States promised to replace losses as quickly as possible. In addition, the United States promised to guarantee the parties against external military interference, whether from Israel, from whom assurances not to exploit the situation were immediately sought and gained, Egypt or the Soviet Union. Various minatory deployments were effected to achieve this latter purpose, of which the most important was the alerting of nuclear bombers of Strategic Air Command. In addition combat aircraft were moved from Western Europe to southern Turkey, and the Sixth Fleet was moved towards the Syrian coast.[4]

Thereafter the situation becomes obscure. A senior American official was despatched on a fact-finding tour and arms were ostentatiously airlifted to some of the potential belligerents. But it soon became evident that in spite of the various promises of American support, and the very real fears of the subversive potential of a Soviet presence in the country, Syria's neighbours were not prepared to take military action.[5] This however was not the end of the matter. As the proposed coalition disintegrated, Turkey, with clandestine American encouragement, emerged as Syria's most determined adversary.[6] Turkish forces were concentrated along the Syrian border as part of a war of nerves intended to try to unseat the Quwatly regime in Damascus,[7] and by September the crisis had developed into a Syrian-Turkish confrontation. At this

relatively late stage the Soviet Union began its own campaign of
minatory diplomacy. Moscow was concerned not only about affording
some degree of protection to the Syrian government, but also with
proving its ability to play a Great Power role in the region and countering
the impression of American firmness.[8] A series of warnings issued
between mid September and late October were backed by dramatic, if
not very convincing, minatory deployments. On 19 September 1957 a
Soviet naval squadron visited Latakia and stayed until 2 October, the
first Soviet warships to visit an Arab port. Three weeks later it was
announced that a senior Deputy Defence Minister had been appointed
to command the Trans Caucasus Military District bordering Iran and
Turkey, and the next day combined exercises including units of the
Black Sea Fleet were officially reported. Yet by the beginning of
November the crisis had petered out.

In retrospect it would seem that American fears had been
exaggerated.[9] But the fact that the Soviet-Syrian connection had not
been as close as it had appeared is perhaps less significant than American
appreciation that, given the unwillingness of its proxies to undertake
military action, Washington was without military access and would
have to accept the status quo. In February 1958 however Syria merged
with Egypt to form the United Arab Republic. This development
precipitated a series of crises in the Arab world, the impact of which was
most immediately felt in the Lebanon. The background is complex:
suffice it here to say that the emergence of the government under the
presidency of the Maronite Camille Chamoun as a strong proponent of
pro-Western alignment, had exacerbated tensions between the Christian
and Moslem communities, the latter looking towards Nasser and the
United Arab Republic.[10] A political assassination in May 1958 precipitated a situation of near civil war and the small Lebanese army lacked
the military capability and the political cohesion to act against the
rebels. After five days therefore, on 12 May, Chamoun sought
assurances from the United States, Britain and France that military
support would be forthcoming within twenty-four hours of any official
request.[11] The British and the Americans believed that there was evidence of Egyptian and Syrian involvement, and they acted swiftly to
mount a display of strength in support of the government. An airlift of
light equipment was reinforced by a display of minatory diplomacy. On
13 May it was announced that the Sixth Fleet's marine contingent was
to be doubled; on 17 May that the Americans were considering sending
troops to the Lebanon, and on 19 May that a NATO naval exercise
scheduled for the western Mediterranean would now take place in the

eastern basin. Meanwhile transport aircraft had been moved to Germany and British forces placed on readiness. But these deployments were only intended to help Chamoun calm the situation. The Americans were extremely reluctant to have to intervene on the ground. They were concerned about creating the impression of interfering in what was essentially a domestic power struggle, and they were anxious about the problems of subsequent disengagement.[12] Intervention was thus made subject to a number of conditions, one of which was that it would have to come from both the Christian President and the Moslem Prime Minister.[13]

In the event broader considerations of regional Middle Eastern politics prevailed over doubts about the viability of the military access afforded the United States by President Chamoun to the conflict between conservatism and nationalism. The Iraqi coup of 14 July 1958 resulted in an immediate Lebanese request for military intervention; the rebels in the Basta 'shrilly announced over the radio ... their day had come' and many Lebanese who had previously remained aloof began to wonder whether they had better not join them before it became too late.[14] Eisenhower's decision to meet the Lebanese request was immediate and amounted almost to a reflex action, although he was clearly aware of the risks involved and there was opposition within the Administration.[15] For all practical purposes the Chamoun regime controlled only 30 per cent of the country, and even the heart of the capital was out of government control.[16] In order therefore to avoid too deep an involvement in a potential quagmire, and against the advice of the military, the American presence was confined to the occupation of Beirut and its airfield and was not extended to the immediate hinterland.[17]

The marines began to land in Lebanon on 15 May, armed with the rather nebulous political brief of seeking to 'stabilise' the situation there.[18] But the operation was primarily an exercise in the restoration of American prestige in the whole region. Eisenhower was concerned to counter the view, which he believed particularly prevalent in Egypt, that fear of possible Soviet reaction had made the United States afraid to conduct a military policy in the Middle East.[19] Thus in addition to the landing of 15,000 American troops in Lebanon, the Western reaction to the Iraqi coup included the despatch of British troops to Jordan, the reinforcement of the British garrison in Libya, and precautionary military movements around the Arabian Peninsula.[20] As a deterrent against possible Soviet intervention, the level of alert of Strategic Air Command was again increased, and the tanker aircraft which would be required to refuel bombers on operational missions were pointedly moved into position.[21] In fact the Soviet Union had also been surprised by the Iraqi coup, and was not prepared for a showdown. Nasser and Khrushchev conferred and Soviet exercises were mounted along the Turkish-Bulgarian borders. As in 1957, these minatory deployments were a bluff and this was made quite explicit to Nasser.[22] Inevitably this meant a loss of Soviet prestige. The failure seriously to counter the Western minatory deployments undermined the reputation that the Russians had built up by their minatory diplomacy of 1956 and 1957, leaving Nasser with the lasting impression that the Sixth Fleet must be considered a key factor in all future foreign policy decisions.[23]

Viewed in terms of its regional objective then, the American minatory deployment was a success, and came to be viewed as such in Washington.[24] The impact of these events in the Lebanon itself is more difficult to determine. By the time the last American troops had been withdrawn on 25 October, only three and a half months after they had first arrived, the situation had indeed stabilised. This may have owed much to the American involvement.[25] Eisenhower was careful to follow up the military landings with the despatch of a special envoy, Robert Murphy. Murphy immediately set about trying to negotiate an agreement whereby presidential elections could be held by the end of July. In this he was helped by the Lebanese capacity for political compromise,[26] but the new president, General Chebab, who as the former commander of the armed forces had originally given the Americans an at best cautious welcome, was now in no hurry to ensure their departure.[27]

The Lebanese problem had not however been solved. In the years after the Six Day War the tensions between the two communities came to be exacerbated by a growing Palestinian presence in the country. The Americans, while still having contingency plans for intervention, and while on several occasions in 1968, 1969 and 1973 being willing to carry out minatory deployments to try to influence the situation 'onshore', recognised that they now lacked effective military access to the country. As Dr Kissinger noted during the civil war of 1975-6, such intervention would require 'a significant United States force. Our judgement is that such an intervention would unify all elements except the Christians against the United States, incur heavy casualties and lead to an open-ended commitment'.[28] The French, who had offered to provide a 5,000-strong peacekeeping force, were similarly wary of the political complications of any military involvement. Their offer was made conditional on its acceptance by all the Lebanese parties. French troops would only be introduced to consolidate a ceasefire and for a limited time period.[29]

Nevertheless both superpowers appear to have sought to exert some military influence in order to contain the situation. In early 1976, prior to the Syrian intervention, Washington had been particularly concerned about the possibility of a Syrian-Israeli clash, and a number of warnings addressed to both parties, while not backed up by any minatory deployments, would have gained weight by America's military status as a superpower.[30] The Soviet Union in early June 1976 mounted a not over-convincing exercise in minatory diplomacy through a short-lived reinforcement of the Mediterranean squadron followed by a diplomatic warning against external intervention.[31] But its primary concern appears to have been the growing conflict between the Palestinians and the Syrian interventionary forces, and there were some reports that Moscow attempted unsuccessfully, to bring about a Syrian withdrawal by manipulating its role as Syria's monopoly arms supplier.[32]

The other crises of conservatism in the eastern Mediterranean have concerned Jordan. After 1956 King Hussein pursued a strongly pro-Western policy and relied heavily on external support to help him surmount a series of internal and external crises in what was a physically insecure and politically unstable state. This came from a number of sources including Saudi Arabia, Iraq (before the 1958 coup), Israel, Britain and the United States. The Israeli role was highly ambivalent. On the one hand Jordan suffered more at the hands of the Israelis than of any other enemy, both in the sense that Jordan lost territory to Israel in 1967, and that it was the Arab-Israeli conflict which led to the internal crisis of 1970. On the other hand the Israelis, who were unwilling to tolerate a radical regime along their lengthy eastern border, implicitly defended the Hussein regime by posing a standing threat to intervene against any radical change in the status quo.

The Israeli problem also complicated the American attitude. While the Americans were willing to support the Hussein regime against internal threat and concomitant external Arab intervention, they did not normally provide a similar guarantee against Israeli incursions, and the transfer of military resources to the Jordanians was limited by considerations of the Arab-Israeli conflict. This inevitably caused strains in American-Jordanian relations, and in 1967-8 and again in 1976 Hussein threatened to turn to the Soviet Union for arms. These flirtations with Moscow however did allow Washington to argue the need for a continued American-Jordanian military resource transfer relationship to the Israelis, on the grounds that additional American arms supplies would be preferable to the political uncertainties resulting from Jordanian arms purchases from the Soviet Union. As a further testimony to the complexities of the American-Jordanian relationship, the Administration on occasion asked the Israelis to persuade Congress not to oppose American military resource transfers to Jordan.[33]

The American defence relationship with Jordan began in 1957 in the wake of the termination of the Anglo-Jordanian defence agreement. In April King Hussein became involved in a power struggle with pro-Syrian and pro-Egyptian factions.[34] The crisis began on 8 April with an apparent attempt at a coup. There followed an army mutiny, the threat of Syrian intervention and rioting which came to a head on 24 April. That day President Chamoun appealed to the United States to save the Hussein regime,[35] an appeal the King himself was unable to make for fear of undermining his internal position. Eisenhower issued a declaration of American support for Jordan's independence and territorial integrity, intended both to reassure Hussein and his conservative neighbours and to warn off interventionary powers. Israel, Syria and Egypt were advised to exercise 'caution and prudence' and avoid any action which might aggravate the situation. These warnings were given weight by a further White House announcement that the Sixth Fleet was moving into the eastern Mediterranean in readiness to act in case of an appeal for help from Jordan. Transport vessels with an 1,800-strong marine contingent aboard anchored off Beirut, while other units carried out air defence manoeuvres on the open seas.[36]

This American minatory deployment was dramatic but brief. On the night of 24-25 April Hussein had installed a new government which was outspokenly monarchist and pro-American, and which proceeded to declare martial law, occupying Amman with loyal troops and dissolving the political parties. The Sixth Fleet was recalled to the western Mediterranean a few days later. The extent of American military influence on the outcome of the crisis is difficult to assess. American action came relatively late. It may have helped to facilitate the formation of the new government on the night of 24-25 April; it may also have strengthened Hussein's hand subsequently and deterred external intervention.[37] But of more immediate consequence, in the view of one observer, was the advice and guidance of pro-Western politicians such as Samir Rifai and Sulaiman Tuquan.[38]

When in July 1958 Hussein appealed to London and Washington for help in the wake of the Iraqi coup, the Americans preferred to leave the operation to the British, promising all aid short of combat troops, most

notably logistic support.[39] The British force, although much smaller
than its American counterpart in the Lebanon, had a similarly nebulous
political role, namely to strengthen the hand of the government, and,
like its American counterpart, succeeded in disengaging itself after a
matter of months, without having become involved in any fighting.[40]
Again in 1963 when widescale rioting led to the dissolution of the
Jordanian parliament and the most serious crisis since the Palestine
war of 1948, some American, and reportedly also British, units were
put on alert.[41]

The deterioration in Arab-Israeli relations of the mid 1960s became a
threat to Israeli security even before the Six Day War. In November
1966, in retaliation against one of a number of Fedayeen raids, the
Israelis launched a major reprisal attack against Samu. This provoked
serious demonstrations against the government, and Hussein came
under pressure to allow the stationing of Syrian and Egyptian troops in
Jordan. In order to forestall the crisis to which this could lead, and also
in a move intended as a rebuke to Israel, the Americans airlifted arms to
Jordan and strengthened their forces in the eastern Mediterranean.[42]
But they did nothing effective for their clients during the Six Day War
and were slow in replacing Jordanian losses afterwards.

By the late 1960s the threat to the monarchy was again in the first
place internal. One of the effects of the Six Day War had been the
establishment of what amounted to a Palestinian state within a state in
Jordan, and a struggle between the King and the Palestinians ensued.
In June 1970 United States troops were briefly placed on alert for the
declared purpose of being ready to protect the lives of American
citizens.[43] The crisis came to a head in September, following the hijacking of three commercial airliners to Jordan. Once again the survival
of the Hussein monarchy was at stake, and with it the stability of the
eastern Mediterranean.[44] What made this crisis particularly acute was
Syrian intervention, and the ambiguous role played by the Soviet Union.
Soviet advisers were known to have accompanied Syrian tanks to the
Jordanian border and were assumed to have had some involvement in
planning the operation.[45] Washington was very much aware that it had
failed to react demonstrably to the build-up of a substantial Soviet
combat presence in Egypt over the preceding months, and that the
Russians had moved SAM missiles into the Canal Zone in contravention
of the recent Egyptian-Israeli ceasefire agreement. It therefore tended
to assume that the Soviet Union was now seeking to interfere by
proxy with an American client, and that the credibility of American
power vis-à-vis the Soviet Union in the Middle East was at stake.[46]

During the early stages of the crisis the United States had two primary objectives: to secure the lives of the airline passengers and to deter Syrian intervention. Shortly after the hijacking, the Sixth Fleet had been moved towards the Lebanese and Israeli coasts. On 16 September, the day after Jordan had been placed under martial law, when intelligence reports already indicated Syrian tanks moving towards the Jordan border, the Americans began a campaign of minatory diplomacy with an off-the-record newspaper interview in which President Nixon suggested that the United States might have to intervene if the Hussein regime were threatened by either Syria or Iraq, and that it might be useful if the Soviet Union were to believe the United States capable of irrational or unpredictable behaviour.[47] The warning had little effect, for Syrian tanks began to move into Jordan on 19 September. For the next two days Washington sought to induce the Syrians to withdraw through a heightened campaign of minatory diplomacy involving some very visible deployments. A selective military alert was ordered, including the 82nd Airborne Division in the United States[48] and airborne units in West Germany, the latter being moved to airfields in a deliberately conspicuous fashion. On 20 September the Soviet Chargé in Washington was warned that unless the Syrians withdrew, Israeli intervention was probable and American intervention possible.

By 21 September the situation in Jordan had deteriorated further, and there was still no sign of a Syrian withdrawal. King Hussein had appealed for help to Israel, Britain and the United States. Five divisions based in West Germany were put on 'full, ostentatious' alert,[49] and the Sixth Fleet was reinforced. But the time was running out for minatory diplomacy. If the Syrians could not be induced to withdraw, they would have to be coerced into doing so, but there was, in the words of a senior Pentagon official, 'good solid reluctance around here to getting involved if we don't have to'.[50] The available military capability for any intervention was in short supply. Because of Vietnam, the Sixth Fleet was short of helicopters to lift its marine contingent ashore. The initial American contingent, plus early reinforcements, would therefore have come from West Germany, where however the Seventh Army was largely mechanised and difficult to airlift.[51] The 82nd Airborne Division had sufficient men properly trained to field only one of its three brigades.[52] Allies were unco-operative and public opinion in the United States would be unlikely to welcome yet another American military involvement only five months after the United States incursion into Cambodia.

The alternative to American intervention was the use of a proxy — Israel.[53] But the Americans could not escape involvement entirely for the Israelis made their intervention conditional on a clear United States undertaking to provide an American air umbrella, against any Soviet countermoves from either the Mediterranean or Egypt. At first the Americans demurred, but as Hussein's position became increasingly critical, they agreed to come to the defence of Israel in the event of Soviet or Egyptian intervention.[54] This co-ordination of American-Israeli policy was deliberately signalled by the movement of an intelligence aircraft from a Sixth Fleet carrier to Tel Aviv for the exchange of air targeting information.[55] It was only at the very last moment that the Jordanians started to get the better of the invading Syrian forces, which then withdrew.

How far United States minatory diplomacy had contributed to these developments again remains unclear. The all-out attack launched by the Jordanians against Syrian forces on 22 September may have been encouraged by assurances of American-Israeli action, and the Syrians themselves were subject to a number of pressures generated by American minatory diplomacy. The then Minister of Defence, Assad, had all along refused to commit the Syrian Air Force in support of the armoured column, whose vulnerability to Israeli and possibly also American attack was becoming increasingly evident. Diplomatic pressure for withdrawal came from the Egyptians and, more important, from the Russians.[56] Indeed officials in Moscow were subsequently reported to have indicated to senior Western diplomats that their attempts to urge restraint on the Syrians, and also on the Iraqis, had been considerably aided by American minatory diplomacy.[57] Yet while Washington played this as a superpower confrontation, seeking to exert pressure on the Syrians primarily via the Russians, there was little evidence of Soviet minatory counterdiplomacy, as there had been in the Six Day War and was subsequently during the Yom Kippur War.[58] The only significant Soviet military moves were the reinforcement of the Mediterranean squadron,[59] but while Soviet warships intermingled with the Sixth Fleet they made no attempt to interfere with the movements of the American warships. Privately the Russians were reported to have appealed to Washington for the superpowers to keep out of Jordan, while publicly Mr Brezhnev warned that any interference in Jordanian affairs was inadmissible,[60] a warning directed at the Soviet Union's own clients, Syria and Iraq, as well as at the United States and Israel.

Both superpowers subsequently increased their forces in the area.

The Soviet Union augmented the Mediterranean squadron and sought to disguise its relatively conciliatory role during the crisis by belligerent declarations.[61] The United States despatched several additional squadrons of F4 fighter bombers to Europe, while President Nixon visited the Sixth Fleet. As an official put it at the time, 'a photo of the President standing under the guns of the Sixth Fleet should be a signal to the Soviets that the Middle East is not a secondary interest to us'.[62] Perhaps more important than this belligerent signal to Moscow was an emergency airlift of military equipment to Jordan which, together with generous American financial aid, helped King Hussein to continue his campaign to clear the country of guerillas.[63] Thereafter and in spite of the Yom Kippur War, Jordan entered a period of unprecedented political stability, and King Hussein's moderating role in the Arab ·world came to be increasingly valued in Washington. Jordanian training and intelligence officers were active in a number of the smaller countries of the Arabian Peninsula; the King was reportedly credited as having helped to bring Sultan Qaboos within the American sphere of influence and with having supplied some aid to the Kurds in Iraq.[64] Some twenty years after the inception of the Jordanian-American relationship, King Hussein was therefore not only still there, but proving himself to be a useful American proxy.

The Western powers, in particular the United States, thus played an important role in shoring up the conservative order in the eastern Mediterranean. In the face of vociferous if mostly token Soviet reaction, minatory deployments and the transfer of a relatively small quantity of military resources helped to ensure the survival of the Hussein regime in Jordan and to bring about a settlement of the 1958 Lebanese crisis. In several cases the United States depended on proxies; the British undertook the 1958 landings in Jordan, and Israel, which constituted a standing guarantee for the political integrity of the Hashemite kingdom, would have undertaken any military action in 1970. During this latter crisis American minatory diplomacy vis-à-vis Damascus was transmitted via, and to some extent reinforced by, the Soviet Union. In each case however the United States relied ultimately on the ability of the local parties to settle their own differences, whether by compromise or by rougher means, and American military policy did no more than to facilitate this process. What it did not therefore achieve was a solution to the deep-seated conflicts within the Jordanian and Lebanese political systems, problems which in the 1970s were seriously exacerbated by the emergence of the Palestinians as a serious local military and political force. Nor, as the abortive attempt of 1957 to destroy the Syrian regime showed, could the United States achieve the restoration of the conservative order once it had been displaced.

Notes

1. Harold Macmillan, *Riding the Storm*, p.280.
2. The United States had apparently however previously explored the possibility of an internally-mounted coup. Patrick Seale, *The Struggle for Syria*, pp.293-4.
3. This is based largely on Eisenhower's account contained in *Waging Peace*, pp.198-203.
4. Ibid. For details of Anglo-American co-operation during the crisis see Macmillan, op.cit., pp.277-86.
5. There were a variety of constraints. Military action would have risked the destruction of the Iraqi oil pipeline across Syria, as well as internal unrest in Iraq, Jordan and Lebanon. In addition there were rivalries between the potential proxy powers.
6. E.J. Hughes, *Ordeal of Power*, pp.253-4. Earlier in the wake of the Suez crisis the Turks had expressed their willingness to consider a preventive strike against Syria. Charles Bohlen, *Witness to History*, pp.435-6.
7. Eisenhower, op.cit., p.203.
8. For Soviet reaction see J.M. Mackintosh, *Strategy and Tactics of Soviet Foreign Policy*, pp.226-8. Also George S. Harris, 'The Soviet Union and Turkey' in Ivo J. Lederer and Wayne Vucinich (ed.), *The Soviet Union in the Middle East* which suggests that both Menderes and Khrushchev had an interest in inflating the crisis for domestic reasons; pp.40-1.
9. Seale, op.cit., p.294.
10. See chap. 10.
11. According to the then American Ambassador, Britain and France had given secret assurances in 1956 of their readiness to preserve the integrity of the Lebanon. 'The only new blank cheque which President Chamoun desired to draw was that of the United States.' Robert McClintock, *The Meaning of Limited War*, p.102. The American Ambassador reported that there was evidence of arms coming in from outside, and referred to radio attacks on Chamoun by Cairo and Damascus. The British were even more forthright. On the day the Lebanese request was received in London, Macmillan noted, 'Nasser is organising an internal campaign there against President Chamoun and his regime. This is partly communist and partly Arab Nationalist. Russian arms are being introduced from Syria, and the object is to force Lebanon to join the "Egyptian-Syrian" combination. In other words, after Austria – the Sudetenland Germans. Poland (in this case Iraq) will be the next to go.' Macmillan, op.cit., p.506.
12. Twice in June 1958 Chamoun asked for American intervention but was discouraged by the American Ambassador. Charles W. Thayer, *Diplomat*, p.76; McClintock, op.cit., p.116.
13. McClintock, op.cit., p.105.
14. Thayer, op.cit., p.79.
15. The decision was reportedly made against the advice of the National Security Council. Apart from the uncertain political situation in the Lebanon, the State Department believed that intervention would result in

the closure of the Suez Canal, the cutting of the IPC pipeline across Syria and serious disturbances in Kuwait. The military also had reservations. The air force reportedly argued that the Middle East was vulnerable to Soviet air power, and the navy was concerned about the length of its supply lines back to the United States. William Polk, *The United States and the Arab World*, p.283; William Quandt, 'United States policy in the Middle East' in Hammond and Alexander (ed.) *Political Dynamics in the Middle East;* Eisenhower, op.cit., p.271; Hughes, op.cit., p.263.

16. Robert Murphy, *Diplomat among Warriors*, p.488.
17. Eisenhower, op.cit., p.275. The dangers of the operation became acutely evident in an incident on 16 July when units of the Lebanese army came close to firing on American troops.
18. N.B. James Cable's description of the situation, 'a threat existed, all the more acute because it was formless, and the outcome seemed likely to be more favourable with the Marines than without them'. *Gunboat Diplomacy*, p.61.
19. Murphy, op.cit., p.485.
20. The exclusion of the French was largely due to American and British concern lest French policy towards Algeria should influence Arab reaction to the Western intervention unfavourably.
21. Eisenhower, op.cit., p.276.
22. See chap. 10. As during the 1957 Syrian crisis, the Soviet Union also invoked its recent advances in the missile race in general terms, but leaving much room for ambiguity by not linking this to specific contingencies. Hannes Adomeit, *Soviet Risk-Taking and Crisis Behaviour*, p.23.
23. George Dragnich, 'The Soviet Union's quest for access to naval facilities in Egypt prior to the June War of 1967' in Michael McGwire, Kenneth Booth and John McDonnell (ed.), *Soviet Naval Policy: Objectives and Constraints*, p.247.
24. Sherman Adams, *First Hand Report*, p.293. The success of the operation may have encouraged the thesis in Washington that the United States could impose stability on the Middle East with a mere show of force. Edward Weintal and Charles Bartlett, *Facing the Brink*, p.53.
25. This seems to be the general consensus of commentators, not only of those involved, see McClintock, p.121, but also of more disinterested parties. See Neville Brown, *Strategic Mobility*, p.75.
26. Polk, op.cit., p.284.
27. Murphy, op.cit., p.497.
28. *Financial Times*, 18 June 1976.
29. *Le Monde*, 24 May 1976. The French offer was first publicly made by President Giscard D'Estaing in May 1976, and repeated by the President the following month during a visit to Paris by President Assad of Syria. Military dispositions were made to facilitate intervention, but the French offer while welcomed by Rightist forces was rejected by the Leftists. The Syrians were reported to have rejected an American suggestion for a four or five nation international force to include contingents from such countries as Norway and Pakistan. *Financial Times*, 27 April 1976.
30. The Americans would appear to have at least delayed the Syrian intervention. It is also arguable that the mission in spring by the United States Special Representative Dean Brown was afforded additional weight by the presence of ships of the Sixth Fleet in the eastern Mediterranean, officially for purposes of evacuating American citizens from Beirut should this become necessary. *International Herald Tribune*. 3-4 April 1976.
31. *Guardian*, 7 June 1976; *Financial Times*, 5 and 9 June 1976.

32. In August the Soviet Union issued a warning against the continuation of an Israeli blockade of the southern Leftist-held Lebanese ports of Tyre and Sidon. *Economist,* 28 August 1976, *Financial Times* and *International Herald Tribune,* 20 April 1977.

33. Zeev Schiff, *A History of the Israeli Army,* p.260. For the impact of the Israeli factor on American arms sales to Jordan before and after the Six Day War, see SIPRI, *The Arms Trade with the Third World,* pp. 540-2. Total American military assistance and sales to Jordan up until 1972 were valued at just over $600 million, compared with nearly $2 billion to Israel over the same period. R.D. McLaurin, *The Middle East in Soviet Policy,* p.107.

34. For an account of the crisis, see Sir Charles Johnston, *The Brink of Jordan,* chaps. 9 and 10.

35. Eisenhower, op.cit., p.194.

36. Keesings Contemporary Archives. The Secretary of the Army stated on American television that the United States troops were ready to parachute into Jordan 'in a matter of days'.

37. John Marlowe, *Arab Nationalism and British Imperialism,* p.151.

38. Joseph Malone, *The Arab Lands of Western Asia,* p.123.

39. Eisenhower, op.cit., p.279. There were difficulties over flights across Israel which the Americans helped to sort out, and American aircraft from carriers in the Mediterranean flew over Jordan in a demonstration of support. *Times,* 18 July 1958.

40. This operation caused considerable anxiety in London. Macmillan noted in his diary on 1 August 1958, 'Our force is too small for any real conflict if, for instance, the Jordanian army deserts the King. Its only use is to strengthen the hand of the Government and provide an element of stability. The danger is that it might be overwhelmed.' Macmillan, op.cit., p.524.

41. *New York Times,* 3 May 1963.

42. Hussein was specifically criticised by other Arab capitals for having failed to defend Jordan properly, a failure which was partially ascribed to his close relations with the United States. Robert Stookey, *America and the Arab States,* p.202; SIPRI, op.cit., p.540.

43. *Washington Post,* 18 June 1970. For American concern over developments in Jordan during the summer of 1970, see Marvin and Bernard Kalb, *Kissinger,* p.192.

44. The Americans were also anxious about the impact of the Jordanian situation on their recent Arab-Israeli peace initiative. If Hussein lost his throne, all chances of sustaining the ceasefire along the Canal and moving politically beyond it would be lost. Robert J. Pranger, *American Policy for Peace in the Middle East, 1969-1971,* p.43-4. See also chap. 8.

45. Kalb and Kalb, op.cit., p.201.

46. Washington 'doesn't know Moscow's intentions but it does know its own credibility is involved'. *International Herald Tribune,* 23 September 1970.

47. Nixon was in fact quoted directly by the *Chicago Sun-Times.* At this stage however the Administration was not seriously contemplating intervention. Kalb and Kalb, op.cit., pp.198-9.

48. This news was deliberately leaked. There was however support within the Administration for a more diplomatic approach to the crisis. Ibid., pp. 200,202.

49. Ibid., p.204.

50. *Washington Post,* 22 September 1970.

51. David Schoenbaum, 'Jordan: the forgotten crisis', *Foreign Policy,* Spring 1973, p.177.

52.   *Washington Star and News,* 19 April 1973. There was particular reluctance in Washington over the deployment of ground troops in a country without a Mediterranean coastline. *Time,* 5 October 1970.

53.   During the crisis the United States relied heavily for intelligence on Israel and Britain. Schoenbaum, op.cit., p.174.

54.   Kalb and Kalb, op.cit., pp.205-7. Already by 21 October marked Israeli reconnaissance aircraft were flying over Syrian positions, and an Israeli armoured unit had been moved up to the northern border, close to the battle area.

55.   Ibid., p.207.

56.   Pranger, op.cit., p.47; Mohamed Heikal, *The Road to Ramadan,* p.98.

57.   *New York Times,* 26 September 1970.

58.   For the view that the Soviet Union may only have intended the Syrian tanks to move as far as the border, but then lost control of their clients, see *Guardian,* 16 October 1973. The Kalbs record the following exchange between Kissinger and the Soviet Chargé, Vorontsov, on 22 September. Kissinger: 'The last time we talked, you told me the Syrians would send no more troops.' Vorontsov: 'We didn't know the Syrians would cross the border; our own military advisers stopped at the border and went no further.' Kissinger: 'You and your clients started it and you have to end it.' Op.cit., p.207.

59.   Whetten gives the following account of superpower naval deployment during the crisis. On 18 September the United States announced the movement of Sixth Fleet elements into the eastern Mediterranean to aid American hijack victims in Jordan. Tass responded by issuing a mild warning that foreign intervention would complicate the international situation, but the Soviet squadron moved into trailing but nonprovocative positions. The United States then despatched four additional destroyers for permanent duty with the Sixth Fleet, bringing the total number of ships to fifty-five. The Soviets also added five surface vessels and five submarines, raising their total to fifty-one. Next, as a show of flexibility, the United States advanced the departure schedule for the relieving carrier and marine task group forces for the Sixth Fleet by one month, giving the fleet three carriers and two marine task groups at the time of President Nixon's visit to the Mediterranean in September.' *The Canal War,* p.428.

60.   *International Herald Tribune,* 24 September 1970.

61.   Wolfgang Berner, 'Die Arabischen Länder' in Dietrich Geyer (ed.), *Sowjetunion, Aussenpolitik 1955-1973,* p.670.

62.   American reinforcements were also a response to the possibility that the Soviet Union might entrench its position in Egypt following the sudden death of President Nasser on 28 September. *Newsweek,* 28 September 1970; *Aviation Week,* 5 and 10 October 1970.

63.   The Deputy Secretary of Defence, David Packard, claimed that the principal lesson of the crisis had been that the United States should emphasise the transfer of military resources to its friends, rather than try to police the world with American troops. He ascribed Jordan's success in defeating the Syrians without American intervention to past American military transfer policy. *Washington Star,* 25 September 1970 and *New York Times,* 26 September 1970.

64.   *International Herald Tribune,* 25 February 1977.

7 ENTANGLING COMMITMENT: THE SOVIET UNION AND THE ARAB-ISRAELI CONFLICT

Since the 1950s the superpowers have become seemingly inextricably involved in the Arab-Israeli conflict. Successive rounds of fighting have come to appear more and more as conflicts between Soviet and American proxies, with the superpowers acting in the role of armourers, protectors of last resort, and also peace negotiators. Not only have Moscow and Washington provided the bulk of their clients' military resources, they also ensured their survival in the face of vital threats, and acted in the role of attorneys, seeking intermittently and sometimes somewhat independently to bring about a settlement.

Yet while the superpowers quickly acquired responsibility, they did not achieve a degree of influence commensurate with their military involvement. They have been able to exert only limited control over the incidence of warfare and the military actions of Arabs and Israelis. Moscow and Washington, while urging and sometimes enforcing restraint on their clients, have all too often found that their own actions have been determined by demands they have been unable to resist, or events which they have been unable to forestall, and which in some cases they have unwittingly helped precipitate. Furthermore they have experienced great difficulty in manipulating the military dependence of their clients as a means of gaining political influence or of working towards a political settlement. The complaint, ascribed to a Soviet ambassador in Damascus, that the Syrians take everything from the Soviet Union except advice, could very readily have been echoed by an American ambassador in Tel Aviv.

Some of these problems have proved more acute for the Soviet Union than for the United States. The Arab-Israeli conflict was initially of tremendous value for the Soviet Union, since it allowed Moscow a political entrée into the Arab world. But the price of this entrée was a de facto alliance with countries which proved politically volatile as well as militarily impatient and incompetent, and whose maximalist objectives the Soviet Union could not afford to support. For the Arabs were not only the revisionist parties to a conflict involving an American client, a client the Soviet Union had in fact afforded early recognition to, and whose surivival the Soviet Union repeatedly declared itself in favour of, but they were also military losers. In consequence the Soviet

Union lost considerable quantities of military equipment and prestige on the Arab-Israeli battlefield and was repeatedly called upon to rescue its clients through the initiation of minatory and even operational deployments.

The sensitivity of the Arab-Israeli conflict to any form of external military intervention was evident the year after the initiation of the Soviet-Egyptian and Soviet-Syrian military resource transfer relationships in 1955. Soviet arms succeeded in spurring on, rather than in deterring, Israeli and Western attack on Egypt,[1] and had provided the Egyptians with only the most limited military capabilities by the time of Suez. Having failed to provide security for its new client through the transfer of military resources before the war, the Soviet Union did little substantive to help once the Egyptians were attacked. Czech and Soviet advisers were immediately withdrawn to the Sudan, much to the relief of the invading allies who had feared that these advisers might be used to fly Egyptian Mig 15s and Ilyushin 28 bombers, for which insufficient Egyptian pilots had been trained.[2] It took as much as a week after the Israeli attack before the Soviet Union attempted to resort to minatory diplomacy, and this remained on a purely verbal level, unsupported by any form of minatory deployment. On 5 November 1956 a vaguely-worded and unconvincing threat of possible nuclear retaliation against Britain and France was issued, while at the same time the Soviet Union proposed joint Soviet-American action to end the fighting. Once the United Nations ceasefire had been accepted, the Soviet Union threatened to send 'volunteers' to compel Britain, France and Israel to evacuate territory they had occupied.[3] But if Soviet minatory diplomacy had little effect on the course of the war, it did create uncertainty in various capitals including Washington and Jerusalem[4] and, more important from the point of view of long-term Soviet objectives, it gained the Soviet Union prestige in the Arab world.[5]

After the war the Soviet Union replaced its client's losses, and a year later the Egyptians were able to declare that their military capability had been restored and even improved.[6] Over the next decade, for much of which the Arab-Israeli conflict was effectively 'on ice', there followed a series of Soviet-Egyptian arms agreements. The most important of these was in 1963, when for the first time the Russians provided modern equipment currently deployed in the Soviet armed forces. These agreements seem to have been designed to provide the Arab confrontation states with a primarily defensive capability. Sufficient tanks and interceptors were supplied to neutralise the offensive threat of

Israeli armour and aviation, but only small quantities of contemporary ground-attack aircraft and tactical rockets, which would have enhanced Arab offensive capabilities. While the Egyptians were given strategic bombers to tie down Israeli fighters in strategic air-defence duties, they were not for example compensated for the subsequent Israeli acquisition of surface to air missiles.[7]

If, as Jon Glassman also argues, the transfer of these military resources was so structured as to give the illusion rather than the reality of over-whelming strategic superiority,[8] the ultimate effect on the Arab-Israeli conflict was in practice nevertheless highly destabilising. The illusion of military superiority helped to give the Egyptians the confidence to go to war in 1967. But the reality ensured that the Arabs would lose and lose disastrously. Little effort had been made to counter an Israeli strategy which relied heavily on the concept of pre-emptive air attack,[9] and the Arabs had received insufficient training to use the military resources they had received effectively.[10]

The Soviet Union bore a more direct political responsibility for the outbreak of the Six Day War, although again the Soviet attempt in the autumn of 1966 and spring of 1967 to manipulate their Egyptian proxies in support of their more vulnerable Syrian ally, was intended largely as an operation in deterrence and constraint. In Feburary 1966 a new and radical Ba'ath regime had come to power in Damascus, and had sought to compensate for its domestic weakness by the pursuit of a militant anti-Israeli policy. This quickly led to Israeli reprisals. Unable to restrain so unstable a regime and unwilling to become actively involved in its defence,[11] the Soviet Union looked round for alternative means of enhancing Syrian security and towards the end of the year promoted a Syrian-Egyptian defence pact. But tension on the Israeli-Syrian border continued. On 7 April 1967 the Israelis shot down six Syrian Mig 21s in an air battle which extended over Damascus, creating panic in the country and raising fears of an impending Israeli offensive.[12] The Soviet Union was forced to take new steps in support of its client.[13] These included a warning of 'serious consequences' should Israeli attacks continue, and an attempt to relieve Israeli pressure on the Syrians through the transfer of inaccurate intelligence to the Egyptians to the effect that an Israeli attack on Syria was imminent. The Egyptians recognised this for the disinformation it was,[14] but not perhaps surprisingly, given that the Russians had also reportedly promised extensive support to Egypt and Syria,[15] they interpreted it as Soviet encouragement to pursue a more actively anti-Israeli policy than had probably been intended. Not only therefore were Egyptian troops massed in Sinai, as the Russians had calculated, but Nasser went on against their expectations to demand the withdrawal of the United Nations Emergency Force and on 22 May to close the Straits of Tiran.

In trying to save the regime in Damascus, the Soviet Union had thus helped to precipitate a crisis it was no longer able to control, although military policy was intensified in the two weeks immediately preceding the war in an attempt to constrain the main protagonists. The Israelis were warned, both directly and via Washington, that the Soviet Union would come to the aid of the Arabs if they were attacked.[16] At the same time a very different message was conveyed to Egypt and Syria, the Soviet Union having reportedly told its clients that they could not count on Soviet support except in the case of direct American intervention. To signal the seriousness of its intent on this score, additional warships were deployed at the end of May into the Mediterranean where they could be used as an interpositionary tripwire force to deter action by the Sixth Fleet.[17]

Soviet minatory diplomacy however failed to prevent war. The Israelis were certainly anxious about the possibility of Soviet inter-vention, but repeated re-examinations of the Soviet threats during the Suez crisis had suggested that these had been taken too seriously at the time, and the Israeli military believed that the battle would be over by the time that Soviet forces could be effectively mobilised. At the worst, the Mediterranean squadron might be moved towards the Israeli coast, where it would probably be faced by the interpositionary presence of the Sixth Fleet.[18] Events proved this assessment to have been sub-stantially correct. Once war began, Israeli forces moved with great speed, and their success caught the Russians by surprise. On 6 June, the day after the outbreak of war, when the Arab air forces had already been destroyed on the ground, the Soviet Union made a half-hearted attempt to restore the status quo ante. It demanded Israeli acceptance of a ceasefire and withdrawal to positions occupied before the Israeli attack, otherwise, Kosygin implied in a message across the 'hotline', the Soviet Union might take action on behalf of its Arab client.[19] But the threat was not accompanied by minatory deployments and had no effect. Only on 10 June, when Israeli action against Damascus seemed imminent, did the Soviet Union resort to a more serious exercise in minatory diplomacy. Against the apparent back-ground of the alerting of Soviet airborne divisions,[20] a note was despatched direct to the Israelis warning of sanctions unless Israeli military activity ceased immediately, while another warning was conveyed to Washington on the 'hotline' to the effect that unless

Israel halted operations, the Soviet Union would take 'necessary actions, including military'.[21] This minatory deployment succeeded in inducing the United States to put pressures on the Israelis not to move against Damascus.[22] Otherwise the Soviet Union maintained a low military profile.[23] In particular it did not resupply its allies during the conflict, although Arab pilots would have been available to fly new aircraft had these been provided.[24]

The Arab defeat in the Six Day War marked a watershed in Middle Eastern politics. The defeat had been a massive one: the Arabs had lost not only vast quantities of equipment[25] but, much more important, territory – Sinai, the Golan Heights and the West Bank. The Soviet Union had been instrumental in that defeat as a result of its long-term military resource transfer policy and its prewar political manoeuvrings. During the war it had restricted its military role to the deterrence of American intervention, an unlikely development in the light of Israeli military success, and to limiting the damage suffered by one of its clients. Inevitably the Soviet Union had lost heavily in terms of prestige, both as a result of the failure of Soviet arms, and its failure to live up to local expectations that it would come to the support of the Arabs.[26] The question was now whether to try to recoup these losses and try to re-establish, and indeed further entrench, its position in the Middle East, or, in the light of the extremely poor performance of the Arab armies and the major effort that any attempt to continue its role in the Arab-Israeli conflict would be likely to involve, to cut its losses.

How seriously this latter option was considered is unclear, although it was reportedly advocated by many Soviet embassies in the Middle East.[27] It would have meant a foreign policy setback at least on the scale of the Cuban missile crisis and, perhaps a secondary consideration, it would have deprived the Soviet navy of its much-coveted bases in Egypt which, as a result of the Arab defeat, the Egyptians now conceded. But the decision to continue support of the Arabs committed the Soviet Union to the formidable task of trying to reverse the Arab defeat, which it had failed to do by its unsupported exercise in minatory diplomacy on 6 June, and to ensuring the survival of its clients in what proved to be recurrent rounds of fighting. The immediate task however was a relatively simple one, the replacement of Arab equipment. Three weeks after the end of the fighting, 130 tactical aircraft had been airlifted to the Middle East[28] and by the end of October 80 per cent of Arab losses had been replaced.[29] This resupply operation was of fundamental importance, because it meant that the Arabs did not have to make peace on the basis of the military situation produced by the war, and its impact was reflected at the Khartoum summit of September, where a policy of no concessions to the Israelis was adopted.[30]

The transfer of arms was augmented by an unprecedented transfer of military skills, in an attempt to establish an effective Arab military capability. A comprehensive retraining of the Egyptian forces was quickly instituted, initially supervised by Marshal Zakharov, a senior Deputy Defence Minister who had accompanied Podgorny to Cairo after the Egyptian defeat.[31] A Soviet military mission was established in Egypt and a large influx of Soviet advisers and instructors took place in the summer of 1967. Russian advisers and technicians were posted to every air and naval base, military training facility and major maintenance depot in the country.[32] There was at least one Russian adviser per squadron in the air force, to whom 100 Russian pilots were assigned. Their role included not only flight training, but also participation in operational training exercises.[33] Egyptian intelligence was reorganised, and in the army Russian advisers and technicians were present at battalion and sometimes company level, apparently supervising day-to-day training and field exercises. By 1969 the entire army command structure had been reorganised on Soviet lines. Russian advisers were also given some responsibility in Egyptian personnel matters, including officer assignments and promotions.[34] In Syria the war was followed by the influx of as many as 1,000 additional Soviet advisory personnel, who took over key posts in training, planning and logistics, from headquarters down to brigade level.[35]

In addition to their improved military resource transfer policy, the Soviet Union also engaged in more demonstrative forms of military support, aimed at reassuring the Egyptians and deterring further Israeli attacks. Almost exactly a month after the end of the war, twelve Soviet warships visited Alexandria and Port Said, the commander of the Soviet squadron declaring on arrival that the Russians were ready to 'co-operate with Egyptian forces to repel aggression'.[36] Soviet warships remained until October, leaving shortly before a celebrated incident when an Egyptian missile patrol boat sank the Israeli destroyer, Eilat. The Israelis retaliated by attacking the missile patrol boats in their home ports, together with the Suez oil refineries. Immediately afterwards, the Soviet ships returned and thereafter maintained a constant deterrent presence.[37] In December a squadron of Tu 16 bombers staged a week's visit to Cairo, making much-publicised flights over the city and carrying out live-bombing exercises in the desert. Another visit was paid, this time to both Syrian and Egyptian airfields in April 1968.[38]

The intensification of Soviet military involvement, while coming together with increased political penetration of both Egypt and Syria, did not however result in a commensurate increase in Soviet control over the conflict. Moscow was quickly made aware that the Syrians and Egyptians wanted a new war, and this demand was to have grave implications for Soviet policy. In late 1968 the Suez front was re-activated and in 1969 Nasser, afraid of allowing the military status quo to solidify into a political fait accompli, launched the War of Attrition. But the Egyptians were as yet in no position to fight an effective action and their air defences proved quite incapable of withstanding the weight of Israeli counterattacks. As the Egyptian position deteriorated, the Russians became more deeply involved in the actual fighting, although they confined themselves to purely defensive operations.

The Egyptians had in fact been trying for some time to get the Soviet Union to take over their air defence system, which had proved so catastrophically inadequate during the Six Day War. The first Egyptian request had been made in late June 1967, during Podgorny's visit to Cairo. Podgorny was reported to have initially agreed, but Soviet acquiescence was withdrawn the same day.[39] Vice-President Sadat later raised the matter during a visit to Moscow, but he too met with a refusal.[40] But by the autumn of 1968 Soviet 'advisers' were operating some SAM and other sites,[41] and when at the end of October the Israelis attacked Naj Hammadi north of Aswan, the Soviet ambassador in Cairo warned that the Soviet Union would be ready to defend the dam. The air defences subsequently built up around it were partially Soviet-manned.[42] The following winter the Egyptians were supplied with SAM 2s operated by Soviet troops drawn from an air defence corps stationed around Moscow.[43] But in July 1969 there was a further escalation in the conflict when the Israeli air force, in an attempt to relieve Egyptian artillery pressure on the Bar-Lev line in Sinai, began a major and highly successful offensive. In the last three months of the year it gained unchallenged air supremacy over the Canal and the approaches to the Nile valley, destroying as many as twenty-four SAM 2 batteries and sixty-seven Egyptian aircraft.[44] By January 1970 a series of deep penetration raids were beginning to threaten the survival of the government, as well as dramatically demonstrating the inadequacy of Soviet training and equipment.

A crisis was clearly at hand, and Nasser now demanded the supply of the more advanced SAM 3 missile. This however meant the provision of Soviet missile crews while Egyptian operators were being trained, as well as the deployment of interceptors. The request probably did not come as a surprise.[45] Already during the previous summer, Soviet advisers were reported to have warned that the war was unlikely to go well and that the Soviet Union was faced with the alternatives of direct combat involvement or complete withdrawal.[46] There was then particular concern about the vulnerability of the Soviet naval facilities in Egypt to Israeli air attack, but the final decision to commit Soviet forces was evidently a difficult one and provoked considerable debate within Soviet decision-making circles.[47] This would be the first time that Soviet forces had been committed in support of a non-Socialist state. Egypt was an ally of uncertain political reliability with a very poor military record. How large would the Soviet military presence have to be and how long would it last? What was the risk of a clash with Israeli aircraft? How would the United States react? How secure could an operation be if the lines of communication ran either across, or near to, NATO territory, and with an American fleet in the Mediterranean?[48]

In the event the Soviet government decided that it did have to take over control of the Egyptian defence system. The survival of Moscow's most important Middle Eastern client was at stake, and the Soviet Union had by now substantial derivatory interests in the conflict. But the Russians acted with considerable circumspection. Before any forces were sent to Egypt, a warning was addressed to Washington, contained in the unusual form of a personal note from Kosygin to Nixon. Short, non-bellicose but firm, it pointed out that the whole of Egypt now appeared defenceless against Israeli attack and that, unless the West were able to restrain the Israelis, the Soviet Union would have no option but to supply Egypt with new weapons.

The political logic of this threat should, in retrospect, have been obvious. But the Soviet warning was less explicit than that of 10 June 1967 or of Brezhnev's message prior to the 'Alert' crisis of 25 October 1973, and the Americans appear to have failed to have appreciated its implications and thus did not act to constrain their clients.[49] The first contingent of Soviet missile crews arrived in March 1970 and began installing SAM 3s around their main supply base and operational centre at Cairo West and Alexandria, as well as around the Aswan Dam.[50] The following month Soviet-piloted Mig 21Js began flying combat patrols over the Egyptian interior.

The Russians were however very anxious to avoid a clash with Israeli aircraft.[51] They were therefore quick to assure Washington that Soviet aircraft would confine their operations to Egyptian airspace,[52] and other steps were taken to ensure that in the event of an aerial confrontation, the Israelis were never in doubt about the nationality of the defending fighters.[53] As late as the end of June American intelligence reports indicated that Soviet pilots had never received orders to 'arm the weapons', even when Israeli aircraft had crossed the Canal on what appeared as potential deep penetration missions.[54] The Israelis were equally concerned to avoid a clash, so long at least that the Soviet pilots stayed outside the highly sensitive Canal Zone.[55] Within days of the beginning of Soviet aerial operations, Israeli aircraft abandoned their mission after making contact with Soviet fighters, and deep penetration raids subsequently ceased. The Russians had achieved their first success without having fired a single shot.

The effectiveness of the Soviet commitment to the defence of the general area of the Egyptian heartland greatly boosted Egyptian morale and forced the conflict back into the Canal Zone where the Egyptians began to try to reconstruct their missile sites.[56] The operation was initially conducted without Soviet participation, but the Israeli counter-attacks were so intensive that the Russians were forced to assume responsibility. Once again they acted cautiously. Contrary to some fears at the time, they did not provide air cover for the construction of the sites and instead adopted a more deliberate and less provocative approach, establishing a systematic logistics base plus adequate ground support facilities with each advance.[57] Israeli air attacks blunted but failed to halt this gradual build-up.[58]

The Israelis were in fact now slowly losing the battle. At the beginning of July the Russians succeeded in consolidating SAM defences within twenty miles of the Canal. There followed what has been described as a Soviet-Israeli conflict in which the Egyptians provided little more than 'muscle and real estate'.[59] Within a month the Israelis had lost seven aircraft and the Russians had demonstrated both the superiority of their air defence technology and the ability of a superpower to sway the battle by sheer weight of numbers.[60] By the end of the month Soviet aircraft were even beginning to operate over the Canal Zone and at this point the Israelis determined to accept the risks of combat, relying no doubt on the quality of their air force and the imminence of the American-negotiated ceasefire. On 30 July Israeli interceptors deliberately baited the Russians by feigning an attack on the Nile valley and then ambushing the Soviet fighters. The Israelis easily outmatched the inexperienced Soviet pilots and shot down five Mig 21s.[61]

The incident was significant. Not only had the Israelis evened the score for their own losses and demonstrated their determination to enter the forthcoming negotiations from a position of strength, they had also undermined the prestige of the Soviet military and underlined the risks of extending the war. Neither side publicised the incident and there were no Soviet threats of retaliation. Soviet pilots avoided contact with Israeli aircraft and the Russians sought instead to augment their much more effective ground-air defence system along the Canal. This despite the fact that it involved the breach of a standstill agreement on missile deployment in the area. The Israelis reacted by refusing to take part in the new round of negotiations which had been envisaged under the second Rogers agreement.[62]

But whatever the immediate political costs, the Russians had for the first time imposed a military stalemate. By the end of the year some 150 Soviet-piloted Mig 21Js and 75 to 85 Soviet-manned missile sites were operational.[63] A full-scale air defence district had been established under a former commander-in-chief of the Moscow air defence district and, in addition to six airfields, Soviet officers were in control of almost all the early warning and missile control systems in Egypt.[64] There were further developments in 1971. Although Soviet combat crews manning SAM sites along the west bank of the Canal were withdrawn during the spring, the advisers and technicians remained.[65] At the same time Soviet air protection of Upper Egypt was extended.[66] By May 1971, when the Treaty of Friendship and Co-operation was signed, the Russians were participating in the air defence of almost the whole country[67] and had deployed some of their most sophisticated air defence equipment.[68] They could do little more without providing offensive weapons or taking on offensive responsibilities.[69]

Hence the Soviet Union was now faced with a serious dilemma. It was deeply involved in Egypt and its military record was not unimpressive. The Soviet Union had succeeded first in deterring and then in defeating the formidable Israeli air threat. But the Egyptians tended to judge the Soviet effort more by what it had not, rather than by what it had achieved. Although Soviet resource transfers, allied to the expanding combat presence in Egypt, had seriously increased the dangers of confrontation, the Americans had refused to respond by pressurising the Israelis into making unilateral concessions. There had in fact been no significant softening in the Israeli bargaining position, let alone any withdrawal from occupied territory. The consequent Egyptian dissatisfaction, which began to become evident in early 1971, drew further strength from Soviet efforts to prevent the Egyptians taking further military initiatives themselves. The Soviet Union could not afford the risk of a renewed war while 20,000 Soviet forces were in the country, and was unwilling to face the consequences of yet another Egyptian defeat with the likelihood of further losses of Soviet equipment and prestige. It had therefore repeatedly urged and enforced restraint on its client.[70] Soviet forces had been placed in control not only of Egyptian air traffic and early warning radar but also in key posts in the army's logistics, maintenance and transport system. The Egyptians had been kept short of ammunition[71] and, according to Mohamed Heikal, Soviet advisers had not discussed operational plans with the Egyptian authorities, nor taken part in the basic studies behind these plans.[72] Most important of all, as far as the Egyptians were concerned, the Russians had refused to provide important offensive weapons such as long-range artillery, armoured personnel carriers, ground-attack aircraft and a 'deterrent' weapon.[73]

The military resource transfer relationship had generated other sources of friction. The Egyptians were not easy customers. They had an exaggerated idea of the military productive capacity of a superpower, and tended to forget that other demands were also being made of Moscow. Moreover the Egyptians' shopping list was constantly changing as the assault plan currently under consideration changed.[74] There was also serious and possibly inevitable tension between the Egyptian forces and the large number of Soviet advisers.

These frictions culminated in the expulsion of virtually all Soviet forces from Egypt. On 8 July 1972 President Sadat told the Soviet Ambassador that he wished the services of Soviet technicians

> to be terminated from 17 July. Soviet arms which were in Egypt should either be sold to Egypt and Egyptians be trained to use them or should be withdrawn . . . Any remaining Soviet forces should be placed under Egyptian command or be withdrawn. Under the terms of the Soviet-Egyptian Treaty of Friendship immediate high level consultations should be initiated. Any technicians who were in Egypt for training purposes and who came before the main body of experts arrived should stay.[75]

The Egyptians took the precaution of moving their forces into position near all Soviet facilities, as well as of controlling fuel supplies to ensure the grounding of Soviet aircraft and of denying senior Soviet officers the use of communications facilities for orders other than those dictated for transmission by the Egyptians. But the precautions proved unnecessary.[76] The Soviet Union was in no position to mount a coup or an operation on the lines of the Czechoslovakian invasion[77] and it may well be that they had anticipated trouble and were in fact quite willing to disengage.[78] In any case they left very quickly and quietly, although they withdrew more equipment and training personnel than Sadat had intended. Over the next few months they concentrated their attention on Syria, where Soviet activity had been stepped up earlier in the year. Israeli reprisal raids against Palestinian guerilla bases deep in Lebanon and Syria, raids which once again demonstrated the poor quality of Arab defences, were followed by a highly publicised airlift of air defence equipment to Syria, presumably as a demonstration of Soviet readiness to support its clients.[79] A significant increase in the number of Soviet training and advisory personnel followed.[80]

The rift with Egypt did not last long. Neither side wanted, or indeed in the Egyptian case could afford, a permanent break, and the Soviet withdrawals had in fact paved the way for re-establishing military relations on a more stable basis. The Egyptians were now free to begin serious planning for a new war – indeed Sadat was subsequently to claim that this had been one of the major reasons for the expulsion.[81] But to fight a war he needed to be assured of arms supplies, and this was something the Russians could contemplate with greater confidence now that they were no longer directly involved in Egypt.

In October 1972 therefore the Prime Minister, Aziz Sidky, visited Moscow;[82] in December a top-level Soviet committee was set up to review the whole question of relations with Egypt,[83] and in February 1973 relations were finally restored during a visit to Moscow by President Sadat's national security adviser, Hafez Ismail.[84] The Soviet Union now began to deliver large quantities of arms. But what is interesting is not just the quantity but also the sophistication and the type of weaponry supplied. For the first time, the Soviet Union began to provide significant quantities of strategic 'offensive' weapons.[85] These included an additional number of Tu 16 bombers armed with Kelt standoff missiles, and, much more important, a limited number of Scud surface-to-surface missiles. The Egyptians had long been calling for a 'deterrent' weapon against Israeli air attack and the provision of the Scuds, some thirty of which were sent to Egypt, where they were placed under Egyptian operational command while being partially serviced and operated by Soviet personnel,[86] was an important factor in the Egyptian decision to go to war. As well as increasing the strategic threat to Israel the Soviet Union also augmented Egypt's tactical offensive capabilities. Soviet deliveries included some 600 additional tanks, over 250 new armoured personnel carriers, anti-tank and anti-aircraft missiles.[87] Arms shipments to Syria also continued at a high level and during the summer of 1973 a complete air defence system which had been promised during a visit by President Assad to Moscow in April was established. This gave the Syrians missile coverage of airspace over Israeli-occupied territory on Golan.[88]

This major change in Soviet military resource transfer policy, coming on top of the years of intensive Soviet training received by the Egyptian and Syrian forces, and the neutralisation of the Israeli air threat through the establishment of one of the densest and most effective air defence systems in the world in Egypt, meant that a limited Arab offensive was now possible.[89] Evidently the Soviet Union had decided either in late 1972 or early 1973 that the risks in facilitating such an offensive were outweighed by the costs of having been seen to have failed to support the Arabs in their priority objective – the reversal of the 1967 defeat. Yet whether Soviet decision-makers expected war to ensue, and if so, within what time period, remains unclear.[90] Certainly the Egyptians made no attempt to disguise their belief in the desirability of a new round of hostilities against Israel, a point Ismail was reported to have emphasised during his visit to Moscow in February 1973, and the public record suggests that, while not endorsing the Egyptian plans for attack, the Russians said nothing during 1973 that might be misunderstood as a condemnation of President Sadat's plans.[91] Nevertheless President Sadat subsequently claimed that the Soviet Union continued to insist that military action should not be considered, and there is other evidence to suggest that the Soviet Union attempted to restrain the Egyptians.[92]

In any case, the military initiative now lay with the Arabs, and at the beginning of October 1973 the Soviet Union was given official indication of the impending Arab attack.[93] Although the initial Soviet response was hesitant, the Soviet Union now had little option but to support its clients. The first Soviet resupply ship left Odessa on 7 October.[94] An airlift, which initially seems to have been confined to non-combat items such as medical equipment, began on or around 10 October and gathered momentum on 12 October, by which time Syrian forces were already under heavy pressure and the extraordinary scale of Arab losses was becoming evident. In all some 15,000 tons of equipment was delivered in 930 missions which stretched over a period of forty days[95] and very much more equipment came by sea, 80,000 tons according to one report.[96] Neither of these operations, it should be noted, was risk-free. The Israelis attacked ports and airfields being used by Soviet ships and aircraft. While they were careful not to attack the ships and aircraft themselves, on occasion Israeli fighters flew alongside Soviet transports as they were making their landing approaches.[97] One ship and one plane were hit as a result of bombing. Other aircraft had to turn away, because they were unable to land at the damaged airfields.[98] In response the Soviet navy was placed off Latakia harbour and SAM sites under exclusive Soviet operation and control were established at Latakia and Damascus, presumably to protect the resupply operation.[99] This presence had its effect, for the Israeli navy was subsequently ordered to avoid attacks on Latakia and Tartus.[100]

Elsewhere in Syria, Soviet personnel played a less obtrusive role. They supervised the firing of Syrian-manned SAMs.[101] Soviet advisers were present in Syrian command posts at every echelon, from the battalion upwards, including supreme headquarters, and they also remained with Syrian ground forces in the zone of combat.[102] Elements of a Cuban brigade were held in reserve for the possible defence of Damascus[103] and North Korean pilots flew combat missions in both Syria and Egypt.[104] In Egypt Soviet forces operated and, shortly before the ceasefire came into effect on 22 October, actually fired a Scud missile against Israeli troops on the Canal[105] and there is some evidence to suggest that the Soviet Union deliberately tried to convey the impression that nuclear warheads for these missiles had been sent to the country.[106]

Soviet minatory diplomacy relied primarily on the Mediterranean squadron and on the alerting of airborne divisions. The Mediterranean squadron was reinforced to a maximum of ninety-six ships including twenty-nine surface combatants and twenty-three submarines.[107] Vessels were deployed to the principal Mediterranean choke points, the Straits of Gibraltar, the Straits of Messina and the Aegean Sea and also in close proximity to the Sixth Fleet operating in the general area south of Crete and Cyprus.[108] In addition to deterring the Sixth Fleet from moving to support action onshore, the activities of the squadron appear to have been aimed at impressing the Arabs and lending credibility to the prospect of Soviet airborne intervention.[109] This latter possibility appears to have caused concern in Washington for much of the war.[110] In the first few days, when Arab forces still appeared to have the upper hand, three Soviet airborne divisions were placed on alert and when, following the successful Israeli counterattack on the Golan Heights, the Syrians appealed for Soviet support, the Soviet ambassador in Washington indicated to Dr Kissinger on 11 October that airborne divisions were ready to go to the defence of Damascus. It was subsequently reported that part of the headquarters staff of a

Soviet division was already in Damascus.[111]

By 15 October the war had begun to turn in the Israelis' favour and on 16 October, the day Israeli forces crossed the Suez Canal, Kosygin flew to Cairo to persuade the Egyptians to accept an in situ ceasefire. Subsequent Soviet diplomacy was conducted against a background of increasing military readiness. Between 16 and 20 October the Mediterranean squadron was increased from twenty-three to twenty-nine surface combatants and a number of amphibious landing craft began to concentrate off Egypt. Three hundred Soviet military personnel arrived in Egypt to try to reconstruct the disintegrating SAM system[112] and a number of Soviet Air Force Mig 25s were also deployed.[113] On 17 or 18 October American intelligence picked up indications that Soviet airborne divisions had been placed on alert, an indication that the existing state of readiness had been heightened, or that the original alert had been restored if, as is possible, it had been cancelled after the earlier Syrian incident.[114] At the same time the Soviet Union sought to gain American co-operation in achieving a ceasefire. On Kosygin's return to Moscow, Dr Kissinger was invited for urgent consultations 'before an irrevocable decision was taken'[115] and at his first meeting with the Soviet leaders the American Secretary of State was warned that they would not allow a repetition of the events of 1967.[116]

Such a development would also have been contrary to American interests and a ceasefire agreement was duly concluded by the superpowers, who then found themselves with the problem of enforcing it on their reluctant clients. The Egyptians had already accepted, but the Syrians were planning a counterattack on 23 October, and in order to gain Syrian acquiescence the Soviet ambassador reportedly ordered a freighter out of Latakia without unloading, as well as the ending of all airlift supplies except for small arms and ammunition. He also reportedly threatened to send home Soviet technicians helping Syria repair and redeploy SAMs.[117] The Syrians gave way, but the Americans failed to persuade the Israelis from encroaching on the ceasefire and the threat posed by Israeli encirclement of the Egyptian Third Army trapped on the east bank of the Canal proved intolerable to the Soviet Union; Kosygin had provided Egypt with an undertaking that the ceasefire agreement would be guaranteed by both superpowers or, if necessary, by the Soviet Union alone.[118] On 24 October therefore the Russians conducted their most serious exercise in minatory diplomacy of the war. United States intelligence had noted, in addition to the military build-up between 16 and 20 October, that the number of airborne divisions on alert had increased to six[119] and that an airborne command post had been set up in southern Russia.[120] In parallel Soviet fighter squadrons were alerted for transfer to the Middle East.[121] It was believed that a sudden drop off in the Soviet airlift might be intended to make aircraft available for troop-carrying. Soviet demands were clearly spelled out in a note from Brezhnev to Nixon. Brezhnev demanded joint United States-Soviet action to enforce the ceasefire, adding,

> I will say it straight, that if you find it impossible to act with us in this matter, we should be faced with the necessity urgently to consider the question of taking appropriate steps unilaterally. Israel cannot be permitted to get away with the violations.[122]

The warning was dramatically retransmitted to Jerusalem via Washington, and under intense Soviet and American pressure the Third Army was saved and a major Arab defeat avoided. Thus the Yom Kippur War can be said to represent an important Soviet contribution to the reversal of the Arab defeat of 1967. In the years prior to the war, and especially in the months before October 1973, the Soviet Union had provided the military resources necessary for an Arab offensive. During the war an emergency resupply operation was mounted, without which it has been estimated that Egypt would have been able to fight for only five days, Syria not even for that long.[123] Once the war began to move against their clients the Soviet Union sought a ceasefire via the United States, a diplomatic operation that was supported by minatory diplomacy. Finally, when the ceasefire failed to hold, it mounted its largest ever minatory deployment in order to save the Egyptian Third Army, and continued over the next few weeks to ensure by means of both military resource transfer and minatory deployments that the Israelis should not take any further action against Soviet clients.[124]

From the Soviet viewpoint perhaps the most important result of the Yom Kippur War was the marked improvement in the climate for a political settlement. But the Russians did not want a settlement negotiated exclusively by the United States, nor can they have welcomed the rapid American-Egyptian rapprochement which accompanied Dr Kissinger's new diplomatic initiative.[125] For in spite of their easing of earlier restrictions on arms transfers and the substantial military support provided during the war, the Russians failed to recoup their political losses in Egypt. The Russian response to this situation was to cut back on arms deliveries and to refuse to reschedule Egyptian debts, the bulk of which had been incurred as a result of previous arms agreements.[126] The Egyptians in turn began to seek to diversify their source of supply, and for the first time in almost twenty years they began to buy military equipment in the West. The deterioration in Egyptian-Soviet relations reached a further stage in March 1976 when Sadat unilaterally abrogated the Treaty of Friendship and Co-operation. As in 1972, neither side however wanted, or again could afford, a complete break. The Egyptians remained very much aware that they depended on the Soviet Union for spares and also for resupply in the event of a new war. They also recognised that any attempt to re-equip their forces entirely with Western equipment would be politically difficult and dangerously time-consuming.[127] At the same time however a substantial legacy of distrust and possibly also antipathy had now been built up between the two countries, and the days when the road to any post in Egypt was said to lie through Moscow, and the Soviet ambassador had donned the garb of former British high commissioners, would seem to be permanently over.[128]

The immediate effect of this deterioration in Soviet-Egyptian relations was to bring about, as it had done previously after July 1972, a closer Soviet-Syrian military relationship. The Syrians, while opposing the Geneva peace conference after the war, were fearful of the possibility of separate Egyptian-Israeli accommodation. The signature of the first Egyptian-Israeli Disengagement Agreement in January 1974 was thus followed by the mounting of a limited war of attrition on the Golan Heights. The Syrian objective was essentially political. They sought to prevent the ceasefire lines from congealing, as they had done after the Six Day War, and, by keeping alive the risk of a new Middle East war, to ensure superpower involvement in a Syrian-Israeli peacemaking process.

This limited, although potentially dangerous, conflict which continued until the signature of the Syrian-Israeli Disengagement Agreement at the end of May 1974, received Soviet support and probably also encouragement. A communiqué issued at the end of Gromyko's visit to Damascus in early March 1974 referred to Soviet military aid for Syria and called for a fixed timetable for Israeli withdrawals from occupied territory. It specifically threatened 'a new eruption of war' that would bring about a 'threat to peace and security in the Middle East and throughout the world' unless Arab demands were met, and within a few days of Gromyko's departure the Syrians began to step up their military activity.[129] Assad visited the Soviet

Union in April 1974, where he appears to have received promises of additional arms supplies and possibly also some more specific assurances of military support in the event of an impending Syrian defeat.[130] Whatever agreements were reached, the role of Soviet military resource transfers in facilitating the Syrian action was clearly evident in the deployment of the latest artillery pieces, T 62 tanks and an impressive array of SAMs around Mount Hermon, where much of the fighting was taking place. Soviet personnel were reported to be fortifying defence lines from the front back to Damascus and operating part of the SAM system around the capital.[131]

This support may well have encouraged the Syrians to keep much closer contact with Moscow during Dr Kissinger's negotiation for a Disengagement Agreement than the Egyptians had done. But its longer-term value is more uncertain. The momentum of arms deliveries, part at least resulting from agreements signed during the Syrian war of attrition, continued for much of the year, and this arms build-up contributed to several crises along the Syrian-Israeli border. In November 1974 the Russians responded to a partial mobilisation of Israeli forces with a naval visit to Latakia, which officials in Damascus were reported to have seen as a demonstration of the Soviet pledge of the previous April.[132] But in Syria, as in Egypt, signs began to appear of a desire to move away from an exclusive reliance on the Soviet Union. These may have owed something to disagreements during 1976 over Syrian intervention in the Lebanon, but they also reflected a broader strategy on the part of President Assad who, already as Defence Minister in the late 1960s, had been critical of the Soviet connection.[133] By the beginning of 1977 Syria had also begun to make arms purchases in the West, and there was evidence of a significant reduction in the number of Soviet advisers in the country.[134]

The immediate cause of this deterioration in Soviet relations with Syria and Egypt lay in the fact that Moscow had been politically outbid by Washington. While the Russians had certainly done much to facilitate the events of October 1973, the political credit for the subsequent Israeli withdrawals went to the American Secretary of State who had conducted the extremely difficult disengagement negotiations. This was not simply because of Dr Kissinger's flamboyant style and persuasive diplomacy, nor because in 1974 and 1975, as in 1957, it was the Americans, not the Russians, who brought about Israeli withdrawals from occupied territory. The Soviet failure to reap the political dividends of its previous military policy probably owed more to the circumstances resulting from the Arab defeat of 1967, a defeat for which the Russians had been in no small measure responsible. At one stage in the late 1960s it did look as though Moscow might be able to turn this defeat to its advantage, by achieving a substantial level of political penetration of both Egypt and Syria and by bringing about a polarisation of the Arab-Israeli conflict. But the Soviet military resource transfer policy, even when allied to a substantial Soviet combat presence in Egypt, proved totally inadequate to bring about an Israeli withdrawal. The very fact of Soviet involvement discouraged the Americans from exerting real pressure on Jerusalem: on the contrary, it encouraged a closer American-Israeli relationship which meant that Soviet resource transfers to Egypt and Syria were almost invariably neutralised by American transfers to Israel, as the Americans sought to maintain a 'balance'. The Russians in fact suffered from the fact that they were both too intimately involved in and at the same time insufficiently deeply committed to the conflict. The pervasiveness of the Soviet military presence in Egypt, in particular the insensitivity of the Soviet advisory corps and those elements of the Soviet military who were pressing for an extension of Russian military facilities in the country, angered the Egyptians, as did the fact that the Russians would not provide the resources which their clients regarded as necessary for a resumption of hostilities.

Clearly then the political balance sheet as it appeared some twenty years after the inception of the Soviet-Egyptian and Soviet-Syrian military relationships showed a significant debit account. Only two major occasions stand out on which the Soviet Union gained any significant political dividends as a result of its military policy. The first of these was in the mid 1950s when the original arms deals with Egypt and Syria served to reinforce the current of anti-Western nationalism in the Arab world, as well as seriously to unnerve Western policymakers. The second was in the wake of the Six Day War, when the large-scale transfer of military resources to the defeated Arab forces resulted in the gain of military facilities in Egypt, and possibly also in Syria. Nevertheless, and this is perhaps the most important point, a combination of military resource transfers, minatory diplomacy and even combat deployments had allowed the Soviet Union to become a key actor in the major conflict of the region, hence giving it the unquestioned status of a Middle Eastern power. In addition, however politically damaging their acts of military omission, the Russians did do a lot for their clients. They saw to it, in 1967, 1970 and in 1973 that no Arab defeat should be crippling, and that vital centres and pro-

Soviet regimes should survive, although they were in practice aided by the United States, which reinforced some Soviet minatory diplomacy vis-à-vis Jerusalem. And while Moscow did not succeed in reversing the Arab defeat, it did help to ensure that the Israeli victory should not consolidate into a political fait accompli. Much the most dramatic operations in this process came in the summer of 1967, with the re-supply of the shattered Arab forces after the Six Day War, and again in 1973, with the supply of offensive equipment prior to and during the Yom Kippur War. But the long-term role played by other transfers of military resources, training as well as arms, and the provisions of an effective air defence system under cover of which the Egyptian attack across the Canal was launched three years later, should not be overlooked.

Notes

1. Jon D. Glassman, *Arms for the Arabs*, p.21.
2. Moshe Dayan, *Story of My Life*, pp. 160, 163.
3. The possibility of sending 'volunteers' had been suggested at a much earlier stage in the crisis during a conversation between Khrushchev and the French ambassador in Moscow. According to one account the Israelis received reports that preparations to send Soviet 'volunteers' were under way. Charles Bohlen, *Witness to History*, pp.433, 434; Michael Bar-Zohar, *The Armed Prophet*, p.247.
4. The Israelis sought French advice over the Soviet threat but while the French offered to share all their resources with Israel, they pointed out that even combined, Israel and France would be unable to resist Soviet intervention. Eban ascribes the Israeli decision to withdraw from Sinai to both American and Soviet pressures. Bar-Zohar, op.cit., p.247; Shimon Peres, *David's Sling*, p.211; Abba Eban, *My Country*, p.208. See also chap. 8.
5. P.J. Vatikiotis, 'The Soviet Union and Egypt: the Nasser years', in Ivo J. Lederer and Wayne S. Vucinich (ed.), *The Soviet Union and the Middle East: The Post World War II Era*, p.126.
6. SIPRI, *The Arms Trade with the Third World*, p. 522.
7. Glassman, op.cit., p.36.
8. Ibid., p.37.
9. Ibid., pp.50, 51.
10. R.D. McLaurin, *The Middle East in Soviet Policy*, p.65.
11. Nadav Safran, *From War to War*, p.276.
12. Shimon Peres, op.cit., p.223.
13. The issue was not simply that of Syrian security but also that of Soviet prestige. 'The humiliating losses inflicted by Israel on the Syrian air force, which had been equipped with the latest Soviet interceptors, would be greeted with great anger in Moscow as virtually a direct affront to the Soviet Union.'Glassman, op.cit., p.38.
14. According to one report the Soviet Union conveyed an Israeli contingency plan for an attack on Syria to Egypt, without however indicating that this

was only a contingency plan. This was not the first time that the Soviet Union had deliberately given false information to the Egyptians that an Israeli attack on Syria was imminent. Similar information had been given in February 1960 and several times during the preceding year. Safran, op. cit., pp.277-8 and Yigal Allon, 'The Soviet involvement in the Arab-Israeli conflict' in Michael Confino and Shimon Shamir (ed.), *The USSR and the Middle East*, p.151. For Egyptian perceptions see Winston Burdett, *Encounter with the Middle East*, p.200.

15. Dayan, op.cit., pp.247, 248. See also Lyndon Baines Johnson, *The Vantage Point*, p.289.
16. Walter Laqueur, *The Road to War*, p.163.
17. Robert Stephens, *Nasser*, p.484, and Burdett, op.cit., p.307. In another incident the Israelis captured or intercepted an Egyptian command order which they interpreted to mean that the Egyptians would attack on 27 May. This information was conveyed to Washington, and from there to Moscow. Thereupon the Soviet ambassador in Cairo was instructed to wake Nasser during the night with a message from Kosygin urging Egyptian restraint. Safran, op.cit., pp. 297, 300, 301; Sir Anthony Nutting, *Nasser*, p.407.
18. Zeev Schiff, *A History of the Israeli Army*, p.159.
19. Burdett, op.cit., p.330.
20. Cited in Glassman, op.cit., p.58. According to a subsequent newspaper report there was intelligence information that a possible airborne operation might be mounted from Bulgaria. This crisis had been preceded on 9 June by a series of minatory statements by Soviet and east European countries. At the United Nations, eastern European diplomats began hinting that 'volunteers' might be sent to the Arab countries. *New York Times*, 16 July 1972, and Glassman, op.cit., pp.56-7.
21. Johnson, op.cit., p.302. The practicality of such an operation is however questionable. The chairman of the Joint Chiefs of Staff is reported to have said: 'We have nothing to fear from Soviet action. The Soviets have no large mobile units to put into action at once in the Middle Eastern war.' Glassman, op.cit. See also Jonathan Turnbull Howe, *Multicrises*, pp.106,107. Howe also argues that had the Soviet Union actually intervened, it would probably have tried to confine its move to a show of strength behind the battlelines.
22. The decision to attack Syria had caused considerable debate among Israeli decision-makers because of Syria's close connection with the Soviet Union. See also chap. 8.
23. See chap. 9.
24. It is not clear why the Soviet Union did not resupply the Arab combatants in any major way during the war. In part this may have been to avoid a possible clash with the Americans, but another factor may have been the practical difficulties of organising a massive resupply operation at short notice. Glassman, op.cit., pp.52, 53.
25. Egypt was reported to have lost about 80 per cent of its arms and military equipment. A.Y. Yodfat, 'Arms and influence in Egypt: the record of Soviet military assistance since June 1967', *New Middle East*, July 1969, p.27.
26. See chap. 10.
27. Reports differ, but it appears that large-scale resupply did not begin until 23 June, three days after a Soviet military mission had arrived in Egypt. Glassman, op.cit., p.53.
28. George Lenczowski, *Soviet Advances in the Middle East*, p.150.
29. Lawrence Whetten, *The Canal War*, p.59.

30. Whetten refers to the decision to rearm the Arabs after the Six Day War as 'one of the most decisive Great Power acts since World War II'. Ibid.

31. Mohamed Heikal describes Zakharov's presence in Egypt as a big Russian concession. *The Road to Ramadan*, p.50.

32. Robert Pajak, 'Soviet Arms and Egypt', *Survival*, July-August 1975, pp.166,167.

33. Yodfat, op.cit., p.30.

34. Pajak, op.cit., p.167.

35. Robert Pajak, 'Soviet military aid to Iraq and Syria', *Strategic Review*, Winter 1976, p.55.

36. James Cable, *Gunboat Diplomacy*, p.146.

37. It was reported that during the summer of 1969 the Soviet Union drew the attention of the Israeli government to the presence of Soviet warships on permanent station at Port Said, and to the danger to which Israel's military activity in the area was exposing them. After 1970 Soviet visits to Port Said became shorter. Among the ships which had been kept permanently at Port Said were minelayers intended to mine the Suez Canal if the Israelis should attempt a crossing. David Vital, *The Survival of Small States*, p.79, and *Christian Science Monitor*, 25 September 1972.

38. *Middle East Record*, 1967, p.26; 1968, p.37.

39. Chaim Herzog, *The War of Atonement*, pp.15, 16.

40. Ibid.

41. Yodfat, op.cit., p.30.

42. Ibid., p.32.

43. Sunday Times Insight Team, *The Yom Kippur War*, p.29.

44. Whetten, op.cit., p.84.

45. This version of events is the one given by Uri Ra'anan in 'The USSR and the Middle East: some reflections on the Soviet decision-making process', in Michael McGwire, Ken Booth and John McDonnell, *Soviet Naval Policy: Objectives and Constraints*. Ra'anan's version, while very detailed, is not footnoted, but is apparently in line with a significant body of evidence gathered by Israeli intelligence and referred to by Yigal Allon in Confino and Shamir, op.cit., p.152. It contrasts markedly with the account given by Heikal in *The Road to Ramadan*, according to which the Soviet Union initially refused Nasser's request. See pp.83-8. Nevertheless the primary issue at dispute is one of timing, and the versions are not necessarily irreconcilable.

46. Ra'anan, op.cit., pp.191-2. Ra'anan states that the plan was mentioned at a Warsaw Pact meeting in November 1969 and that thought was given at one stage to the inclusion of symbolic eastern European contingents in the Soviet force.

47. Ibid., pp.194-8. See also Ilana Dimant-Kass, 'The Soviet military and Soviet policy in the Middle East, 1970-1973', *Soviet Studies*, October 1974, p.509.

48. Ra'anan, op.cit., and Dimant-Kass, op.cit., p.513.

49. Marvin and Bernard Kalb, *Kissinger*, p.192.

50. General Peled was quoted as saying that these were the central areas of Soviet activity in Egypt; the Israelis had never bombed them and, he implied, they never would. *New York Times*, 30 March 1970.

51. See Heikal, op.cit., p.86.

52. *Times*, 7 May 1970.

53. Heikal, op.cit., p.90.

54. *International Herald Tribune*, 23 June 1970. For other evidence of Soviet constraint see Dimant-Kass, op.cit., p.511, and *New York Times*, 5 August 1970.

55. Don Horowitz, 'The Israeli concept of national security and the prospects for peace in the Middle East' in Gabriel Sheffer (ed.), *Dynamics of a Conflict*, p.239.
56. Whetten, op.cit., pp.108-9.
57. Ibid.
58. The Israelis were also making periodic probes into the presumed Soviet defensive areas in an attempt to measure Soviet combat proficiency and intentions.
59. Whetten, op.cit., p.110.
60. The Chief of the Israeli Air Staff was quoted as saying that 'if we ever have to fight the Russians we ought to do damn well at the beginning. But the trouble is, they are so many and we are so few for the long pull'. *Washington Post*, 10 August 1970.
61. Horowitz, op.cit., pp.251-2, Schiff, op.cit., p.251 and Whetten, pp.127-8.
62. Whetten, op.cit.
63. *Strategic Survey 1970*, p.47.
64. Pajak, 'Soviet Arms and Egypt', *Survival*, July-August 1975, p.170.
65. Whetten, op.cit., pp.192-3.
66. Whetten cites a statement issued in *Pravda* on 28 February 1971 complaining about the lack of progress towards a settlement and warning that the alternative to progress would be renewed fighting which would require continued Soviet assistance. Another explanation advanced at the time was that the Soviet action was a response to repeated hints that in the case of renewed fighting, Israel might retaliate against targets in the Nile valley. Whetten, op.cit., p.162, and *New York Times*, 18 April 1971.
67. The defence clauses of the Treaty were vaguely worded, but they were played up by the Arab media and also by Soviet military organs. *Red Star* declared that the Treaty exerted pressure on the United States and Israel 'in order to force them to comply with the Egyptian demands for withdrawal of all the Israeli forces from the occupied territories'. Dimant-Kass, op.cit., p.516.
68. Deliveries in 1971 included some of the latest Soviet electronic control and command equipment. Particularly notable were several types of secure data transmittal systems linking air-defence headquarters with radar facilities, aircraft, anti-aircraft guns and missile systems. Pajak, op.cit., p.168.
69. Whetten, op.cit., pp.166,167.
70. During 1968 Nasser's son-in-law, Hatim Sadiq, revealed that Soviet arms deliveries had been made conditional on assurances that Egypt would not risk another conflict with Israel until her forces were fully prepared. According to the Chinese, Soviet arms sales to the Arabs 'had four no's attached to them: (a) no selling of offensive weapons, (b) no permission to use the weapons sold to recover the lost territories, (c) no adequate supply of ammunition and spare parts, and (d) no delivery to the buyer of certain weapons sold (that is operation of advanced weapons would be by Soviet personnel only)'. *Middle East Review*, 1968, p.37. Glassman, op.cit., p.114.
71. According to Sadat, the Soviet Union failed to replace ammunition expended during the War of Attrition. Speech in the People's Assembly, 14 March 1976. Summary of World Broadcasts, pt.4. The Middle East and Africa, ME/5160.
72. Heikal, op.cit., p.156. Glassman states that Soviet-assisted tactical planning for cross-Canal operations began in the post-1970 period. Op.cit., p.109.

73. According to Sadat, Nasser had been promised delivery of a 'deterrent' weapon during his visit to Moscow in January 1970. Summary of World Broadcasts, op.cit. Other evidence suggests that during 1970 the Soviet Union did significantly augment Egypt's tactical offensive capabilities. Glassman, op.cit., p.109.

74. Heikal, op.cit., p.167.

75. Heikal, op.cit., pp.171, 172. At one stage the Russians proposed that they should retain an office in the Egyptian Ministry of Defence for the chief Soviet expert only, plus a staff of around eighty, to supervise questions of co-operation on training. The Egyptians refused, seeing this as an attempt to maintain a military mission under another guise. Ibid., p.175.

76. Bulloch, *The Making of a War*, pp.185-7.

77. See Oded Eran and Jerome Singer, 'The exodus from Egypt and the threat to the Kremlin leadership', *New Middle East*, November 1972, p.22.

78. According to Al Nahar, Brezhnev had told Sidky on 13 July that the Soviet Union had proposed the withdrawal of experts and advisers on four occasions. I.F. Stone, 'Where was Nixon when Sadat gave the Russians the boot?', *New York Review of Books*, 31 August 1972. See also Ra'anan, op.cit., pp.968,969, and Heikal, op.cit., p.112.

79. See Robert Freedman, *Soviet Policy towards the Middle East since 1970*, pp.93-4.

80. Glassman, op.cit., p.97. It has been claimed by a friend of Sadat that Soviet experts who had been in Egypt were transferred to Syria. 'Egypt approved this Syrian stand, in fact supported it, because the national interests required the continued existence of Soviet experts in the region.' *Al Ahram*, 31 October 1975, cited in Uri Ra'anan, 'The Soviet-Egyptian "Rift" ', *Commentary*, June 1976, pp. 31-2.

81. Sadat has variously been quoted as saying, 'I expelled the Russians to give myself complete freedom of manoeuvre' and 'I was making sure that no one could claim that what we did in the future was inspired by the Soviets'. Sunday Times Insight Team, *Insight on the Middle East War*, pp.32, 33 and interview with *Newsweek*, 25 March 1974.

82. This was followed by the resumption of the supply of spare parts for the Egyptian air force and the return of some SAM 6 missiles withdrawn in July. Glassman, op.cit., p.96.

83. Yaacov Ro'i, *The USSR and Egypt in the Wake of Sadat's 'July Decision'*, p.35.

84. Glassman, op.cit., pp.98-100.

85. The high level of sophistication of equipment had a major impact in the early stages of the war. According to Geoffrey Kemp and Robert Pfaltzgraff, 'The Soviet Union had made available to the Arabs some of its most advanced electronic warfare equipment, and its use surprised both the Israelis and the United States. The Arabs were initially able to intercept Israeli communications on an unprecedented scale, and they located and attacked very quickly the principal Israeli ground and airborne command and control centres. At the same time, the Arabs employed a range of countermeasures that, in the early hours of the war, almost totally disrupted Israeli tank communications. Similarly the Israeli Air Force initially faced formidable problems in its air-to-air and air-to-ground communications.' 'New technologies and the geo-strategic environment' in Geoffrey Kemp, Robert Pfaltzgraff and Uri Ra'anan, *The Other Arms Race*, p.143.

86. Glassman, op.cit., p.113. Previously the Soviet Union had made the supply of a 'deterrent' weapon dependent on the condition that operational

control would remain with the Russians, a condition the Egyptians rejected. Heikal, op.cit., p.118.

87. For details of weapon shipments see Glassman, op.cit., pp.112-15 and Ra'anan, op.cit., pp.33,34. Nevertheless at the outset of the war the Egyptians were short of spares, some complete weapons systems and a wide range of ammunition. Elizabeth Monroe and A.H. Farrar-Hockley, *The Arab-Israel War: October 1973,* p.32.

88. The Sunday Times Insight Team, *The Yom Kippur War,* p.72.

89. For a favourable assessment of the impact of Soviet training on Arab military performance, see Dayan, op.cit., p. 417.

90. There is no clear evidence on this score. Arnold Hottinger argues that the primary purpose of Soviet arms deliveries during 1973 was to give weight to Egyptian insistence on the need to liberate occupied territories, and that the Soviet Union appears to have envisaged this as being the result of a diplomatic rather than a military operation. Galia Golan concludes however that, while the Russians were indirectly aware of Arab plans, they were not party to them, and that there was no direct collaboration or planning for the war. In contrast Lawrence Whetten claims that the Russians accepted Egyptian plans for a limited war during Ismail's visit to Moscow in February and that several Soviet officials were kept informed about Arab war planning. Arnold Hottinger, 'The Great Powers and the Middle East' in William Griffith (ed.), *The World and the Great Power Triangles;* Galia Golan, *Yom Kippur and After,* pp.71-2; and Lawrence Whetten, *The Arab-Israeli Dispute,* pp.24-8.

91. Glassman, op.cit., pp.98-104.

92. *International Herald Tribune,* 4 April 1974. And it appears from Heikal's account that the Egyptians were concerned lest the Soviet Union should in some way stop their clients from going to war. The Egyptians would seem to have been particularly fearful lest their interests be sacrificed to Soviet-American detente. Op.cit., p.24. See also Golan and Glassman, op.cit.

93. Golan, op.cit., p.69. According to Heikal, the Soviet reply on 4 October was that 'the decision *when* to fight must be for Sadat alone to take'. Heikal, op.cit., pp.24-5, 34. (author's italics).

94. Glassman, op.cit., p.130.

95. General P.K. Carlton, cited in *Armed Forces Journal,* August 1974. At its peak up to 100 flights per day were made to Arab countries, and considerable flexibility was shown in responding to the day-by-day needs of the combatants. Pajak, op.cit., p.170, and *Armed Forces Journal,* July 1974.

96. Pajak, op.cit., p.170. Soviet deliveries to Egypt alone included some 100 fighter aircraft, nearly 200 Soviet amphibious armoured personnel carriers, over 100 artillery pieces, large numbers of SAMs and anti-tank missiles, and some 600 tanks which reportedly allowed the Egyptians to reconstitute two armoured divisions. Ibid., and Ra'anan, op.cit., p.34.

97. Glassman, op.cit., p.130.

98. Zeev Schiff, *October Earthquake,* p.167.

99. Schiff refers to the convergence of Soviet missile boats on the harbour, ibid., p.197, and Glassman to the positioning of a destroyer to provide anti-submarine protection for Soviet ships entering the harbour, op.cit., p.134.

100. Schiff, op.cit., p.197.

101. *Sunday Times,* 19 May 1974.

102. Glassman, op.cit., p.134.

103. Although the Syrians did not want to use non-Arab troops in combat. *International Herald Tribune*, 3 February 1976.
104. The North Koreans however reportedly sought to avoid aerial combat. Schiff, op.cit., p.253.
105. Glassman argues that this was probably sanctioned by 'some relatively authoritative Soviet echelon', op.cit., p.138.
106. This is suggested by two pieces of intelligence information. During the war American intelligence detected nuclear material aboard several ships passing through the Bosphorus, which subsequently called at Egyptian ports. American reconnaissance satellites also showed pictures of what some analysts believed to be nuclear warheads next to the Scud missiles. On balance however it seems unlikely that such warheads were actually sent to Egypt, although the Soviet Union may well have wished to give the impression that they had been. *Washington Post*, 21 and 22 November 1973. Glassman, op.cit., p.163, and Sunday Times Insight Team, op.cit., p.411.
107. Admiral Thomas Moorer, *United States Military Posture for Fiscal Year 1975*. The Soviet naval build-up in the Indian Ocean, where the Soviet squadron was increased from its normal size of less than six warships to a maximum of ten surface combatants and four submarines, was on a much smaller scale and, according to the head of the CIA, William Colby, was a response to the unanticipated American build-up in the area. But Soviet ships appear to have been either involved in, or at least in the vicinity of, the Egyptian blockade of the Straits of Bab el Mandeb. *SIPRI Yearbook 1975*, p.69; Congressional Record, 22 March 1975; Golan, op.cit., p.134.
108. Whetten, op.cit., p.108.
109   See Elmo R. Zumwalt, 'The lessons for NATO of recent military experience', *Atlantic Community Quarterly*, Winter 1974-5, p.459.
110. See Kalb and Kalb, op.cit., pp.470-1.
111. Schiff, op.cit., p.195. See also chap. 8.
112. Sunday Times Insight Team, op.cit., pp.370-1.
113. Schiff, op.cit., p.264.
114. Glassman, op.cit., p.161.
115. *Observer*, 28 October 1973.
116. Sunday Times Insight Team, op.cit., p.378.
117. Ibid., p.400.
118. Kalb and Kalb, op.cit., p.490.
119. Thus some 50,000 combat and 100,000 support troops were reportedly on the alert. According to press reports at the time, aircraft involved in the airlift had been diverted to the Soviet Union, close to bases where the airborne divisions were located and there were also signs of troop trains moving towards the airfields. *New York Times*, 26 October 1973, and Golan, op.cit., p.122.
120. Kalb and Kalb, op.cit., p. 488. The Soviet Union may also have feared the possibility of a 'crazy' Sharon attack on Cairo.
121. *Aviation Week*, 29 October 1973, and Schiff, op.cit., p.289. The two brigades of Scuds were now also deployed east of Cairo. Interestingly, Schiff also notes that the Soviet Union appeared to be doing little to conceal its preparations.
122. *New York Times*, 10 April 1974.
123. Glassman, op.cit., pp.130-1.
124. The main build-up of Soviet naval forces in the Mediterranean occurred after the Alert crisis and the Soviet alert was not immediately deactivated.
125. For an assessment of Soviet interest in a settlement see Golan, op.cit., pp. 129-31.

126. This became evident within a matter of months after the war. However the cutoff in arms supplies was not complete and deliveries on a limited scale continued to be made both directly from the Soviet Union and indirectly via Algeria, Eastern Europe and possibly also Syria. Some 200 Soviet military technicians continued to service the computers controlling the Egyptian SAM system. Pajak, op.cit., p.171; Ra'anan, op.cit., p.34; *Strategic Survey 1974*, p.19; *Neue Zuricher Zeitung*, 22 August 1974, and *Daily Telegraph*, 18 March 1976.
127. Ra'anan, op.cit., p.30.
128. In a radio and television address on 3 February 1977, following riots for which the authorities held the Communists responsible, Sadat said, 'There was a time in 1968, 1969 and 1970 before Abd an–nasir's death when it was openly said that the road to any post in Egypt was through Moscow. This is a fact. The Soviet Ambassador here in Egypt donned the garb of the British High Commissioner of old times and later the one-time British Ambassador Killearn and worse. How so? It is because the power centres were, before Abd an–nasir's death, in control of the Ministries of the Interior, Information and its means and all the press and culture. The Army was with them.' Survey of World Broadcasts, pt.4, The Middle East and North Africa, ME/5431.
129. Freedman, op.cit., p.139, and *Times,* 28 March 1974.
130. Golan, op.cit., pp.213-14, and *Guardian,* 17 April 1974.
131. *Times,* 29 April 1974 and *Daily Telegraph,* 18 May 1974.
132. *New York Times,* 19 November 1974.
133. In March 1969 Assad had openly accused the Soviet Union of interfering in Syrian internal affairs and of supplying obsolete and substandard arms. *Daily Telegraph,* 17 March 1969.
134. *International Herald Tribune,* 4 March 1977. The number of Soviet advisers in Syria was reported as having been substantially reduced from a peak of around 3,500 after the war to nearer 1,800.

8 ISRAELI SECURITY: THE AMERICAN DILEMMA

Seen from Washington, the problem of Israeli security has clearly separable military and political dimensions. The military dimension, Israel's ability to defend itself against Arab or Soviet attack, has presented the United States with problems of relatively manageable proportions. Israel has maintained continuous military superiority over its neighbours. It has won every round of fighting at least against the Arabs, between 1948 and 1973, and, with the possible exception of the first few days of the Yom Kippur War, neither the security of its vital centres nor its survival has ever been seriously in doubt. The Israelis have espoused the doctrine of self-help and looked to the United States primarily for the supply of military resources. American minatory deployments have only been necessary in the face of potential Soviet intervention. Operational deployments have never been required.

Yet, while a valued military proxy, Israel cannot be said to have proved a model American client. The political basis of its security problem, the search to bring about an Arab-Israeli settlement which would significantly reduce the likelihood that Israel would be subject to attack, has led to recurrent strains in American-Israeli relations. Whereas American policy has sought to persuade Israel to trade territory for political legitimacy, the Israelis, whose intense sense of insecurity has its roots deep in Jewish history, emphasised the importance of military strength and the retention of strategically defensible borders in preference to a settlement of uncertain long-term viability. To try to overcome this formidable obstacle, with its critical complications for American interests in the Arab world, Washington has tried, although with only limited success, to fashion its support for Israel's military security into an instrument for both pressure and reassurance vis-à-vis Jerusalem.

It was not however until almost two decades after the foundation of the Jewish state that its security became a priority issue in Washington. The Israelis had searched widely for political and military allies. At various stages in the 1950s they had sought to join the Commonwealth, the EEC, NATO and even the proposed European Defence Community.[1] But Israel's main defence relationship, beginning in the early 1950s and lasting until the Six Day War, was with France. Close collaboration developed in the fields of strategic planning, the exchange of intelligence and weapons research, and France became Israel's principal arms supplier.[2] Hence the United States was relieved of the embarrassing task of transferring military resources to Israel and, when in 1956 Suez for a short time forced a more active American involvement in the Arab-Israeli conflict, this followed a course which the Israelis could scarcely find satisfactory but which, with variations, was to be repeated during subsequent rounds of Arab-Israeli fighting. The United States sought to prevent Soviet intervention while at the same time containing the Israeli victory.

Even though it was recognised that any direct Soviet intervention would be extremely difficult,[3] the Administration was concerned over the possibility of some form of Soviet military reaction.[4] The American Ambassador in Moscow advised of a possible Soviet countermove against Iran, and in Washington threats to send Soviet 'volunteers' to the Middle East were treated seriously.[5] The Americans responded with a warning that any military action against Britain and France would meet with armed American opposition, and with a gradual increase in the state of readiness of American forces.[6] Naval reinforcements were despatched to the eastern Mediterranean, where the Sixth Fleet was positioned midway between Suez and Cyprus, with destroyer screens out and combat aircraft up in a demonstration of evident readiness.[7]

With the failure of its allies to act quickly enough to present the world with a fait accompli, American pressure was soon also exerted to bring about a ceasefire and then withdrawal. By 7 November 1956 the Israelis were being alternately cajoled and bullied. Cajoled by promises of greater American concern for Israeli security after a withdrawal from Sinai, and bullied by warnings that the world was on the brink of a third world war, and that the United States would acquiesce in Israel's expulsion from the UN and in the imposition of economic sanctions.[8] These pressures had their effect. Jerusalem was already concerned about Soviet threats, and the occupation of Sinai had not in itself been a priority Israeli objective in the campaign. Where the Israelis were not prepared to give way without a further struggle was over control of the Gaza strip and Sharm el Sheikh at the mouth of the Straits of Tiran. Thus the conflict continued into 1957 between a United States which was concerned over the damaging effect of Israeli intransigence on oil supplies and increasing Soviet influence in the Middle East,[9] and an Israel determined to retain what it regarded as the most important economic and military fruits of its victory. The eventual result was a compromise solution in which the French played an important role.[10] In February and March 1957 the

United States, in association with France and Britain, declared that no nation had the right to prevent free and innocent passage in the Gulf of Aqaba.[11] Given these assurances, the Israelis finally evacuated their forces from the eastern coast of Sinai.

Thereafter the Israelis were to seek closer co-operation with the United States. In October 1957 Ben Gurion proposed co-ordination of Middle Eastern policy between Israel on the one hand and the United States and NATO on the other. In addition he suggested American aid for the enlargement of Israeli ports and airfields so that Israel could serve as a base for the United States in an emergency, and that the United States should promise to go to Israel's assistance if she were to be attacked by Syria or Egypt. The Americans appear to have demurred, but after the American landings in the Lebanon in July 1958, Eisenhower assured Ben Gurion that the United States would similarly come to the aid of Israel if she were threatened and asked for help.[12]

In the early 1960s Israel received additional, although never formal, American assurances. In 1962 President Kennedy told the then Israeli Foreign Minister, Mrs Meir, that the United States and Israel were de facto allies and in 1963 Kennedy provided the Israeli Prime Minister with a written assurance of Israel's territorial integrity, amounting to a virtual guarantee. The following year Eshkol was told by Kennedy's successor that the United States would 'not be idle if Israel is attacked',[13] and Israeli leaders were repeatedly assured that in case of need they could rely on the Sixth Fleet. The United States was also beginning to supply Israel with important weapons systems, such as the Hawk surface-to-air missile and the A4 Skyhawk ground-attack fighter. Indeed by the mid 1960s the United States was coming increasingly to look upon Israel as a valued military proxy in the Middle East, and from 1965 the two countries carried out joint periodical surveys of the military situation in the region, which reportedly went beyond the routine exchange of information and came close to joint military planning.[14]

The closure of the Straits of Tiran in May 1967 faced the Americans with the problem of honouring their ten-year-old commitment to uphold free navigation.[15] But given the competing military demands of Vietnam and the hostile attitude on the part of Congress towards further American military involvements abroad, the Administration was loath to take any unilateral action. The alternative was a British proposal for an international declaration reasserting the right of free passage through the Straits of Tiran, supported if necessary by an international naval force. This plan however proved both militarily and

politically impractical. Although it was believed that the force would
not meet with Egyptian resistance, military planning in Washington
proceeded on the assumption that American forces would be operating
in an area where they might encounter Soviet opposition. This pointed
to the need for a substantial rather than a token force,[16] but there was
a shortage of ships and allies. Only Australia and the Netherlands
agreed to participate. The British, whose role Washington regarded as
politically important,[17] became increasingly reluctant to become involved. Argentina, Canada, Italy, Japan and New Zealand were willing
to take part only on condition that the operation would be under the
auspices of the United Nations, which would have left it open to Soviet
political interference.

Israeli diplomacy in the weeks prior to the war however was concerned with more than the question of whether the Americans would
take action to re-establish the status quo in the Gulf of Tiran. In
addition to an attempt to probe whether Israel could expect American
military support in the event of attack, the Israelis were anxious
to ensure that should they need to take unilateral military action, they
would not again be opposed by Washington, as they had been in 1956.[18]
They therefore took careful note of President Johnson's warning that
Israel 'will not be alone unless it decides to act alone', and presidential
messages on 23, 26 and 28 May were a major factor in postponing the
Israeli decision to go to war.[19] But the Israelis also took note of the
subsequent waning of American pressure with the failure of the proposal for the Red Sea Regatta to materialise, and the attack on 5 June
was probably launched on the basis of the assumption that the Americans
would neither interfere nor allow the Soviet Union to interfere.[20]

In fact the United States also contributed indirectly to the success
of the Israeli pre-emptive strike. It was reported that much of the
American intelligence effort in Egypt prior to the 1967 crisis had been
geared to Israeli needs.[21] Moreover since the Egyptians believed that
they would risk American intervention were they to strike first, they
rejected the idea of a pre-emptive strike, thereby allowing the Israelis
to destroy the bulk of the Arab air forces on the ground on 5 June.[22]

Thereafter American military influence was confined to the
deterrence of Soviet intervention in what Washington perceived not as
a local conflict, but as a 'stage in a process which threatened the
security of Europe and the United States in fundamental ways'.[23] The
Sixth Fleet was used to counter Soviet minatory diplomacy. On 6 June,
in response to Kosygin's demand for Israeli acceptance of a ceasefire
and withdrawal to positions occupied before the war, the Fleet was

moved closer in to the Israeli coast and another aircraft carrier was despatched to the Mediterranean.[24] The second and more important crisis occurred on 10 June following Soviet threats of intervention in the event that Israeli forces should attack Damascus. In spite of the practical difficulties in deploying Soviet military units into Syria, Soviet minatory diplomacy during the crisis had again succeeded in creating serious uncertainty in Washington about Moscow's intentions.[25] The Americans reacted by changing the cruising pattern of the Sixth Fleet. Previously ordered to remain at least 100 miles off the Syrian coast, the restriction was now reduced to 50 miles as a signal that the United States was, in Johnson's subsequent words, 'prepared to resist Soviet intrusion in the Middle East'.[26] At the same time, the Americans re-inforced the Soviet warning against further Israeli action against Syria, and this American pressure may have influenced the Israelis not to press their attack as far as Damascus.[27]

This final intervention to limit the extent of the Israeli advance not-withstanding, the Americans had done much to affect the politico-military environment in which the Israeli victory had been possible. This does not appear to have been the result of any deliberate policy. In so far as the Americans can be said to have encouraged the Israelis to go to war, they did so because of their own inability and unwillingness to intervene, although they did expect the Israelis to win easily and some elements within the Administration may not have regretted the prospect of an Egyptian and Syrian defeat.[28] But Israel's occupation of the West Bank was probably another matter, and the scale of the Arab defeat was to have far-reaching consequences for American policy. Had the Russians not mounted their subsequent resupply operation, the Israelis might have been able to trade occupied territory for an immediate peace settlement. In the event however the Israelis held on to territories which for the first time in their history provided them with strategically defensible borders. This policy was soon to exert its own price. The post Six Day War borders could only be retained at the cost of renewed hostilities, which soon resulted in direct Soviet intervention, and the Israelis therefore found themselves faced with a much more formidable military threat than they had done prior to 1967. Partly for this reason, but partly also because French arms supplies were now cut off, Israeli security became increasingly dependent on the United States.

Given the effectiveness of the Israeli forces, the United States could, at least until the Yom Kippur War, fulfil its de facto guarantee through the transfer of military resources — for the most part arms, but also military technology and intelligence.[29] American military policy sought to maintain a 'balance' in which the superior size of the Arab populations was offset by military technology, which effectively meant that the Americans maintained the predominance of Israeli air power. Israel, in the words of a senior State Department official, must be able 'to defend itself against a co-ordinated Arab attack . . . The United States is committed to an Israeli edge which will permit it to win under such an attack',[30] and, he might have continued, to win without the necessity for American intervention. But the policy of maintaining a 'balance' was also intended to prevent war. It sought to ensure that the Israelis, whom the Americans now suspected of possessing nuclear weapons,[31] would not resort to a pre-emptive attack, and to deter an Arab attack on Israel.

In practice the concept of an Israeli strategic edge proved ineffective as a stabilising factor. The Arab sense of grievance was too deep,[32] and their ability to manipulate the military resource transfer policy of their own patron was ultimately too effective, for any given military Israeli capability to deter attack in the absence of movement towards a settlement. Both the War of Attrition and the Yom Kippur War were launched in the face of very considerable odds. And by 1973, far from being able to defend themselves against co-ordinated Arab attack, shortages of ammunition and ineffective tactics in the face of highly sophisticated Soviet weaponry meant that the Israelis were quickly in serious trouble. Moreover, where the Israeli edge had made itself felt, most notably during the War of Attrition, it had helped to precipitate a development contrary to fundamental American policy objectives in the region, namely the first large-scale Soviet combat incursion into the Middle East.

The American response to this development was curiously fatalistic. For some three months after the introduction of Soviet combat crews into Egypt, there was little sign of any positive American reaction. Only when the Soviet presence had reached major proportions[33] did the Administration begin to resort to minatory diplomacy. On 26 June Dr Kissinger did say that the United States was trying 'to expel the Soviet military presence, not so much the advisers, but the combat pilots and the combat personnel before they became so firmly established'.[34] A few days later President Nixon warned that the United States would not allow the security of Israel to be endangered, and that the risks of a superpower confrontation in the Middle East were very real.[35] But American minatory diplomacy was not backed by any minatory deployments and, *pace* Dr Kissinger, the Americans failed to expel the Soviet combat forces, which remained in Egypt for another two years.

Thus, in sharp contrast to the situations on 10 June 1967 and 25 October 1973, the Americans effectively accepted a major Soviet military incursion into the Middle East. For it was one thing to counter a Soviet threat of military action intended to halt Israeli action against a Soviet client. Under such circumstances the risks of American counter-minatory deployments were limited, partly because Washington could subject the Israelis to sufficient pressure to ensure that they refrained from taking whatever military action Moscow found intolerable. But if, as in early 1970, Israeli military action continued[36] and Soviet forces were introduced gradually and quietly, Washington was faced with the much more difficult task of expelling Soviet forces in situ. Such minatory action had been mounted against Soviet nuclear forces in the Western Hemisphere in 1962, but eight years later the United States was politically unprepared and militarily ill-equipped to mount a Cuba-style exercise thousands of miles from its home base. The costs and risks were too high, while domestic opinion, which had been deeply disturbed by American action against Cambodia in April 1970 was un-likely to be favourable, and little support could be expected from the European allies.[37]

The alternative[38] was to try to depolarise and defuse the conflict through a political initiative. Great power talks on a possible settlement had been going on for much of the previous year and had reached the stage where two comprehensive treaties for Israel, Egypt and Jordan had been drafted. Although developments in the War of Attrition had caused the Soviet Union to withdraw its co-sponsorship of the treaties, the Americans had pressed on unilaterally. But they met with strong resistance from Jerusalem, since Secretary of State William Rogers' public declaration of December 1969 that a final settlement 'should not reflect the weight of conquest and should be confined to insub-stantial alterations required for mutual security' conflicted directly with Israel's territorial concept of security.[39]

The Americans reacted to this obduracy by seeking to capitalise on their de facto guarantee of Israeli security. Already by the end of 1969 Washington was stalling on some Israeli arms requests,[40] and the Soviet intervention greatly enhanced American leverage[41] and helped to give the peace initiative high priority status in Washington for much of 1970.[42] Nevertheless the exercise was not easy. Washington had good reason to be careful how it manipulated its arms transfer policy. With the Soviet air force now in Egypt, Jerusalem was sensitive to the implicit message that American military support would be dependent

on a favourable response to the American diplomatic initiative of 25
June 1970 which called for a ceasefire along the Canal and talks under the
auspices of the United Nations special mediator, Gunnar Jarring.[43]
Moreover the decision to supply the 100 A4 and 25 F4 Phantom
aircraft, for which the Israelis had been pressing, could have led to an
escalation in the fighting, and would certainly have undermined the
American peace initiative vis à vis the Arabs.[44]

At the same time however Washington remained fully aware that
they must continue to compensate for Israel's sense of insecurity. There
was the danger that otherwise the Israelis might escalate the conflict out
of sheer desperation before the balance of power appeared to move
irrevocably against them, and there were the problems of divisions
within the ruling coalition. Thus aircraft losses were quietly replaced,[45]
and electronic countermeasure equipment against Soviet SAMs was
made available.[46] And when towards the end of July 1970 the Israelis
rejected the American proposal, Washington sought to inject greater
flexibility into the Israeli position by spelling out the strongest commitment so far offered by an American Administration.[47] A presidential
note of 23 July promised additional arms and provided assurances that
the United States would maintain a balance against the Soviet military
presence in the Middle East and that American forces would remain in
the Mediterranean. The note even suggested that some kind of American-
Israeli military relationship, possibly a formal alliance, could be arranged
after the signature of a peace treaty.[48]

Given these new assurances, as well as the fact that the Administration was no longer pressing for an Israeli withdrawal, Jerusalem reluct-
antly acquiesced.[49] The ceasefire which came into effect on 8 August
1970 marked the success of an important American diplomatic initiative,
which helped to defuse the dangerous situation along the Canal,
and to contain the Soviet military incursion into Egypt.[50] By the
autumn, following the confrontation in Jordan between King Hussein
and the PLO, which had dramatically underscored Israel's value as a
regional proxy, American arms were arriving in Israel in large quantities.
But although the Israelis had by now refused to participate in the
Jarring talks, Washington had not abandoned its attempts to seek a
political settlement, and the Israelis therefore continued to be subjected
to American pressure via the manipulation of the military resource
transfer relationship. The sale of F4s was suspended in July 1971, when
the existing economic and military aid agreement expired.[51] This was
an attempt to soften the Israeli negotiating position, although the
Administration was also at the time concerned lest new sales result in

increased supply of Soviet arms to Egypt.[52] But by the end of the year
the American tactics had changed, from a stick to a carrot approach.
While the United States had previously refused to enter into long-term
commitments over arms supplies for fear that these would reduce
leverage over Jerusalem,[53] Washington now for the first time agreed on
the transfer of military technology.[54] Moreover the United States
promised more F4 and A4 aircraft as an inducement towards Israeli
acceptance of the proposed 'proximity' talks.[55]

While the Israelis accepted 'proximity' talks, the Egyptians refused
and no progress towards a political settlement was made until after the
Yom Kippur War.[56] Indeed it was not until then that the United States
was in a position to put sufficient pressure on the Israelis to bring about
any significant concessions. The 1973 war, like the 1970 Soviet incursion
into Egypt, initially placed the Americans in a difficult position and, as
in 1970, American military support for Israel was not unqualified. The
immediate problem lay in the fact that the United States found itself
on the side that did not best serve its material interests.[57] The Administration feared an oil embargo and at the outset it was also concerned
at the prospect of yet another massive Israeli victory, which could only
help to repolarise the Arab-Israeli conflict and create conditions in
which a negotiated settlement became more difficult than ever to
achieve. To try to contain these problems the Administration sought
in the first few days to adopt a low military profile. It denied Israeli
requests for large-scale arms shipments,[58] and sought to encourage a
similar Soviet restraint over arms supplies to the Arabs and to gain
Soviet co-operation in an attempt to bring about a ceasefire.[59]

Egyptian unwillingness to accept a ceasefire and the growing
momentum of the Soviet airlift however forced a reappraisal of policy
at the end of the first week. But the subsequent abandonment of the
low profile did not prevent the United States from achieving and
harmonising its basic objectives: the neutralisation of Soviet military
policy, the survival of Israel, and the limitation of any Israeli victory.
The neutralisation of Soviet military policy depended on both military
resource transfer and minatory diplomacy. The decision to launch a
major resupply operation, beginning on 14 October 1973,[60] was largely
a response to the Soviet airlift. The war had come to be seen as a conflict
between superpower proxies, and America's determination to ensure the
viability of its client was clearly signalled in the message to Congress
accompanying the Administration's 19 October request for $2.2 billion
aid for Israel, in which President Nixon stated that, while the United
States was trying to stop the war as quickly as possible, 'prudent

planning also requires us to prepare for a longer struggle'.[61]

The deterrence of direct Soviet operational deployments was primarily a function of minatory diplomacy. This was resorted to five days after the beginning of the war. In response to Soviet minatory support for Syria on 11 October, Dr Kissinger warned that the United States would not want the Soviet Union to take any irresponsible action in the Middle East, and this warning was backed by the movement of units from the Atlantic to the Sixth Fleet.[62] Again on 16 October, against the background of a rapid naval build-up in the Mediterranean, Dr Kissinger hinted that if the Russians deployed troops in the Middle East, the United States would do likewise,[63] and this message was much more dramatically articulated on 25 October, in response to the Soviet attempt to enforce the ceasefire agreement by the threat of direct intervention. The Administration ordered a worldwide alert at Def. Con 3, 'troops placed on standby and awaiting orders'.

Although the 82nd Airborne Division at Fort Bragg was alerted for possible deployment in the Middle East, an extra carrier despatched to the Mediterranean, and the Sixth Fleet moved south of Crete where it was in a position to interpose itself between Soviet amphibious vessels in the Mediterranean[64] and their possible theatre of combat, the Alert was primarily intended to trigger unusual activity and communications at American bases, activity which would instantly come to the attention of Soviet intelligence.[65] The question is in fact not why the United States believed it necessary to transmit a signal of intent to resist a Soviet military encroachment into the Middle East, but why the signal was such a strong one. Nuclear forces had not been alerted in connection with the Middle East since the Syrian and Lebanese crises of the late 1950s, which had occurred during a much more acute phase of the Cold War. On 10 June 1967, when the Soviet Union had threatened to intervene on behalf of Syria, the American counter-minatory deployment had been confined to the repositioning of the Sixth Fleet. But the Soviet involvement in the Yom Kippur War had been on a much larger scale than during 1967. Washington had been deeply concerned about the size of the Soviet resupply operation, the early alert of Soviet airborne divisions, the unprecedented presence of Soviet-operated Scud surface-to-surface missiles in Egypt[66] and the fact that the Mediterranean squadron outnumbered the Sixth Fleet.[67] Decision-makers were also very worried lest the credibility of American policy should be undermined by Watergate, which was coincidentally entering a particularly acute phase.[68]

The security of Israel vis-à-vis the Arabs was almost exclusively a

function of military resource transfer.[69] By the time the American resupply effort gained momentum, the Israeli armoury had been very
seriously depleted.[70] At its height the American airlift was flying 1,000
tons of equipment per day, of which 700-800 tons was ammunition.[71]
C5A Galaxy transports, then barely out of the experimental stage,
capable of carrying two M60 tanks together with other long-range
transport aircraft, reportedly delivered some equipment direct to the
airfields in Sinai.[72] American personnel were sent to Israel to help
with the problem of processing such a large volume.[73] In all, some
50,000 tons of military equipment was delivered during and after the
war, of which 22,395 tons was airlifted over a 32-day period.[74]

The American commitment to the survival of Israel was not however synonymous with American support for another Israeli victory.
On the contrary, the Americans, who were concerned to keep their lines
of communication open to both sides in the conflict, wanted a military
stalemate, even possibly a limited Israeli defeat.[75] This was most clearly
evident at the beginning of the war, when Washington stalled on Israeli
arms requests at a time when the Israeli forces had suffered serious
reverses, and again at the end, when the Israeli army had regained the
initiative and was operating on the west bank of the Suez Canal. But
by then Dr Kissinger had in effect become the 'ultimate quartermaster
of the Israeli army', capable of controlling its operations by modulating
the flow of supplies.[76] When the superpowers had finally reached agreement in Moscow for a ceasefire, and Mrs Meir received a personal letter
from the American President asking that Israel should cease operations,
Jerusalem realised that it had little option but to comply.

The crisis that now arose concerned the enforcement of the ceasefire. Fighting quickly broke out again along the Canal, where the Israelis
completed the encirclement of the Egyptian Third Army.[77] This situation was intolerable to Washington, not only because of the consequent
risk of superpower confrontation so dramatically reflected in the Soviet
minatory diplomacy of 24 October, but also because it threatened to
undermine the favourable negotiating conditions which the outcome of
the conflict so far had created.[78] Over the next week therefore
Jerusalem was subjected to very heavy American pressure. The immediate problem was to ensure that the Israelis did not destroy the Third
Army. Already the day after the ceasefire had theoretically come into
effect, Dr Kissinger reportedly told the Israeli Ambassador in Washington
that Israel would be unable to count on American military support if,
as a result of its actions, the war were to continue.[79] This warning
evidently failed to have its effect and the Americans used the 'Alert'

crisis as a means of reinforcing Soviet minatory diplomacy vis-à-vis Jerusalem, in order to make it quite clear to their client that further provocations would have grave implications for American interests far beyond the area of immediate hostilities.[80]

Once the ceasefire had been effectively established in the wake of the 'Alert' crisis, attention turned to the resupply of the Third Army. Jerusalem wished to make this dependent on the return of Israeli prisoners; Washington wanted the immediate opening of a supply corridor. The Americans again repeated their warning that they would not be able to support the Israelis if their hardline policy were to result in a renewal of hostilities, but the Americans now added a new ultimatum: unless Israel opened a corridor to the Third Army, the Americans themselves would supply the Egyptians. This, according to Dr Kissinger, was to pre-empt a Soviet supply operation, which would seriously weaken American prestige in the Arab world. The threat was under-lined by the diversion of transport aircraft from the Israeli airlift to European bases in preparation for an airlift to Egypt and the preparation of logistic supplies for a sustained airdrop.[81] Under intense pressure the Israelis again gave way, but they were now under more general notice that the extent of future American military aid would be dependent on their willingness to co-operate with Washington over political developments in the Middle East.[82]

This did not of course mean that the United States was about to reverse its traditional support for Israel. The Americans continued to make good Israeli losses, and immediate Israeli concern over the Egyptian blockade of the Straits of Bab el Mandeb was eased by the activities of an American task force which had been sent into the Indian Ocean shortly after the end of the war. In December an American carrier was operating in the vicinity of the mouth of the Red Sea, while its aircraft periodically circled over Egyptian and Israeli ships there.[83] It did however mean that Washington was determined to take advantage of the political conditions created by a war the outcome of which American military policy had helped to shape. The prospects for a settlement were more favourable than at any time since before the Six Day War and the Americans could now capitalise on their military relationship with Israel in order to bring about the concessions necessary for the improvement of American-Arab relations, the reduction of Soviet influence and the enhancement of Israeli political security.[84]

This process lasted nearly two years and resulted in the signature of two Egyptian-Israeli and one Syrian-Israeli Disengagement Agreements. With the ties between Moscow and Cairo substantially loosened,

Washington was less inhibited in pressurising the Israelis than it had been during the interwar period,[85] while the Israelis, who had been shocked by the revelation of the extent of their dependence on the United States during the war, were again sensitive to pressure. Dr Kissinger repeatedly emphasised the risks inherent in an exclusively territorial concept of security by implying that continued political inflexibility over the long run risked the erosion of American military support. The Israelis were warned not to manoeuvre the United States into a position of political isolation with them,[86] and his warnings were underlined by the imposition of occasional restrictions on arms deliveries.[87]

At the same time Washington once more showed itself ready to compensate for territorial concessions through the provision of additional military resources and various assurances of long-term support. By the end of 1976 the Israelis had completed their postwar emergency re-equipment programme and had obtained over $5 billion worth of arms from the United States,[88] the Americans providing between 60 and 70 per cent of the equipment of the Israeli armed forces. Not only had these been expanded since the war, but the major weaknesses exposed during October 1973 had been remedied and their qualitative superiority over the Arabs re-established.[89] These military resource transfers were in part the result of commitments entered into by the United States during Dr Kissinger's step-by-step diplomacy. By far the most comprehensive of these was contained in the memorandum of agreement accompanying the second Sinai Disengagement Agreement of September 1975.[90] Thereby Washington pledged itself to be 'fully responsive, within the limits of its resources and Congressional authorisation and appropriation, on an ongoing and long-term basis to Israel's military equipment and other defence requirements, to its energy requirements and to its economic needs'.[91] In addition the United States formally committed itself to consult with Israel if Israeli security were threatened by a 'world power',[92] agreed to conclude within two months plans for a military supply operation to Israel in the case of an emergency situation, and committed itself to station 200 American civilian personnel to man early warning systems in Sinai. These would provide information on any infringements of the agree-ment to both Israel and Egypt, as well as to the United Nations Emergency Force established after the Yom Kippur War. The military value of this commitment apart,[93] the presence, in the words of Defence Minister Shimon Peres, 'of even a symbolic group of American technicians would serve as a (deterrent) for either side'.[94]

Israeli security then was clearly to be a long-term American responsibility. It had become a priority issue for Washington only after the end
of the worst phase of the Cold War, and, perhaps ironically, the problem
had developed in part out of Israel's military strength. The Six Day War,
while it had demonstrated Israel's value as a regional proxy, had left a
highly destabilising territorial and political legacy. From the late 1960s
onwards therefore the United States was faced with an increasing and on
occasion embarrassing Israeli demand for the transfer of military
resources. The Israeli military 'edge' which the United States helped to
maintain alienated important elements in the Arab world and in 1970
precipitated a major Soviet military incursion into the Middle East, an
incursion which the United States failed effectively to counter.

These developments did not of course prevent the United States
from ensuring that the security of Israel should not be threatened by
either Arab or Soviet attack. But they clearly complicated the task of
providing for Israeli military security and led Washington to place a much
greater emphasis than Jerusalem on the political dimensions of the
problem. There thus developed a certain community of tactical interests
between the United States and the Soviet Union. This was evident not
only in the intermittent process of superpower negotiations over a
settlement, but also in an interaction between their military policies
which worked in favour of a modus vivendi. The United States was
able to constrain Soviet support for Arab offensive operations against
Israel and, acting sometimes directly and sometimes thus indirectly via
the Soviet Union, to help bring about a general realisation that the
existence of an independent Jewish state in the Middle East was an
irreversible fact. Conversely however the United States on occasion
retransmitted and reinforced Soviet minatory diplomacy vis-à-vis
Jerusalem, in order to limit the extent of Israeli military incursions
into Arab territory. It also capitalised on Soviet military support for
the Arabs, most notably in 1970 and after the Yom Kippur War, in its
attempts to induce a more flexible Israeli bargaining position.

Yet American attempts to place Israeli security on a firmer political
basis through the manipulation of military policy have met with only
limited success. Paradoxically, the United States proved most successful
in the aftermath of Suez, when American-Israeli links were relatively
weak. Moreover when the Israelis did make concessions, as in 1956 and
1957 and again between 1974 and 1975, they did so on issues which
they did not regard as being of vital importance for their security[95] and
in response to pressures which combined both the carrot and the stick.
Granted that this combination was probably the most effective means

of dealing with the inflexibility in Israeli policy induced by the deep sense of insecurity, while at the same time exploiting Israeli dependence on the United States, there remains some doubt over the skill with which American policy was executed. While Washington experienced difficulty in pressurising a valued proxy with an important political constituency in the United States, there was a strong case for applying such pressure. Jerusalem did respond to American warnings, for it was all too conscious of its international isolation.[96] As Mrs Meir remarked, 'It is difficult to say no to the Americans; who else remains to supply us with arms?'[97] Thus the question is whether the United States did not prove too reluctant to apply pressure through threatening to withhold or diminish resource transfers, and too ready to offer military assurances in order to create a greater sense of self-confidence over security, and to compensate for actual or mooted concessions. For it is clear that such resource transfers did not necessarily inject flexibility into the Israeli bargaining position,[98] and instead sometimes they helped fuel the regional arms race. But there is also a more fundamental problem. Could any quantity of externally-supplied military resources, plus even the most binding of American assurances, prove a convincing substitute to the Israelis for such tangible security assets as territory and, more ominously, for Israeli-produced and Israeli-controlled nuclear weapons?

These problems became very evident during and after the process of step-by-step diplomacy. The Americans paid heavily for their success, although the Israelis withdrew from only 10 per cent of the territories occupied in 1967, and all of the more intractable issues were carefully skirted. But once again it was evident that Jerusalem was sensitive to pressure, and something at least of any long-term success of American efforts must depend on a combination of firmness and continuity of effort, qualities which neither the American domestic political environment nor the organisation of the United States foreign policy-making machinery makes easy.

Notes

1. Shimon Peres, *David's Sling*, pp.146-8.
2. For details of Franco-Israeli military co-operation see Sylvia Kowitt Crosbie, *A Tacit Alliance: France and Israel from Suez to the Six Day War*, pp. 19-21, 104-105, 168-9, 180.
3. In the view of the Chairman of the Joint Chiefs of Staff, Admiral Redford, the only way by which the Soviet Union could intervene directly would be through long-range air strikes with nuclear weapons, a contingency judged very unlikely. Dwight Eisenhower, *Waging Peace*, p.91.

4. Eisenhower was concerned that following the Hungarian uprising the Soviet Union might be willing to undertake 'any wild adventure'. The Russians 'are scared and furious as Hitler was in his last days. There is nothing more dangerous than a dictatorship in that frame of mind'. Ibid., p.90.

5. Charles Bohlen, *Witness to History*, pp.433-4. This was partly because during the Korean war American officials had incorrectly dismissed Chinese threats to send volunteers.

6. Eisenhower proposed the recall of personnel on leave, 'an action impossible to conceal which would let the Russians know – without being provocative – that we would not be taken by surprise'. *Waging Peace*, p.91.

7. Rear-Admiral J.C. Wylie, 'The Sixth Fleet and American diplomacy' in J.C. Hurewitz (ed.), *Soviet-American Rivalry in the Middle East*, p.55,56.

8. Abba Eban, *My Country*, p.147, and David Ben Gurion, *Israel – A Personal History*, p.509.

9. Sherman Adams, *First Hand Report*, p.225.

10. For an account of the critical French role, see Crosbie, op.cit., pp.91-2. Bar-Zohar argues that one of the reasons the Israelis accepted the French proposals to solve the Gaza and Sharm el Sheikh problems was fear of offending France and hence risking a cutoff of French arms supplies. *The Armed Prophet*, p.253.

11. 'The United States', declared President Eisenhower on 20 February 1957, 'was prepared to exercise this right itself and to join with others to secure general recognition of this right.' Michael Howard and Robert Hunter, *Israel and the Arab World: The Crisis of 1967*, p.8.

12. Bar-Zohar, op.cit., p.257. Robert St John, *Eban*, p.329. Israel had already sought an American defence guarantee before Suez.

13. Cited in Robert J. Pranger and Dale Tahtinen, *Nuclear Threat in the Middle East*, p.4. Following the presidential assurance, the visiting Israeli delegation to Washington was given a briefing on the international situation including a detailed review of United States capabilities to intervene in regional conflicts, as an indication that American promises 'were backed by power'. The Americans also undertook to give 'serious consideration' to their readiness to come to Israel's aid if she were attacked. Peres, op. cit., p.106.

14. Jon Kimche, *Palestine or Israel: The Untold Story Why We Failed*, p.251.

15. The State Department was also anxious to achieve a reopening of the Straits for fear that a failure to reverse the Egyptian fait accompli would strengthen Nasser's position in the Arab world, leading to a possible Nasserist takeover in the oil states. William Quandt, 'United States policy in the Middle East' in Hammond and Alexander (ed.), *Political Dynamics in the Middle East*, p.520.

16. Eugene Rostow, *Peace in the Balance*, p.363. Among other military problems were the provision of air cover and the difficulties of undertaking operations under attack in the confined Red Sea region. Jonathan Howe, *Multicrises*, p.68.

17. Howe argues that the unusually heavy dependence on British support was as much psychological as it was military. True, the British had forces south of Suez, but there was also Congressional concern that any operation should be international rather than unilateral, and the general sensitivity about becoming the world's gendarme. The importance attached to British support declined once the Red Sea Regatta failed to materialise, but as the possibility of Soviet intervention increased during the war, the British naval presence in the Mediterranean assumed greater importance. Ibid., pp.89, 125-6.

18. Moshe Dayan, *Story of My Life*, p.263, Zeev Schiff, *A History of the Israeli Army*, p.154, and Robert St John, op.cit., p.426.

19. Lyndon Baines Johnson, *The Vantage Point*, p.293, and Michael Brecher, *Decisions in Israel's Foreign Policy*, p.322.

20. Ibid., p.421.

21. Abdul Lateef, 'America, Israel and the Arabs', *Pakistan Horizon*, vol. XXVII, no. 1, 1974, citing the then chargé d'affaires in the American Embassy in Cairo, p.23.

22. Nasser overruled military proposals for an Egyptian first strike because of the risk of bringing the United States into the war. An Israeli first strike on the other hand was calculated to keep the United States out. Theodore Draper, 'From 1967 to 1973: the Arab-Israeli Wars', *Commentary*, December 1973, p.35.

23. Eugene Rostow cited in 'The Near East conflict', House of Representatives Committee on Foreign Affairs, Subcommittee on the Near East, July 1970, p.315. cf. also Johnson, op.cit., p.288.

24. Winston Burdett, *Encounter with the Middle East*, p.330.

25. Howe, op.cit., pp.106, 107, and Johnson, op.cit., p.302.

26. Ibid.

27. *New Middle East*, June 1970, p.50. See also Dayan, op.cit., p.304. According to Johnson's account, he informed Kosygin over the 'hotline' that the Americans had been pressing the Israelis to make the ceasefire completely effective and had received assurances that this would be done. This American pressure probably defused the crisis. But it may also have been exactly what the Soviet Union had intended, and it is arguable that American action convinced the Soviet Union that such minatory diplomacy could be a highly effective instrument of military policy under similar circumstances. Johnson, op.cit., p.303, and Jon Glassman, *Arms for the Arabs*, p.58.

28. For evidence that the Israelis may have received encouragement for their move against Syria at the end of the war, see St John, op.cit., p.462.

29. The intelligence relationship was a mutually profitable one, whereby the American and the Israeli intelligence services were reported to have co-operated against Soviet and other mutual intelligence targets, and the Americans benefited from Israeli intelligence-gathering and other activities, not only in the Middle East but also in Africa. See inter alia *Christian Science Monitor*, 6 December 1973, *Guardian*, 25 February 1977, Marvin and Bernard Kalb, *Kissinger*, p.455, and Sunday Times Insight Team, *The Yom Kippur War*, pp.103, 112-13.

30. 'The military balance of power in the Middle East: an American view', *Journal of Palestine Studies*, Spring 1972, pp.5,6. Nevertheless the term 'balance' was inherently ambiguous and capable of different interpretation within the Administration. But it was of course semantically useful in American-Arab relations because of the impression of restraint in American arms supply policy which it sought to convey. Robert J. Pranger, *American Policy for Peace in the Middle East*, p.27.

31. According to a report which appeared in the *New York Times* on 18 July 1970, American policy in the Middle East had for at least two years been conducted on the assumption that Israel either had, or could quickly assemble, nuclear weapons.

32. In Dayan's words, 'Israel is only one operative move away from all the Arab capitals, less than one hundred kilometres from Cairo, Damascus, Amman and Beirut. We have no aggressive intentions. But our presence along these borders . . . is more than just a challenge to the countries around us — it virtually imperils their foundations.' Shabtoi Tereh,

Moshe Dayan, p.341.

33. By 30 June there were some 120 Soviet-manned Mig 21Js, between 45 and 55 SAM3 sites and 8,000 missile crews in Egypt. *Strategic Survey 1970*, p.47.
34. Kalb and Kalb, op.cit., p.193.
35. 'The sudden blunt talk by the President' had reportedly taken much of the bureaucracy by surprise. *Washington Post*, 11 July 1970.
36. See chap. 9.
37. See the article by Stewart Alsop in *Newsweek*, 3 August 1970.
38. American policymakers had been divided on the correct American response. The JCS reportedly favoured the prompt supply of more aircraft to Israel and a visit by the Sixth Fleet. *Newsweek*, 8 June 1970.
39. Mrs Meir went so far as to say on 30 December 1970 that the American proposal 'would constitute a grave threat to our very existence'. Cited in Shlomo Slonim, *US-Israeli Relations, 1967-1973*, p.20.
40. Ibid., p.21.
41. In the words of a former Administration official, 'Creative policy that initiates as well as reacts . . . requires enormous effort; such effort was expended within the United States government during the first nine months of 1970 as the entire National Security Council system (comprising State, Defence, CIA and the NSC staff) worked to forge a political and military policy that achieved significant results for peace by August 1970.' Robert J. Pranger, op.cit., p.56.
42. *Washington Post*, 8 June 1970. Yair Evron, *The Middle East*, p.116.
43. In this the Americans also manipulated the Soviet risk factor, implying to the Israelis that they would be very reuluctant to provide additional aircraft until after a ceasefire. At the same time Washington sought to manipulate its military resource transfer relationship with Israel by inferring to Moscow and Cairo that it would have to provide Israel with extra F4s unless the ceasefire was accepted. Whetten, op.cit.., p.112.
44. Secretary of State Rogers remarked at a press conference on 25 June that 'it would not be useful to discuss publicly military assistance for Israel', *Newsweek*, 6 July 1970.
45. See Pranger, op.cit., p.24.
46. Israel had a more extensive knowledge of, and access to, American electronic countermeasure technology than any other American ally. *Aviation Week*, 19 October 1970.
47. Nixon's personal letter proved the turning point in the Israeli decision to accept the American proposal. It included copious assurances regarding the American attitude to the Israeli negotiating position. The extent of the various assurances may be seen in the light of the view ascribed to Joseph Sisco, that Israel would never make concessions until militarily invincible. Michael Brecher, 'Israel and the Rogers peace initiative', *Orbis*, Summer 1974, pp.414, 425; Edward R.F. Sheehand, 'How Kissinger did it: step-by-step diplomacy in the Middle East', *Foreign Policy*, Spring 1976, p.9.
48. Whetten, op.cit., pp.116-17. These assurances were renewed in November when Foreign Minister Eban visited Washington.
49. Six right-wing Gahal ministers resigned from the government as a result. Ibid., pp.117, 119.
50. But the risk of a confrontation between Israeli and Soviet aircraft was not entirely removed until the Soviet expulsion from Egypt in July 1972.
51. State Department officials were quoted as saying that there would be no sale of F4s because the Soviet Union was exercising restraint over its arms shipments to Egypt. *International Herald Tribune*, 17 November 1971.
52. *New York Times*, 4 August 1971.

53. The Americans were also trying to use assurances of support as a means of getting concessions. In summer Sisco visited Jerusalem in an attempt to persuade the Israelis to withdraw from the Canal and allow Egyptian troops back onto the east bank. Israeli sources were quoted as saying the Israelis were assured the Americans could rush 100 F4s to Israel in a matter of days if as a result the Egyptians tried to retake the rest of Sinai. *New York Times,* 20 September 1971.

54. Whetten, op.cit., p.203.

55. Evron, op.cit., p.217. But not until four days after Israel announced its decision to accept negotiations did the United States unofficially announce the sale of forty-two F4s and ninety A4s to be supplied over a three-year period. Whetten, op.cit., p.207.

56. How much urgency there was behind the American attempts by this stage is also questionable. The Americans do not seem to have taken Sadat very seriously and, with the Russians out of Egypt, the incentive for a major diplomatic initiative must have been further reduced. After the Soviet expulsions Nixon sent a secret message to Sadat pledging that the Administration would concentrate on the Middle East once the American presidential election and the Vietnam peace negotiations were over. Matti Golan, *The Secret Conversations of Henry Kissinger,* p.145; Edward R.F. Sheehan, op.cit., p.9; Marvin and Bernard Kalb, op.cit., p.424.

57. Elmo R. Zumwalt, 'The lessons for NATO of recent military experience', *Atlantic Community Quarterly,* Winter 1974-5, p.450.

58. For an account of this highly sensitive political exercise, see Walter Laqueur and Edward Luttwak, 'Kissinger and the Yom Kippur War', *Commentary,* September 1974.

59. Golan, op.cit., p.46.

60. Limited arms supplies had been sent before 14 October, including air-to-air missiles and electronic countermeasure equipment. The latter was accompanied by American technicians. *Flight,* 22 November 1973, and Sunday Times Insight Team, op.cit., p.275.

61. Kalb and Kalb, op.cit., p.483.

62. Schiff, op.cit., p.196. At the outbreak of war the Sixth Fleet was placed on full combat ready status (Alert 1). One aircraft carrier and three destroyers were sent to take up stations in the Soviet patrolling grounds between Crete and Cyprus, the second carrier subsequently being brought east from Barcelona. Sunday Times Insight Team, op.cit., p.271.

63. Whetten, op.cit., p.287. N.B. a similar comment by Dr Schlesinger. *New York Times,* 19 October 1973.

64. 'Those storm-beaten Ships, upon which the Arab armies never looked', United States Naval Institute Proceedings, May 1975.

65. Ray S. Cline, 'Policy without intelligence', *Foreign Policy,* Winter 1974-5, pp.128,129. But something of the scale and implication of the operation is suggested by the inclusion in the Alert of Air National Guard air defence squadrons, indicating that the Administration was moving to counter a direct Soviet nuclear threat to the United States. *Aviation Week,* 29 October 1973.

66. The presence of the Scuds resulted in 'some high-level communications' with the Soviet Union. *Washington Post,* 21 November 1973. See also Glassman, op.cit., p.163.

67. The Sixth Fleet, while outnumbered, had the advantage of integral air support and retained an edge in firepower. But this assessment was not unanimously shared within the United States Navy. Admiral Zumwalt subsequently claimed that the superior numbers enjoyed by the

Mediterranean squadron, the possibility of deploying air cover from bases in Egypt, Syria, Yugoslavia and the Crimea, combined with the American difficulties in acquiring basing rights, meant that the United States had no military option but to acquiesce in the Soviet ultimatum of 24 October. Glassman, op.cit., p.162; *Guardian*, 31 July 1975.

68.   On 10 October Vice-President Spiro Agnew had resigned, on 12 October the Court of Appeal had ruled that the President must hand over the White House tapes to the Special Prosecutor, Archibald Cox, and on 20 October Nixon dismissed Cox. This was immediately followed by the resignation of the Attorney General, Elliot Richardson. Officials were quoted as saying that the Alert grew out of a feeling in the Administration of being besieged, partly because of Watergate, but also because of the 'suspicious nature' of President Nixon and Dr Kissinger. *Washington Post*, 28 November 1973.

69.   On 17 October Kissinger told a delegation of visiting Arab foreign ministers that there would be no American intervention in the fighting unless there was 'violation of the territory of Israel proper'. Mohamed Heikal, *The Road to Ramadan*, p.234.

70.   At the time the large-scale American airlift began, Washington believed that Israel was close to defeat. *Times*, 31 October 1973.

71.   *International Herald Tribune*, 3 December 1974.

72.   Sunday Times Insight Team, op.cit., p.376.

73.   Amnon Sella, *What will the Next War be Like?* p.11.

74.   General P.K. Carlton, *Armed Forces Journal*, August 1974. The equipment ranged from rifle ammunition to underwear, from blankets to combat aircraft. But the Israelis received only a small proportion of the arms they requested. Laqueur and Luttwak,op.cit., p.39, and Dayan, op.cit., pp. 421-2.

75.   Kalb and Kalb, op.cit., p.479, Sunday Times Insight Team, *Insight on the Middle East War*, p.132.

76.   Laqueur and Luttwak, op.cit., p.39.

77.   For this however Dr Kissinger may bear some responsibility. While in Jerusalem on his way back from Moscow, several of his comments were open to interpretation as an indirect go-ahead for the encirclement of the Third Army. Golan, op.cit., pp.86-7.

78.   The Americans had already given assurances to both the Arabs and the Soviet Union that the United States would not allow the Israelis to destroy or starve the Third Army. Golan, op.cit., pp.89, 104. See also Heikal, op. cit., p.233.

79.   Ibid., p.88.

80.   Whetten, op.cit., p.293. Dayan is also quoted as saying that Washington 'passed on to us evidence that Soviet airborne forces were preparing to intervene directly to save the Egyptians Second and Third Armies. Unless Israel accepted a ceasefire forthwith, the United States would not stand in the way of the Soviet Union'. *Observer*, 16 December 1973.

81.   Golan, op.cit., pp.105-6, 108; Dayan, op.cit., p.448, and Lawrence Whetten, *The Arab-Israeli Dispute*, p.32.

82.   Golan, op.cit., p.109.

83.   In Dayan's words, 'the hint was enough'. Op.cit., pp.458-9.

84.   Sheehan argues that Washington had for the first time succeeded in formulating an 'Arab policy', the essence of which was an American commitment to work for a settlement which would take Arab interests into account, on the condition that the Arabs understood that the United States would not abandon Israel. Op.cit., p.17.

85.   Although the Israeli lobby continued to constitute an important constraint

on the pressure Washington could bring to bear on Jerusalem. Ibid., p.67.

86. *Washington Post,* 21 March 1976. Of the negotiations leading to the Syrian-Israeli Disengagement Agreement, Golan notes, 'Israel was conducting negotiations not only with Syria, but also primarily with the United States. If an agreement was not achieved with Syria, it was essential to Israel that Kissinger should leave the area without holding Israel to account for the failure — which could have severe implications in the field of military and political aid.' op.cit., p.210.

87. At the end of 1973; in summer 1974 when Dr Kissinger was investigating the possibility of an interim agreement with Jordan; and most prominently in the summer of 1975 following the breakdown of Dr Kissinger's initial attempt to negotiate a second Egyptian-Israeli Disengagement Agreement.

88. *Financial Times,* 22 December 1976.

89. Some indication of the economic value of American military assistance may be gathered from the fact that in 1975 Israeli defence expenditure amounted to 15.9 per cent of the GNP, a figure which would have risen to 26.8 per cent had American assistance not been available. *Military Aspects of the Israeli-Arab Conflict,* pp.180, 219; *Financial Times,* 21 January 1977; Sheehan, op.cit., p.66.

90. The Israeli draft for the 'Memorandum of Understanding' amounted to a formal political and military alliance, but the wording was watered down by the United States, so that with the exception of the clause concerning oil supplies, which the Administration regarded as constituting a legally binding commitment, the document was in general a statement of intent, involving the good faith of the United States. While Dr Kissinger was able to tell a Congressional committee that nothing in these assurances went significantly further in America's commitments and understandings with Israel than had been the practice in the past, Israeli officials claimed that the memorandum was 'much more than the general understanding of friendship that has existed between Israel and the United States until now'. Sheehan, op.cit., p.60; Hearings, Senate Committee on Foreign Relations, 'Early Warning System in Sinai', October 1975, pp.223, 237; *Washington Post,* 2 September 1975.

91. This commitment was similar to that given in a 'Memorandum of Understanding' which had accompanied the First Israeli-Egyptian Disengagement Agreement. However, a secret addendum of the 1975 Memorandum read, 'The United States is resolved to continue to maintain Israel's defensive strength through the supply of advanced types of equipment, such as the F16 aircraft. The United States government agrees to an early meeting to undertake a joint study of high technology and sophisticated items, including the Pershing ground-to-ground missiles with conventional warheads, with a view to giving a positive response. The United States administration will submit annually for approval by the United States Congress a request for military and economic assistance in order to help meet Israel's economic and military needs.' Sheehan, op.cit., p.34, and *Washington Post,* 16 September 1975.

92. The original draft of this clause, a draft which the Administration had first accepted, laid down that in the case of the involvement of a foreign power there would be automatic active counterinvolvement, i.e. military, by the United States. Golan, op.cit., pp.248, 249.

93. It has been argued that the stations were made largely irrelevant by the weapons provided to Israel as part of the agreement. The United States 'seems simultaneously to have installed a warning system for the last war and provided weapons for the next'. Robert J. Pranger and Dale R.

Tahtinen, *Implications of the 1976 Arab-Israeli Military Status,* p.12.

94. Sheehan, op.cit., p.61. Cf. also Dr Kissinger in Hearings, op.cit., p.219.
95. Dennis Chaplin, 'Material controls and peace: the Middle East', *Journal of the Royal United Services Institute,* March 1976, p.35.
96. Suez reportedly convinced Ben Gurion that without American support or acquiescence, Israel would not again be able to take bold action. Bar-Zohar, op.cit., p.256.
97. Cited in Brecher, *Orbis,* op.cit., p.419. See also Dayan, op.cit., p.465.
98. This dilemma was aptly summarised by Dr Kissinger. 'When I ask Rabin to make concessions he says he can't because Israel is weak. So I give him more arms, and he says he doesn't need to make concessions because Israel is strong.' Sheehan, op.cit., p.66.

9 THE RISKS OF SUPERPOWER CONFRONTATION

Every major Middle Eastern crisis, and in particular every round of Arab-Israeli fighting, has raised the spectre of superpower confrontation. What Washington and Moscow have feared is a clash between their forces in or in the vicinity of the Middle East, a clash which could lead to a nuclear exchange. This danger was already perceived during the mid 1950s when the Cold War was still acute. It was revived nearly a decade later with the outbreak of the Six Day War, the initial Soviet reaction to which displayed what an American official has described as 'almost frantic anxiety'.[1] In later years the Nixon Administration frequently drew an analogy between the contemporary situation in the Middle East and that existing in the Balkans prior to the First World War, warning that the conflicts of the region could prove a catalyst for Great Power conflict in the same way that the rivalries of the Balkans had done over half a century earlier.

How real was this prospect? The risks should not be exaggerated. The crises of the Middle East were less dangerous than those over Berlin in the late 1950s and early 1960s or over Cuba in 1962. Minatory diplomacy between Suez and the Yom Kippur War involved a large element of drama and bluff. In quite a number of cases deployments should be seen as attempts to impress allies or intimidate adversaries, rather than as tokens of serious interventionary intent. Even the highly publicised American alert of 25 October 1973 was subsequently described by an American official as having been harmless from the military point of view,[2] and the same may well have been true of Soviet minatory diplomacy during the Yom Kippur War. It remains unclear what military role the several airborne divisions alerted during the early stages of the war could have played in the defence of Damascus, and what the Americans apparently feared at the time of the Alert crisis was not so much a major Soviet military incursion into the Middle East as the deployment of some kind of symbolic force. This would have been intended not to intervene in the fighting but as an answer to an appeal already made by Sadat, and to re-establish a Soviet military presence in the country. But the incident was really remarkable only for its scale: there was nothing unusual in Middle Eastern minatory diplomacy being articulated by forces which were only of superficial or limited military relevance to the conflict in which they might conceivably find themselves engaged.[3]

Yet however little intention the superpowers actually had of intervening, the anxiety which these crises caused was genuine. The incidence
of crisis and warfare was high. Events proved extremely unpredictable,
clients were often perceived to be in imminent danger or dominoes
looked as though they might be about to fall. Under such circumstances
there was an inevitable danger of a superpower clash. Minatory deployments were usually countered in some form, and after the mid 1960s
both superpowers were operating naval forces in close proximity to
each other in the Mediterranean. Until the signature of the Agreement
for the Avoidance of Incidents at Sea in 1972, minor although
potentially dangerous incidents between their respective ships and aircraft were relatively frequent.[4] In crisis the two fleets were kept under
more careful control. But it was then that they sought to interpose
themselves between their adversary and the Middle Eastern coastline
and, during the Yom Kippur War, the Sixth Fleet was, in the words of
an American commander, 'targeted for instant attack from multiple
points' by the Mediterranean squadron.[5]

Minatory diplomacy directed against the adversary superpower was,
as this incident illustrates, in some measure based on a manipulation
of the risks of nuclear war, and deliberately sought to generate a sense
of uncertainty and danger. Neither superpower could ever be sure how
its adversary would act. On the American side, where most of the
evidence is available, such uncertainty over Soviet intentions trans-
cended any appreciation of the limitations of Soviet interventionary
capabilities. Washington was not entirely disposed to dismiss the Soviet
threat to send 'volunteers' to the Middle East during the Suez crisis.
There was anxiety at the time of the main Soviet minatory deployments
of the Six Day War, partly at least because the Russians did not appear
to have decided among themselves what to do.[6] Again at the time of
the 1973 Alert crisis, Washington was concerned that 'hawks' in Moscow
might be gaining ascendency over the 'doves'.[7]

But if such uncertainty made for the kind of situation which Dr
Kissinger was once reported to have described as 'murderously
dangerous',[8] the record suggests that the real danger lay in the
possibility that the superpowers might mismanage their minatory
diplomacy vis-à-vis one another, or that they might in some way be
dragged onto the Middle Eastern battlefield. That could have been the
result of a deliberate attempt by a client to manoeuvre its patron into
the fighting, although Egyptian claims at the beginning of the Six Day
War that American and British aircraft had participated in the Israeli

attacks on Arab airfields were rejected by the Soviet Union, which had its own ways of monitoring the military situation. But the Russians could not eventually avoid being dragged into the War of Attrition, and over the two years that their combat units were operating in Egypt the danger of a superpower clash in the Middle East was greater than at almost any other period. The catalyst was seen as lying in a major Soviet-Israeli conflict. Towards the end of the war Washington became concerned that the Israelis, faced with a growing Soviet involvement in the sensitive Canal zone, might launch a pre-emptive strike against Cairo while they still retained air superiority.[9] Jerusalem was in fact very anxious to avoid a deeper entanglement with the Russians but at the same time it was also worried about where and when the Soviet intervention would stop. The danger, as outlined by Dayan in late June 1970, lay rather in Israel's inability to stand alone if the Russians entered the war in full force.[10]

This was the first indication by a senior Israeli figure that direct American intervention might become necessary, and subsequent evidence suggests that the possibility was accepted in Washington, albeit more readily once the ceasefire along the Canal had come into effect. Assurances of American support in the event of Soviet action were given at the time of the Jordanian crisis of September 1970, and during talks in Washington in December the Israelis were given the impression that if the Russians came in, then the Americans 'would not stay out'.[11] According to one report in 1971 the Administration had considered the possibility of sending American-piloted F4 Phantoms to defend Israeli airspace in the event of Soviet attacks on Israeli bases in Sinai.[12] These dangers were of course reduced by the Egyptian expulsion of Soviet forces in July 1972. But the Yom Kippur War again raised the spectre of the superpowers being drawn into the fighting. The Russians certainly professed themselves to be concerned that this might happen as a result of the unprecedentedly heavy involvement of both America and the Soviet Union in resupply operations,[13] and the danger was rather more dramatically underscored by the initial American failure to ensure Israeli observance of the ceasefire agreement.

By 1973 a new factor had begun to influence superpower behaviour. Rumours of an Israeli nuclear capability had been in circulation since the late 1960s, but according to an unconfirmed report in 1976 the Israelis actually assembled a number of nuclear devices during the first few days of the Yom Kippur War, when they were still under very heavy pressure from the Arabs.[14] This may explain why the Russians sought to give the impression that they had shipped nuclear warheads for Scud

missiles to Egypt, as well as part of the reason for the sense of acute
crisis in Washington at the time of the Alert. Much of this is speculative,
but there is good reason to believe that the existence of regional nuclear
capabilities must increase tension during crises. It places a premium on
the need for the superpowers to be able to discipline their clients.
Assuming that only the Israelis have a nuclear capability, the immediate
burden of this task would probably fall on the Soviet Union, which
would in effect be responsible for seeing that the Arabs did not press
the Israelis to the point where they felt compelled to make use of their
nuclear option. But Moscow would probably also expect Washington
to exert pressure on the Israelis to refrain from using, or even threatening to use, their nuclear option. These dangers must make the superpowers especially sensitive to their clients' security requirement, the
Americans needing to ensure that the Israelis do not resort to nuclear
weapons out of a feeling of desperation and abandonment, the Russians
to assure their clients against the dangers of engaging in any hostilities
against an adversary with a nuclear potential. One of the more pessimistic
scenarios envisages a pre-emptive nuclear attack by a regional power
on its adversaries, that would result in retaliation of some kind by one or
both of the superpowers.[15]

Even in the absence of destabilising developments on the battlefield,
the superpowers have reason to fear that they might stumble into a clash
either as the result of miscalculation on their own part or out of sheer
bad luck. There is always the danger of an incident or of a misreading of
signals. The initial response in Washington to the attack on the intelligence-gathering ship Liberty during the Six Day War was to believe that
the Russians had been responsible.[16] and once Israeli responsibility had
been established the Joint Chiefs of Staff proposed a retaliatory air
strike against the bases from which the Israeli attack had been
launched.[17] Had this latter proposal been carried out, it might have
raised serious doubts in Soviet minds as to the firmness of the American
commitment to Israel, doubts which might have influenced Soviet
behaviour during the subsequent crisis on 10 June. One instance where
there is evidence that minatory intent was overestimated is in the
American interpretation of certain Soviet military moves immediately
preceding the Alert crisis.[18] This was an additional factor contributing
towards the American counterdeployment, the vehemence of which
reportedly greatly worried the Russians,[19] and which, had the Israelis
not immediately been brought to comply with Soviet demands, might
have created an atmosphere in which the mutual interpretation of
signals became increasingly difficult.

Given then that Middle Eastern crises have involved an appreciable if
not a prohibitive risk of nuclear war, what have the superpowers done
to prevent a clash between their forces? At the level of preventive
diplomacy the record is patchy. Attempts were made to remove the
political causes of regional conflict and after the Six Day War a good
deal of effort was invested in the search for a settlement of the Arab-
Israeli dispute. In 1968 and 1969 these efforts took the form of two-
power talks which reflected a real willingness on the part of the superpowers to seek a modus vivendi in a conflict which did not directly
involve vital interests but which had been recognised as being potentially
very dangerous. The breakdown of the two-power talks was followed by
a variety of American initiatives about which Moscow was kept more or
less informed by Washington. But the Soviet attitude towards a settlement remained ambivalent, at least until the Geneva peace conference
of December 1973 and neither superpower proved either able or willing
to impose a settlement on its clients.

The alternative and much less satisfactory approach to preventive
diplomacy has been the attempt to control the outbreak of war. On the
American side this has for the most part been a question of assuring the
Israelis of America's continued commitment to their security and
survival, and of ensuring that the regional balance of power remained
such as to obviate any perceived Israeli need for pre-emptive military
action. This inevitably meant showing considerable sensitivity towards
Israeli perceptions of their own security requirements, and Israeli arms
requests were frequently supported by the argument that the stronger
the country was the more unlikely it would be that it would have to go
to war. But Washington rarely provided all that the Israelis asked for,
and decisions on resource transfers were sometimes influenced by the
hope that restraint on the American side would be matched by Moscow.
The Americans exercised an additional degree of constraint over their
clients by virtue of the oft-repeated warning that pre-emptive military
action could endanger American support in the ensuing conflict. These
warnings were clearly registered in a small country which was becoming
increasingly conscious of its military dependence on the United States,
and their effectiveness was reflected in the Israeli decision to forego
a pre-emptive strike on the eve of the Yom Kippur War.[20]

There was however a clear limit to what the Americans could achieve
in this field. Although Washington's appreciation of the balance of
power on the eve of the Six Day War was less alarmist and proved more
accurate than that of the Israelis, the Americans were quite unable to
persuade Israel that there was in fact no need to resort to immediate

military action. Subsequently certain factions in Washington encouraged the Israelis to pursue their own military solution in order to relieve the Americans from the need to shoulder yet another military burden in addition to Vietnam.[21] After the Israelis had won their massive victory the American ability to prevent the outbreak of another war was limited by their failure to bring about any substantive progress towards a peace settlement and the success of American preventive diplomacy was thus increasingly dependent on the degree of constraint which the Russians were able or willing to exert on their clients. The Russians had of course sought to exert some pressure on Cairo and Damascus to prevent the initiation of hostilities immediately before the Six Day War, and their anxiety in the years after the war to prevent either a Syrian or an Egyptian attack was pressed to the point of straining relations with both countries.[22] In October 1970 the Egyptians were quite specifically warned that the battle should not be resumed until all Soviet advisers had left the country. Sadat's repeated requests for offensive weapons during the 'Year of Decision' were refused,and the Egyptians were advised not to attack Israel within either her pre or post June 1967 borders.[23] Even when these diplomatic pressures were relaxed in 1973, the Russians continued to stress the need for a political settlement of the Arab-Israeli conflict and to exert a degree of constraint in their arms supplies. Deliveries in the months prior to the war, while substantial, failed to come up to Egyptian expectations. At no stage were the Arabs provided with sufficient arms to undertake an overwhelming offensive against Israel, and the delivery of Scuds to Egypt was confined to some thirty missiles, a number insufficient to affect the outcome of the war in Egypt's favour.[24] Deliveries to Syria were only made after the Yom Kippur War and the missiles were reportedly controlled under a 'double-key' system, which allowed the Russians a final say over their use.[25] Thus the war which the Russians facilitated in 1973 could have been regarded as a relatively 'safe', because limited, operation.

What the Russians, like the Americans, succeeded in doing therefore was to postpone rather than to prevent war, and the brunt of preventing a superpower clash thus fell on the manner in which they conducted themselves in crisis. Here the evidence suggests considerable circumspection. Superpower intervention only became a serious possibility when a client's regime or vital centres were threatened. Major deployments, whether minatory or operational, were almost invariably confined to attempts to maintain the status quo. This was relatively more acceptable to the adversary superpower than any attempt to revise the status quo by direct military means. Moreover the adversary superpower was normally allowed time to constrain its client from pursuing whatever actions might now be expected to precipitate a superpower confrontation or worse. A definite pattern of superpower behaviour emerges from the crises between 1967 and 1973. The minatory initiative was taken by the superpower whose client was in danger. In each case its adversary reacted by mounting some kind of counterdeployment to deter actual intervention, while at the same time putting pressure on its own client to desist, pressure which sometimes included the warning that the client was in danger of precipitating a third world war.[26] And desist they did. On 10 June 1967 and 11 October 1973 the Israelis refrained, under Soviet-American pressure, from attacking Damascus. On 8 November 1956 and 25 October 1973 they refrained under similar circumstances from continued military action against the Egyptian forces. In September 1970 the Syrians, under American pressure retransmitted by their Soviet patrons, withdrew their forces from Jordan. To speak of ground-rules determining the circumstances in which a superpower might intervene[27] or threaten to intervene without precipitating a clash, might be going too far. But there would certainly seem to have been a semi-explicit code of conduct reconciling vital regional interests with the more imperative need to avoid a nuclear exchange.

Where the superpowers did deploy forces near or into the combat area, they usually acted with great caution. At the time of their intervention in the War of Attrition, the Russians went to some lengths to reassure Washington about the defensive nature of their operation, and for much of the summer of 1970 at least, to avoid a clash with Israeli aircraft. During the Yom Kippur War Soviet military personnel in Syria kept out of the immediate zone of combat, and refused Egyptian demands to fire Scuds against the landing of American supplies in Sinai.[28] The Russians avoided giving publicity to such deployments and when, as during both the War of Attrition and the Yom Kippur War, they incurred casualties or met with serious Israeli 'provocation', they were careful to avoid responding in a manner which might worsen the crisis.[29]

In the Mediterranean both Washington and Moscow took care to keep their naval forces clear of the zone of combat, partly in order to avoid incident, but partly also to signal an absence of interventionary intent. At the outbreak of the Six Day War American marines were allowed shore-leave on Malta while, with the exception of the two incidents on 6 and 10 June, the Sixth Fleet was kept more than 100 miles off the Syrian coast. Soviet naval deployments both in terms of ship movements, with the majority of vessels continuing routine exercises, and of the make-up of the Mediterranean squadron, which lacked an amphibious component, were also regarded as indicative of an intention to avoid involvement.[30] At the beginning of the Yom Kippur War the Russians withdrew their warships from Egyptian ports and the Mediterranean squadron was moved from the immediate battle area to positions south of Crete. In spite of the precautions against American intervention, the overt Russian posture was described by the Americans as being 'restrained and considerate', and conveyed the impression that the squadron was taking some care to avoid incidents.[31] The Sixth Fleet likewise avoided the battle area and shunned publicity.[32]

It was perhaps fortunate that the crises of the late 1960s and early 1970s which involved a much greater danger of Soviet intervention than those of the mid 1950s, coincided with a general improvement in Soviet-American crisis management techniques. The 'hot-line' installed after the Cuban missile crisis was first used during the Six Day War,[33] and the subsequent evolution of detente was acknowledged by both Russians and Americans to have eased relations during the Yom Kippur War.[34] It certainly facilitated the superpowers' search for a ceasefire which had begun immediately after the outbreak of the war and culminated with the negotiations in Moscow between Dr Kissinger and the Soviet leadership and the jointly sponsored Soviet-American ceasefire resolution in the Security Council, Resolution 338. This, like previously negotiated ceasefires in 1967 and 1970, succeeded in terminating the conflict precisely at the stage where the danger of a superpower confrontation appeared likely to increase dramatically.

The timing was of course no coincidence. The very magnitude of the risk can be seen as one of the major factors reducing the likelihood of a superpower clash, since it enforced restraint and constituted one of the few interests shared by both Washington and Moscow in the Middle East. Considerable efforts were made to reduce the risk factor. Preventive diplomacy proved an important element in both Soviet and American Middle Eastern policy and the fear in Cairo that the Soviet Union might subordinate Egyptian interests to the wider dictates of detente was not without foundation. But the superpowers did not succeed in eliminating the danger of a clash. They showed themselves willing to live with a relatively high level of risk and to learn the complicated and dangerous sign language of crisis management. While ready to exert heavy pressure on their clients in the face of imminent superpower confrontation, the containment of risk was only occasionally an absolute priority of policy. Neither superpower was ready to go to the extreme of seriously considering disengagement, nor to exert the substantial and continuous pressure necessary for the achievement of an Arab-Israeli settlement or a permanent avoidance of war. Such policies, to be effective, would have required a much higher level of superpower co-operation than in fact existed, as well as a greater willingness to subordinate regional interests to the demands of nuclear safety.

These options were certainly not regarded as being open to the United States. They would have meant putting the vital interests of key allies at risk and placing a question-mark over the credibility of alliance commitments worldwide. The Soviet Union was also unwilling to endanger its recently established position in the Middle East, not only because this was valued for its own sake, but because substantial derivatory interests had come to be involved. The reduction of the risk factor, and in particular preventive diplomacy, involved not only a weakening of Soviet-Arab relations, but also laying Moscow open to Chinese and Third World criticisms of superpower collusion. In addition of course it risked a potential strengthening of the American position in the region. These classic problems of Soviet-American rivalry could only be ameliorated, not solved, without, that is, a substantive change in the nature of Soviet-American relations.

Notes

1. George Ball, *New York Times*, 28 June 1970.
2. Ray S. Cline, 'Policy without intelligence', *Foreign Policy*, Winter 1974-5, pp. 128-9.
3. Galia Golan, *Yom Kippur and After*, pp.121-2.
4. For an account of such incidents see *New York Times*, 22 October 1970.
5. Jon Glassman, *Arms for the Arabs*, p.162.
6. Jonathan Howe, *Multicrises*, pp.125, 364.
7. *Observer*, 28 October 1973, and Golan, op.cit., p.131.
8. In response to the news that Soviet airborne divisions had been alerted in the early days of the Yom Kippur War. Marvin and Bernard Kalb, *Kissinger*, pp.470-1.
9. *Washington Post*, 16 July 1970.
10. *Washington Post*, 12 July 1970.
11. Moshe Dayan, *Story of My Life*, p.369.
12. *New York Times*, 20 September 1971.
13. Mohamed Heikal, *The Road to Ramadan*, p.245.
14. *Guardian*, 5 April 1976.
15. See Robert Pranger and Dale Tahtinen, *Nuclear Threat in the Middle East*.
16. Howe, op.cit., pp.102-3.
17. Patrick McGarvey, *CIA: The Myth and the Madness*, p.17.

18. See Glassman, op.cit., pp.172-3, and Cline, op.cit., p.133.
19. *Washington Post,* 30 November 1974.
20. See Kalb and Kalb, op.cit., pp.460-1.
21. Lawrence Whetten, *The Arab-Israeli Dispute,* p.8.
22. For the impact on Soviet-Syrian relations, see Charles McLane, *Soviet-Middle East Relations,* p.90. For Soviet-Egyptian relations, see chap. 10.
23. Heikal, op.cit., pp.112, 117; *Strategic Survey 1971,* pp.36-7; Whetten, op.cit., p.39.
24. Glassman, op.cit., pp.115-16, 190-1. During the Yom Kippur War the Russians are reported to have leaked their refusal of an Algerian request for strategic bombers, in order to indicate to the West their intention to observe crucial restraints in their resupply operation.
25. *Neue Züricher Zeitung,* 22 August 1974.
26. Warnings to this effect were delivered to the Israelis at the time of Suez and at the end of the Yom Kippur War.
27. It is interesting to note that some officials in Washington initially took the view that the Soviet intervention in the War of Attrition was a relatively mild response to the critical threat posed to Egypt by the Israeli deep penetration raids. *Washington Post,* 14 May 1970.
28. Golan, op.cit., p.87.
29. Including the incident on 30 July 1970 when 5 Soviet Mig 21s were shot down, the accidental bombing of the Soviet cultural centre in Damascus during the Yom Kippur War, and Israeli interference with the Soviet resupply operation to Syria.
30. Howe, op.cit., pp.70, 79; Lyndon Baines Johnson, *The Vantage Point,* p.302. During the latter stages of the War of Attrition the Sixth Fleet reportedly received orders to remain twenty-five miles off the Egyptian coast in contrast to the normal limit of three miles. *New Orleans Times Picayaune,* 25 July 1970.
31. Golan, op.cit., p.80, and Glassman, op.cit., p.162.
32. *New York Times,* 9 November 1973.
33. Inter alia to explain to Moscow why bombers had been despatched from the Sixth Fleet carriers following the attack on the Liberty. The 'hotline' was apparently not used during the 1973 Alert crisis. *New York Times,* 21 November 1973.
34. For Soviet views, see *New York Times,* 16 November 1973.

10 THE COSTS OF MILITARY POLICY

The superpowers have incurred much lower costs than any assessment of the risks as they appeared at the time might lead the observer to expect. This was largely because they managed to avoid the two most serious dangers inherent in interventionary politics in the Middle East – the risk of a clash discussed in the previous chapter and that of being dragged into a Vietnam-type situation. This latter danger proved most serious in the case of the Yemen and Egypt, but extended also to a number of other situations. Tacit guarantees or small-scale transfers of military resources helped to establish derivatory interests which, as much as a decade later, were regarded as necessitating minatory and operational deployments. These were the situations in which clients were militarily outclassed by their local adversaries or, in the case of intrastate conflicts, lacked the popular support necessary for political survival. The superpowers then faced an awkward choice. They could either disengage at the cost of losing an ally and incurring prestige losses of possibly more than purely regional significance. Alternatively they could increase their support, an option which further entrenched derivatory interests without affording assurance of eventual success.

This dilemma at various points faced both Washington and Moscow. It weighed heavily, although in the event not decisively, with the Eisenhower Administration during the 1958 Lebanese crisis and has been cited as an objection to a series of subsequent military relation-ships, including the deepening American involvement with Israel and the burgeoning resource transfer relationship with countries in the Gulf. The Russians, who witnessed the embroilment of their principal client in the Yemen between 1962 and 1967, reportedly advised Egyptian disengagement some time before the Six Day War.[1] In turn Soviet embassies and military advisers warned of the risks of re-equipping the Arab armies after their defeat in 1967 and also of taking on a major role in the air defence of Egypt. For a time in the late 1960s it did indeed look as though the Soviet Union was being sucked deeper and deeper into the Arab-Israeli conflict, but partly because air defence was an art they well understood[2] and partly also because, as the events of 1970 showed, the Russians were prepared to take decisive action, the situation was brought under control.

Thus costs, while frequently a reflection of a military policy

174

determined by developments on the ground, rather than by superpower preferences, were never inflated by disaster. They fall broadly into three categories — resource costs, foreign policy costs and domestic costs. The most tangible of these are resource costs. Many of the military resources transferred to the Middle East have been supplied either free of charge or at below free market value, and there is evidence that significant inroads have been made, particularly since the Six Day War, on military stocks, skilled manpower and scarce combat units.

Military involvement in the Middle East has probably been a greater economic burden on the Soviet Union than on the United States. Reliable figures for the cost of military aid and operational and minatory deployments are not available but it has been estimated that between 1955 and 1970 Soviet military equipment supplied to Egypt, Syria and Iraq represented between 2.5 per cent and 4.4 per cent of Soviet defence production.[3] Thereafter with the growing emphasis on the supply of new as opposed to surplus equipment, aid to Egypt alone may have reached 5 per cent of Soviet defence production.[4] How much of this equipment was paid for is unclear. Until the early 1960s the Egyptians paid for arms with cotton and rice. In 1965 however payment was suspended and an arms debt of $460 million written off. From then until 1973, when oil-producing states began to fund Egyptian and also Syrian arms purchases, the Egyptians may have paid little for Soviet military aid, although the services of the Soviet advisers in Egypt were paid for in hard currency, and a substantial debt was amassed.[5]

From an economic point of view the difficulties in securing 2 per cent to 5 per cent of Soviet military production for the Middle East may have been much greater than the actual percentage figure implies. There may well have been short-run pressures on production capacity and resultant delays on deliveries to high-priority domestic sectors.[6] The Soviet economic base was only half as large as that of the United States so that any confrontation demanding the same military effort bore twice as heavily on the Soviet Union. But to maintain some kind of military balance, Egypt had to deploy a much larger army requiring much greater quantities of equipment than did the Israelis, and until 1973 at least, was much less able to finance its defence requirements.[7] This may partly explain why aid to the Middle East has been unpopular in the Soviet Union,[8] and the economic burden of military involvement appears to have been one of the reasons behind the divisions within the Soviet leadership over the whole question of military involvement in the Middle East.[9]

The cost of military policy also bore on the Soviet and Warsaw Pact armed forces. Although the arms originally supplied to the Arabs had been obsolescent, from the early 1960s onward deliveries included weapons which would have been of value in the European theatre.[10] This process was accelerated in the aftermath of the Six Day War, and in the spring of 1971 new types of air defence equipment not yet in general use in the Soviet Union were deployed in Egypt.[11] The scale of Arab losses during the initial stage of the Yom Kippur War horrified the Russians,[12] and the Soviet resupply operation drew heavily on Soviet and Warsaw Pact reserve stocks.[13] Yet, given the high rate of Soviet defence production during the early 1970s, including tank production of 3,000 units per year,[14] such demands were probably tolerable. Much more compromising was the poor performance put up by Soviet military equipment in Arab hands, and the fact that many items of sophisticated Soviet equipment were either captured by the Israelis and then turned over to the West or, as in the case of Egypt following the Egyptian-Western rapprochement, made directly available to the Western defence community.[15]

American resource costs are rather better documented, both the costs of resource transfer and of minatory deployments. The cost of the 1958 Lebanon operation was given as $200 million,[16] that of the deployment of an extra aircraft carrier and other ships to the Mediterranean during the September 1970 Jordanian crisis as $50 million.[17] Total United States military assistance and sales to the Middle East between 1946 and 1972 were valued at $11.696 billion,[18] a figure which however it might be as wise to regard as an indication of order of magnitude rather than an exact total. Israel was subsequently granted very large sums in terms of both grant aid and long-term military credits. On the other side of the account, resource transfers to the Gulf made a significant contribution to the American balance of payments, to employment in the United States, and to reducing the unit costs of various items of equipment purchased by the American forces.

The main burden of these costs was thus felt not by the economy but by the American armed forces. The early 1970s were a period of stagnant defence budgets, and the heavy demands for military resources from Israel and Iran resulted in shortages in the American forces. In the case of Iran, the problem was centred on the sizeable training missions necessary to support the major expansion of the Iranian forces, which drew on technical skills, many of which were in short supply in American units.[19] The Arab-Israeli conflict proved a drain on American combat stocks. In 1970 F4 aircraft delivered to Israel to compensate for losses being incurred during the War of Attrition came from USAF inventories[20] and the following year senior officers were reported to be concerned that the continued drawing on production inventories might weaken the United States combat strength in Europe and the Mediterranean.[21] The problem became acute with the Yom Kippur War, after which the Defence Department had difficulties in meeting Israeli arms requirements while at the same time modernising United States forces.[22] Equipment sent during the war was in part withdrawn from active units (including thirty-four F4E aircraft from Air Force squadrons), and in part from combat stocks maintained in Europe for troops which would be airlifted from the United States in the event of an emergency in the NATO theatre. According to one report tanks supplied comprised nearly 10 per cent of the total American tank force.[23] Concern was again voiced in the Department of Defence at the time of the second Egyptian-Israeli Sinai Disengagement Agreement, that Israeli defence requirements were being given priority over those of the United States[24] and the United States Annual Defence Report for the fiscal year 1977 stated that $16 billion was to be spent over the next 5-8 years in replenishing worldwide reserve stocks depleted by the 1973 emergency airlift.[25]

Foreign policy costs, the detrimental impact of military policy on foreign policy objectives both in and beyond the Middle East, are an altogether more complex subject. The superpowers have constantly had to weight the costs of providing military support against those of withholding it. For once involved in the region the failure to provide military support when, reasonably or unreasonably, such support is expected by clients, has bred resentment, and in some cases has created doubt over the reliability of the superpower as an ally or patron, and its formidability as an adversary.

These costs of military omission have not proved overbearing for the United States, although given that its whole forward security system depends on maintaining the credibility of some forty alliances, Washington has been hypersensitive about its reputation as a good ally. Such costs that have been incurred have been confined to the Northern Tier and have been the result of conflicts between American friends. Since the early 1960s American-Turkish relations have been periodically strained by the Cyprus dispute. In 1964 President Johnson attempted to manipulate Turkey's security dependence on the United States and NATO as a means of preventing a Turkish invasion of the island, and in a letter to the Turkish president warned that Turkey's allies had 'not had a chance to consider whether they have an obligation to protect Turkey against the Soviet Union if Turkey takes a step which results in

Soviet intervention without the full consent and understanding of its NATO allies'.[26] When ten years later Turkey did invade, Congress imposed a ban on arms supplies in order to force the Turks into making concessions. Not surprisingly these incidents did cause damage. The arms embargo resulted in a loss of American intelligence, reduced the combat capabilities of a NATO country[27] and, like Johnson's threat of 1964, undermined the credibility of the American guarantee in Turkish eyes. They also added weight to an inherent Iranian scepticism regarding the reliability of the assurances they had received within both the CENTO and the bilateral Iranian-American framework.[28]

The Soviet Union has been more continuously and seriously embarrassed by the costs of military omission. Although the largely theatrical minatory deployment during the Suez and 1957 Syrian crises gained Moscow credit in the Arab world, much of this was subsequently lost by the Soviet failure to match Western deployments in the aftermath of the Iraqi coup. A rather more serious reaction followed on the Six Day War, with protest demonstrations outside Soviet embassies in Cairo, Baghdad, Beirut and Khartoum.[29] The Egyptians in particular were furious because they had refrained from opening hostilities on Soviet advice and because the Soviet Union had not come to their aid during the war. As Eric Rouleau remarked, 'Just as they were convinced that the Sixth Fleet would intervene on behalf of Israel should the need arise, it seemed natural to them that the Russian army would land in Egypt to aid the Egyptian forces.'[30] This the Russians may well have realised and, according to Sadat, a letter promising aid was delivered to Nasser while he was actually making his resignation speech immediately after the war.[31] But while the Russians did make good much of their prestige losses as a result of their subsequent resupply operation, the dilemma of weighing up the risks of military support against the potential political losses inherent in military constraint became a standing issue for Soviet policymakers for the next six years. The denial to the Egyptians of a major offensive capability involved substantial costs in terms of Soviet-Egyptian relations. It helped to precipitate the Soviet expulsions in July 1972 and to bring about the curtailment, and subsequent loss, of base facilities. It was also a factor in the Egyptian decision after the Yom Kippur War to diversify its arms supplies to the West. Similar restrictions over military resource transfer caused some strain in Soviet-Syrian relations,[32] and in the early 1970s Soviet relations with Iraq suffered as a result of Moscow's unwillingness to afford the Iraqis unqualified support in their disputes with Iran.[33]

The willingness to incur these costs of military omission was of course a result of the realisation that support might involve even greater dangers. Given the political fragmentation of the region, it was difficult even to transfer military resources without causing some friction. At the very last this meant complicating other bilateral relationships, but it could also mean something more serious. As had already become clear in the early 1950s, military resource transfers risked generating local arms races and, as the chain of events leading to the 1956 Sinai campaign showed, war. This the Russians subsequently recognised and Khrushchev, in defending the limited nature of the Soviet response to the Iraqi coup, subsequently told Nasser that, 'knowing your impulsiveness we feared that our unlimited support of your belligerent sentiments might have prompted you to take military action .. and might have been interpreted by you as our agreement to take military action'.[34] Another problem arose where large-scale Soviet advisory corps were established. In Syria relations between the military and the Soviet advisers were relatively, although not entirely, trouble-free.[35] This was not however the case in Egypt where the advisory corps was much larger and where it was also authorised to issue orders, a situation which caused deep resentment within the Egyptian armed forces. The Egyptians also felt that the Russians failed to understand local conditions, to which much Soviet training and equipment was unsuited, and suspected them of exploiting their Egyptian assignment for their own training purposes.[36] In turn the Russians found the Egyptians too impatient to appreciate their slow and thorough training methods, and were unwise enough to betray a patronising manner and evince a near racist scorn for their hosts.[37] When the Soviet-Egyptian Treaty of Friendship and Co-operation was finally abrogated, one Egyptian newspaper described the 20,000 advisers and troops who had been expelled nearly four years earlier as an army of occupation, while Sadat was to compare the behaviour of the then Soviet Ambassador Vinogradov unfavourably with that of past British High Commissioners.

The Americans also quickly ran into political difficulties. In the early and mid 1950s the United States had shown considerable sensitivity towards the susceptibilities of Arab nationalism, most notably when Washington ostentatiously dissociated itself from the Anglo-French Suez expedition. But the subsequent American espousal of the conservative cause reflected an underestimation of the force of nationalist feeling and of the intense regional suspcion, if not downright hostility, existing towards the West.[38] The use of the Sixth Fleet in the April 1957 Jordan crisis gave rise to cries of 'gunboat' diplomacy and placed the United States in the eyes of many Arabs in a position barely distinguishable from that which the British had just been forced to relinquish.[39] In the Lebanon, President Chamoun's acceptance of the Eisenhower Doctrine was viewed by Moslems, and even by some Christians, as a violation of the National Convention of 1943, which had laid down the principle of neutrality in foreign affairs.[40] The result was to polarise yet further the growing conflict between the two communities, thus contributing to the exacerbation of tensions which eventually ended with the American landings in July 1958.[41]

Military resource transfers caused other problems. The dangers involved in the Gulf programmes which included unprecedentedly large advisory corps of whom the unflattering term of 'white-collar mercenaries' was used, became the subject of much debate in the United States. But as of the mid 1970s the costs actually incurred had not so far proved substantial, certainly much less so than the resource transfer relationship with Israel, which risked not only polarising the Arab-Israeli conflict but damaging American interests in the Arab world. This latter fear had long served to constrain American policy. It accounts for Washington's unwillingness to respond to repeated Israeli requests for arms during the 1950s, and for some of the subsequent disagreements between Washington and Jerusalem after the Six Day War. Washington was constantly having to take into consideration Arab reaction when determining its policy over major arms requests. This was particularly notable during late 1969 and 1970 when the Americans, who had been privately warned that they risked a break in diplomatic relations with several moderate Arab regimes as well as hostile reaction throughout the Arab world,[42] stalled on Israeli requests to supply 100 A4 Skyhawk and 25 F4 Phantom aircraft. The decision in November 1971 to provide technological support for the Israeli arms industry was influenced by the erroneous belief that the transfer of technology was less 'visible' and hence less damaging to American interests in the Arab world.[43] By 1973 resource transfers were beginning to have a direct impact on American oil interests. One account attributes the Saudi linkage of oil with American policy towards Israel during the spring of 1973 to King Feisal's anger over the announcement of the supply of additional F4s to Israel at the same time as Sadat's national security adviser, Hafez Ismail, was in Washington.[44] Fears over American oil supplies were strong enough by the time of the outbreak of the Yom Kippur War for the Secretary of Defence to tell the Israeli Ambassador that the United States would only deliver F4 aircraft at the rate of one and a half per day and that deliveries would stop after a couple of days in order to 'read' Arab reaction before further shipments were decided upon.[45] In the event of course the situation on the battlefield and the Soviet airlift dictated a different policy. But the American fears had not been misplaced. The imposition of the oil embargo followed shortly after the inauguration of the American airlift and although the Saudis appear to have been willing to grant the Americans a period of grace until the end of November, they rapidly changed their minds following the announcement of the $2.2 billion of aid made in the last week of the war.[46] By 1976 the Americans found themselves in the potentially embarrassing situation of acting as the major arms supplier to both Israel and to Jordan and Saudi Arabia, while also being under pressure to begin a significant military resource transfer relationship with Egypt.[47] Such a situation could cause complications in the event of renewed fighting because of the need for resupply.[48]

Outside the region, military policy has incurred foreign policy costs in the form of strains on alliance systems and on the development of detente. The crises of 1956 and 1973 were both dramatic and unpleasant and more frequent repetition might well have been damaging to the cohesion of the alliance. But the immediate conflicts between perceived priorities of interests, while unfortunate, did not seriously undermine the overall purposes of the transatlantic alliance. Eisenhower's likening of Suez to 'a family spat', while no doubt something of an understatement, does put the Suez and Yom Kippur incidents in perspective.[49] Similarly, while the Middle East was in the late 1960s and early 1970s the most frequent and probably the most dangerous theatre of superpower confrontation, Middle Eastern crises do not appear to have seriously undermined the long-term attempts by the superpowers to work out a safer relationship with one another. While the Egyptian and Jordanian crises of 1970[50] and more significantly the Yom Kippur War did raise doubts in the United States about the prospects for detente, at a governmental level at least they did not result in any excessive or lasting strains on bilateral relations. Dr Kissinger was anxious to emphasise Soviet restraint during the earlier stages of the Yom Kippur War, and even the airlift was not regarded as going beyond the limits set by detente.[51] Thus the war did not substantially impede ongoing negotiations. Most notable of all, the SALT talks continued uninterrupted, as did talks over future collaboration between Soviet and American space scientists and a visit to the United States by a Soviet delegation to negotiate a new agreement on Siberian natural gas.[52] The Administration was evidently reluctant to impose economic or other sanctions on the Soviet Union in areas unconnected with the immediate crisis because of the high value it attached to the need for seeking a modus vivendi with its nuclear adversary.[53]

Yet the war was not entirely without costs to detente. It gave encouragement to domestic critics of the relationship on both the Soviet and the American side.[54] Certain elements of public and Congressional opinion took a less tolerant view of Soviet behaviour during the war than the Administration had done, and this was one of the factors behind the waning of Congressional support for the Mansfield Resolution, which had called for reductions in the number of American troops stationed in Western Europe.[55] Moreover there were inevitable limitations to the Administration's toleration. As Dr Kissinger noted at the time of Angola,

> the essence of the United States-Soviet relationship, if it is to proceed to a genuine easing of tension, is that neither side will seek to obtain unilateral advantage vis-à-vis the other, that restraint will govern our respective policies, and that nothing will be done which could escalate tense situations into confrontation between our two countries ... these principles of mutual relations are not simply a matter of abstract good will. They are the very heart of how two responsible Great Powers must conduct their relations in the nuclear era. It must be clear that when one Great Power attempts to obtain a special position of influence based on military intervention, and irrespective of motive, the other power will sooner or later act to upset this advantage.[56]

Inevitably some of the costs of military policy have fed back directly into domestic political and economic systems. Any military actor in the Middle East dependent on the region economically is vulnerable to sanctions. This the British found at Suez and were again very conscious of during the crisis immediately preceding the Six Day War, to the point indeed of becoming extremely reluctant to press their earlier plan for an international force to maintain free navigation through the Straits of Tiran. According to Dr Kissinger, the 1973-4 oil embargo cost the United States one million jobs and 1 per cent of the national output, while adding at least 5 percentage points to the price index. Predictions of the cost of future oil embargoes foresaw much more serious damage.[57] But the superpowers, unlike their European predecessors, avoided the most dangerous domestic political costs, the costs of military failure. In Britain, Suez caused a major domestic political crisis, while in France, where the political system was much weaker, it was a contributory factor to the fall of the Fourth Republic eighteen months later.[58]

The superpowers suffered no comparable debacle, although the Six Day War did cause a minor crisis in the Soviet leadership,[59] and the coincidence of Watergate with the Yom Kippur War led some officials to fear during the first week of the war that public realisation that the United States was holding back on Israeli arms requests could endanger the Nixon Administration.[60] Even without the incubus of a domestic crisis on the scale of Watergate, an American administration would find any failure to honour the de facto American guarantee to Israel both costly and potentially dangerous in domestic political terms.[61]

This last example again underlines the point that costs are inherent in interventionary politics in a region as politically and militarily unstable as the Middle East, and that the choices frequently fall between trading off one kind of cost against another. A policy of restraint, whether in terms of meeting clients' requests for military resources or in mounting minatory and especially operational deployments, may prove less costly than one marked by greater adventurism, but penalties are still liable to be incurred. Nevertheless, enjoying the prestige and the resources which are part of the attributes of superpowers, as well as a certain degree of good luck, the United States and the Soviet Union did manage to avoid the extreme penalties of disaster, and the costs which they did incur, while hardly insignificant, could not be regarded as prohibitive. Military policy has on occasion been counterproductive in terms of regional interests. It has had detrimental effects on superpower alliance systems and to some extent also on their mutual relations, a subject of increasing concern after the mid 1960s. In addition there were some damaging costs to the domestic economy and to the stability of governments. But the impact of these costs has fallen rather differently on the two superpowers. The United States was perhaps the most vulnerable, because of the dependence of its main allies on Middle Eastern oil and also because of the Israeli connection. In addition the Americans suffered from a shortage of military resources during the early and mid 1970s, a shortage which however, given the size of its economic base, could be rectified without too much difficulty. The Soviet Union on the other hand appeared to possess the necessary military resources, but it paid a higher domestic political price for providing them and was more frequently embarrassed by the military demands of its clients.

Notes

1.   *Middle East Record*, 1967, p.30.
2.   In contrast to the American failure to come to terms with guerilla warfare in Vietnam.
3.   Gur Ofer, 'The economic burden of Soviet involvement in the Middle East', *Soviet Studies*, January 1973, p.336. But as a percentage of conventional defence production the figure may have been much higher, as much as 7.5 per cent for Egypt alone.
4.   Ibid., p.337. According to a 1971 State Department report, Egypt had received from 3 per cent to 16 per cent of total Soviet inventories of various ground and air equipment. Glassman, *Arms for the Arabs*, p.198.
5.   Ofer, op.cit., p.334. Heikal, *The Road to Ramadan*, p.65. Subsequently the Russians received hard currency for arms as well. For an account of methods of payment for equipment delivered during the Yom Kippur War, see Glassman, op.cit., pp.146, 229.
6.   Ofer, op.cit., p.341.
7.   Ibid., p.342.
8.   But this may be more a reflection of a general resentment against the diversion of scarce resources abroad at a time of low Soviet living standards.
9.   Lawrence Whetten, *The Canal War*, p.367.
10. Glassman, op.cit., p.29.
11. Whetten, op.cit., p.162.
12. Heikal, op.cit., p.245.
13. Reports at the time suggested that by the early 1970s the Soviet Union had pre-positioned large stocks of military supplies in Eastern Europe. Capability for quick combat readiness had been a constant preoccupation of Soviet military writings for some years. Glassman, op.cit., p.229.
14. *Financial Times*, 8 April 1976.
15. *Financial Times*, 22 June 1976.
16. Robert Murphy, *Diplomat among Warriors*, p.497.
17. *New York Times*, 9 October 1970.
18. R.D. McLaurin, *The Middle East in Soviet Policy*, pp.106,107.
19. *International Herald Tribune*, 3 January 1975.
20. Ibid., 13 July 1970.
21. *New York Times*, 4 August 1970
22. *International Herald Tribune*, 21 November 1974. This was apparently the background to several comments by the Chairman of the Joint Chiefs of Staff, General Brown, who on one occasion described Israel as a 'burden' to the United States.
23. Other weapons supplied in quantities large enough to cause concern to the American military, included armoured personnel carriers, TOW anti-tank missiles, Shrike anti-radar missiles and Maverick air-to-ground missiles. In the words of an Israeli account, 'a relatively small army had thinned out the warehouses of a Great Power to danger point'. *Washington Post*, 18 November 1974, 29 December 1975, and Zeev Schiff, *October Earthquake*, p.205.
24. *Aviation Week*, 15 September 1975.
25. *Scotsman*, 28 January 1976.
26. Cited in Ferenc Váli, *Bridge Across the Bosporus*, p.130.
27. In early 1977 General Haig, Supreme Allied Commander in Europe,

described the Turkish forces as operating at less than 50 per cent of their capabilities as a result of the embargo. *International Herald Tribune*, 2 March 1977.

28. So did America's refusal to aid Pakistan during the 1965 Indo-Pakistani war.
29. *Middle East Record*, 1967, p.16.
30. Cited ibid.
31. Speech in the People's Assembly, 14 March 1976. Survey of World Broadcasts pt.4, The Middle East and Africa, ME/5160.
32. For Syrian complaints over Soviet arms supplies see *Arab Report and Record*, 1-15 August and 1-15 December 1972. For evidence of Syrian demands for improved fighters to cope with Israeli aircraft, see Hélène Carrère d'Encausse, *La Politique Soviétique au Moyen Orient, 1955-1975*, p.248.
33. See Robert Freedman, *Soviet Policy towards the Middle East since 1970*, p.70.
34. Mohamed Heikal, *Nasser — The Cairo Documents*, pp.123, 128.
35. *Neue Züricher Zeitung*, 24 August 1972, and *Guardian*, 28 September 1973. Assad was also reported to have come under some pressure to follow Sadat's example and expel the Soviet advisers.
36. Heikal, *The Road to Ramadan*, pp.179-80. Heikal refers to the variable quality of the Soviet advisers and to suspicions that the Russians were using Egypt as an all-weather training ground for pilots. This thesis was allegedly supported by the Egyptian air force's bad accident record: between 1968 and 1971, sixty-eight aircraft with Soviet or Egyptian pilots were lost during training flights.
37. Edgar O'Ballance, *The Electronic War in the Middle East*, p.33, and P.J. Vatikiotis, 'Notes for the assessment of the Soviet impact in Egypt', in Michael Confino and Shimon Shamir (ed.), *The USSR and the Middle East*, p.288.
38. Alexander L. George and Richard Smokes, *Deterrence in American Foreign Policy: Theory and Practice*, pp.326,327.
39. Ibid., p.332.
40. Ibid., p.341.
41. Fear that direct American military intervention would over the long term undermine the Hussein regime was one of the reasons for American reluctance to intervene directly at the time of the September 1970 Jordan crisis. Marvin and Bernard Kalb, *Kissinger*, p.199.
42. *Washington Post*, 8 and 15 June 1970.
43. *New York Times*, 14 January 1972; Whetten, op.cit., pp.204, 207.
44. Feisal had reportedly urged Sadat to expel the Russians in order to get the US to put pressure on Israel for territorial withdrawals. Sheikh Rustum Ali, *Saudi Arabia and Oil Diplomacy*, pp.107,108.
45. Kalb and Kalb, op.cit., p.474.
46. Sunday Times Insight Team, *Insight on the Middle East War*, pp.180-1.
47. Following the signature of the second Egyptian-Israeli Disengagement Agreement President Ford declared that the Administration had 'an implied commitment' to supply some military equipment to Egypt. *Washington Post*, 25 and 27 September 1975.
48. The United States would obviously be reluctant to resupply both sides during a war, but a failure to resupply the Arabs might increase the likelihood of the imposition of an oil embargo.
49. Dwight Eisenhower, *Waging Peace*, p.107. More serious damage was done in 1956 to the more precarious Franco-American relationship. Similarly Soviet policy during the Six Day War caused serious strains within the

Warsaw Pact, even though there was no significant Soviet military involvement. Whetten, op.cit., Appendix 1, 'Eastern European reactions to the
June War: a case-study in Soviet foreign policy compartmentalisation.'

50.   *New York Times*, 15 October 1970.

51.   Galia Golan, *Yom Kippur and After*, pp.93-4.

52.   Ian Smart, 'The superpowers and the Middle East', *World Today*, January
1974, p.14. The Americans did however try to slow down discussions at the
Conference on Security and Co-operation in Europe, a proposal their
European allies opposed.

53.   This was spelled out more clearly at the time of Soviet and Cuban
involvement in Angola. In Dr Kissinger's words, 'The limitation of
strategic arms is . . . a permanent and global problem that cannot be
subordinated to the day-to-day changes in Soviet-American relations.'
Times, 15 January 1976.

54.   Golan, op.cit., p.248.

55.   Phil Williams, 'Whatever happened to the Mansfield Amendment?' *Survival*,
July-August 1976, p.149. After the war the Administration felt it necessary
to postpone introduction of a Bill giving most favoured nation trading
status to the Soviet Union.

56.   *Times*, 15 January 1976.

57.   Address to the National Press Club. Washington, 3 February 1975.

58.   General André Beauffre, *The Suez Expedition*, p.127.

59.   Whetten, op.cit., p.366. See also *New York Times*, 3 February 1971.

60.   The Kalbs quote a high State Department source as saying 'There were
enough people in the country just looking for a breach of confidence in
foreign affairs, above and beyond Watergate. We had always told the
Israelis, "When the chips are down, we're with you." Well, the chips were
down and it looked as though we were not with them.' Op.cit., p.475.

61.   N.B. the view that if the United States were to allow the destruction of
Israel it would loose the 'poison of guilt and hatred, of rage and recrimina-
tion' within the United States. *International Herald Tribune*, 19 March
1970. Significant political repercussions could also be expected in Western
Europe. In addition, it should be remembered that there are some 30
million Moslems living in the Soviet Union, many near the Chinese border.
For the view that Soviet policy in the Middle East affects not only the
attitude of the individual nationalities towards Moscow, but also the
relationships of the nationalities towards each other, see 'Soviet involvement in the Middle East', Hearings, House of Representatives, Committee
on Foreign Affairs, Subcommittees on Europe and the Near East, 1971,
pp.66-7.

11 CONCLUSIONS AND IMPLICATIONS

In contrast to the record of European predecessors, there was only one major occasion on which superpower combat forces have been committed to the Middle Eastern battlefield. Operating beneath the nuclear umbrella, Moscow and Washington have largely confined themselves to the pursuit of minatory diplomacy and the transfer of military resources. Since the Second World War the United States, and from the mid 1950s also the Soviet Union, have made very large transfers of military resources to the Middle East. They have been used as a means of providing security for local clients, of acquiring and paying for military facilities or political influence, and of manipulating the regional balance of power. They have also been used in order to facilitate the objectives of proxies, whose military access in the region has usually been greater than that of their patrons. In general military resource transfers have been seen as a means of acquiring indirect military influence in the Middle East, while at the same time trying to keep political costs and military risks to a minimum.

Up to a point these purposes have been fulfilled. But the success of resource transfers has depended very much on circumstances. As the Arab-Israeli conflict has so dramatically underlined, certain regional conflicts were far too intractable to be contained simply through an externally-manipulated military balance. Moreover the resources transferred were not always appropriate to the military needs and capabilities of the recipients. There was a tendency, particularly on the part of the Soviet Union, to provide too many arms and too little accompanying training, to emphasise the military balance as it appeared on paper rather than the combat capabilities of regional states. This was not entirely the superpowers' fault. Both Washington and Moscow experienced considerable difficulty in fending off excessive arms shopping lists tendered by their clients, lists which frequently took little account of the problems of operating and maintaining sophisticated equipment in a region where the level of technological education was generally low, and where skilled manpower was at a premium. But the superpowers in turn sometimes compounded the problem by providing training and equipment designed for the European rather than for the Middle Eastern battlefield. In the case of the Arab-Israeli conflict Soviet resource transfer policy actually contributed to the outbreak of several rounds of fighting, and to the Arab defeats. Thereupon Moscow discovered that, just as in the case of the United States in Vietnam, low-level military resource transfers had given rise to derivatory interests which now became an important determinant of policy. The result was a series of superpower confrontations, a major resupply operation in 1973 with which the Israelis tried to interfere, and even from 1970 to 1972 the deployment of Soviet combat troops. Clearly resource transfer could not be regarded as a risk-free policy.

Moreover, despite the dependency of the recipients on the superpowers for spares, training and new weaponry, it is quite evident that arms do not necessarily buy influence. Where recipients and supplier share a common purpose, well and good. But where they do not, and in particular where, over the passage of time, purposes come to diverge, the superpowers cannot be sure that the military resource transfer relationship will allow them to apply sufficiently effective sanctions to bring their clients back into line. To attempt, as the Soviet Union did, to seek the change or constrain Egyptian policy through the denial of military resources was a dangerous and difficult policy.[1] Dangerous because it bred distrust and resentment in bilateral relationships, and because the recipients, often simply by virtue of the fact that they afforded the external powers military access, could retaliate against their patrons. Difficult because the recipients could often turn elsewhere for arms. These might not always be available in the necessary quantities, qualities or within the timescale the recipient required, but the very threat to look elsewhere was frequently an effective means of deterring patrons from seeking to manipulate military resource transfer relationships in this way. Only in the case of Israel is there evidence that the manipulation of a military resource transfer relationship had any significant effect in changing a client's policies. And Israel is an unusual case both because after 1967 it had no major alternative arms supplier and because the United States was very careful to manipulate Israeli security policy through the use of the carrot as well as the stick.

In contrast to military resource transfer, minatory diplomacy would seem to have offered the superpowers a more consistently successful, even if a sometimes rather more dangerous and ambiguous instrument of military influence. While minatory diplomacy involved a large element of bluff, and military planners were very conscious of the existence of a number of constraints, including shortages of readily available interventionary forces and the risks of committing small symbolic units in a potentially operational environment, the threat of force has carried considerable weight. In their minatory dealings

with Middle Eastern countries, Moscow and Washington have traded
heavily on their status as Great Powers. Even the strongest of Middle
Eastern states have maintained a healthy respect for the discrepancy
between their own military resources and those of a superpower, and it
was widely believed, in some cases mistakenly, that the United States
and the Soviet Union were readily capable of bringing overwhelming
force to bear in the region.[2]

In their minatory dealings with each other, the superpowers have
sought to manipulate the risk of nuclear warfare to the point at which
the adversary superpower decided to refrain from military intervention
or disciplined its clients to constrain their military actions. On at least
three occasions, in August 1957, July 1958 and October 1973, nuclear
forces, each time American, were involved in the alert. In all major
Middle East crises, and in particular during and after the Six Day War,
the primary channel of communications was that between Washington
and Moscow. This channel was undoubtedly safer than any exclusively
direct minatory communication between a superpower and the regional
client of its adversary. But it was also sometimes the only feasible
method of communication, either because of an absence of diplomatic
relations, or because Middle Eastern countries lacked the necessary
intelligence equipment to monitor minatory signals emitted by various
forms of extra-regional alert.

The impact on the Middle East of these modes of extra-regional
military policy has been substantial and extensive. Practically every
Middle Eastern country has depended on arms and training from outside the region. There is virtually no regional capital where foreign
and security policy has not been influenced, often decisively, by the
promise of some form of external support or by the threat of intervention. For many years Britain, supported by the United States, helped
maintain the stability of the Gulf. To the north Washington underwrote
the security and independence of those countries lying along the Soviet
periphery. In the eastern Mediterranean the Americans ensured the
survival of the conservative order in Jordan and Lebanon, and sought to
solve Israel's security problem. The Soviet Union provided the military
resources to underwrite Nasser's pan-Arab policies and to give the Arabs
a military option in their conflict with Israel. It also ensured the survival
of Syrian and Egyptian regimes and vital centres. But the impact of the
superpowers on the Arab-Israeli conflict was largely a function of the
interaction of their military policies. The relative equilibrium, even
stalemate, which they have tended to impose, was a result not only of
their rivalry but also of a shared, if not always an equally strong,

interest in a political settlement less unfavourable to the Arabs than the military status quo established by the Six Day War. Washington several times reinforced and retransmitted Soviet minatory diplomacy vis-à-vis Jerusalem, not simply in order to contain the risks of confrontation, but also to limit the extent of Israeli military victories which the Americans themselves found embarrassing. In 1970, as during and after the Yom Kippur War, Washington willingly exploited the opportunities created by increased Soviet military support for the Arabs in order to pressurise the Israelis into making concessions.

Yet if the superpowers have helped to stabilise the Arab-Israeli conflict, their methods of doing so have frequently appeared highly destabilising. Here and elsewhere they have grafted their own rivalries on to essentially regional disputes. The Middle East in consequence sometimes came to appear to be little more than another theatre for superpower conflict by proxy, in which it was assumed, frequently erroneously, that the actions of regional proxies were always a faithful reflection of the purposes of their patrons. Local crises were turned into superpower confrontations, provoking one Beirut cynic to remark that the Great Powers had so many 'vital' interests, it was a wonder that they survived at all.[3] In addition competitive resource transfers fuelled arms races in the eastern Mediterranean and in the Gulf, and Middle Eastern countries have been able to acquire an increasingly costly and destructive array of modern weaponry which has done much to determine the pattern of the Arab-Israeli conflict.

These are but two of the reasons why any evaluation of the efficacy of military policy from the point of view of the superpowers is so complex. The historical record suggests that in spite of the constraints imposed by the balance of nuclear terror, and indeed to some extent because of it, force remains, if in circumscribed form, a viable instrument of policy. Without doubt military policy, and the prestige which goes with it, have been a sine qua non for those external powers who have sought to exert any substantial measure of influence over events in a highly volatile region. As Gromyko disparagingly commented about the United Nations Special Mediator in the Arab-Israeli conflict, 'There is nothing wrong with Jarring, except that he has no navies in the sea and no missiles in the air.'[4] Nevertheless the Soviet record, as much as any, indicates that military policy is but an imprecise instrument of control, and that it is suited, at least under the circumstances prevailing in the Middle East, to the achievement of only limited categories of objectives. Military policy has been at its most effective where it has been used to underwrite the status quo, most notably in interstate conflicts. But, and the reservation is an important one when it comes to placing the military instrument in its proper perspective within the wider framework of foreign policy, it has not of itself usually allowed the superpowers to establish conditions of stability within the region. On the contrary, the purpose of minatory deployments has frequently been simply to shore up the status quo in times of crisis. Very occasionally this has allowed a client to eliminate opposition, as King Hussein effectively did in September 1970. More often such minatory deployments did little more than contribute to the establishment of conditions in which a settlement might prove easier to achieve over the long term. Alternatively they bought time. But the value of doing so depended on how quickly and resolutely they were followed by political initiatives. The marines sent to the Lebanon in 1958 were quickly followed by the despatch of an American special envoy to help negotiate a political settlement, and the carefully modulated American military policy during the Yom Kippur War was succeeded by Dr Kissinger's step-by-step diplomacy. But such initiatives were not automatic, nor were they always successful. Clients proved recalcitrant, political problems intractable and, as crises receded, so did the sense of urgency which appears necessary to impel any major peace-seeking initiatives.[5] The history of the Arab-Israeli conflict, as well as the recurrence of troubles in both Jordan and Lebanon, is ample testimony to the greater ability of the superpowers to contain, rather than to solve, conflicts.

Other significant limitations on the efficacy of military policy have been its restricted role in the defence of oil interests and the failure of the superpowers to achieve decisive revisionist objectives. This failure has been most marked in the case of the Soviet Union, given that it was essentially a revisionist power in Middle Eastern terms. The obvious exceptions are the early Soviet arms sales to Egypt and Syria,[6] but the highly favourable circumstances of which the Soviet Union first took advantage did not lend themselves to indefinite exploitation. Ironically the Soviet Union achieved much more in altering the political balance in the Arab world by means of relatively small arms deals in the 1950s, than by the vast later military resource transfers to the Egyptians and Syrians, intended to reverse the Arab defeat of 1967. The American record here is also unimpressive. Possibly the transfer of small quantities of military resources to the Kurds via Iran in the early 1970s may have helped to weaken the Iraqi government. But this achievement is relatively insignificant in comparison with the failure of American minatory diplomacy and military resource transfers to persuade Syria's neighbours to move against the allegedly pro-Communist regime in the late summer of 1957, or the failure of the United States to 'expel' the Soviet military presence in Egypt between 1970 and 1972. The most that American military policy achieved in this latter instance was to contain the extent of the Soviet military incursion, and to add to the constraints on Soviet military resource transfer to Egypt, constraints which did serve to sour Soviet-Egyptian relations.

These limitations on the efficacy of military policy were an inevitable result of the peculiar conditions under which it was pursued. The superpowers were operating in a very complex and highly volatile political environment. They were not imperial powers in the traditional sense. They had few troops on the ground, they did not exercise sovereignty within the region, they were not allowed the benefit of the rights enjoyed by their European predecessors under the so-called 'unequal treaties'. Many of the necessary requisites of military policy, both political and military, were in short supply, and there was the critical problem imposed by the fact of mutual rivalry. Both Moscow and Washington found themselves in a position in which any dramatic strategic advantage achieved either by themselves or by their clients would in all likelihood be countered or neutralised by the adversary superpower. There were few parallels in the Middle East for the situation in Angola in 1975, where the Soviet-backed MPLA was able to achieve a relatively easy victory because the United States was unwilling to sustain resource transfers to its opponents. In addition the risks inherent in superpower confrontation had led to the development of tacit understandings which specifically limited minatory or other deployments to the defence of the status quo.

What conclusions can then be drawn about the relative value of military policy to Moscow and Washington? Without question military policy has allowed the Soviet Union to become a Middle East power, a status which postdates the 1955 arms agreement with Egypt. While Moscow cannot control events in the region, it can certainly influence them and also constrain the influence exercised by others, at least in the eastern Mediterranean. But the price has been high, and the long-term dividends gained from a substantial military investment must, particularly in the case of Egypt, seem disappointingly small. Part of the problems derived from the fact that Soviet military access to the Middle East originated not only from the anti-Western sentiment of the radical states of the eastern Mediterranean, but also from their conflict with Israel. It was this latter involvement which required a major and totally unforeseen transfer of Soviet military resources to the region, as well as a succession of minatory, and even one combat, deployment.

But the problems went beyond what proved to be an injudicious choice of allies: in a region where military access was at a premium, the Soviet Union, like the United States, had after all to take its clients where it could find them. Soviet military resource transfer policy was also for many years poorly designed to meet the real military needs of its clients and, when the Soviet military presence was expanded after the Six Day War, the behaviour of the Soviet military, in particular of the advisory corps in Egypt, proved insensitive and inflexible. That was in part an error in political psychology, but more fundamentally it reflected an absence of any real community of long-term interests between the Soviet Union and its principal clients. The Soviet Union sought military bases and political influence, demands which the radical states, still highly conscious of their recent historical experience with the British and French, were very unwilling to concede. In turn the Soviet Union was stinting in its support for the Arabs' priority objective, the reversal of the 1967 defeat.

It is in fact arguable that, after the anti-Western mood of the mid and late 1950s had subsided, military policy became a more suitable instrument for the United States than for the Soviet Union. American purposes in the Middle East were essentially those of a status quo rather than of a revisionist power. The Americans had the advantage not only of more extensive military access than the Soviet Union, most notably in the Arabian Peninsula-Gulf area, but also of having clients who, either because they kept out of fighting or because they showed much greater military competence, made smaller and more manageable military demands on their patron. Moreover, in view of the greater importance of their interests in the region, American policymakers must have found it easier to justify the relatively high-risk level inherent in military policy than could their Soviet opposite numbers. The doubts about American military policy have centred on the inability of the United States to solve regional conflicts, most notably the difficulties the United States has experienced in attempting to put Israeli security on a firmer political basis, and the suspicion, which may partially reflect the much greater amount of information available about American than Soviet decision-making, that the United States has tended on occasion to over-react and to dismiss non-military approaches to problems too readily.[7]

These conclusions may help us to identify some of the factors which will determine the future role of external military policy in the Middle East. It seems probable that the constraints on military policy will increase rather than decrease. The growth in size and sophistication

of regional armouries suggests that direct military intervention by
external powers is liable to become even more difficult and
dangerous than it has been. That indeed has been the object of
much of American military resource transfer policy to the region, but
under certain circumstances American freedom of action may also be
constricted. It is for example debatable whether the United States would
still be able to consider mounting an invasion to protect oil supplies
in the 1980s, once the Saudi armed forces absorb the large quantities
of equipment currently on order from the United States. Such
considerations also raise questions about the future efficacy of minatory
diplomacy. Defence planners are liable to become even more cautious
about deploying limited forces into a heavily armed region in which
high-value targets, such as aircraft carriers, may become increasingly
vulnerable to the armed forces of those regional states armed with
precision-guided munitions.[8] Moreover the availability of more, and
more lethal, arms could result in Middle Eastern capitals feeling less
vulnerable when they find themselves victims of superpower minatory
diplomacy. In consequence the superpowers may suffer a diminution of
the prestige on which they have in the past relied in order to overawe
local states into refraining from pursuing a particular course of
action.

A further constraint on external military policy arises from the
continuing decline in the availability of military access. The demand for
externally-supplied military resources is unlikely to continue at the
high rate of the early and mid 1970s, especially once the expansion of
regional arms industries gets seriously under way. But in the short to
medium term these industries will depend on the transfer of extra-
regional technology, and even over the long term it is difficult to
envisage any Middle Eastern country becoming self-sufficient in its
arms supplies. More important is the increasing ability of some Middle
Eastern countries to do without, or at least with much less, external
military support than previously. This tendency is most marked in the
Gulf, where ample revenues are available to finance the development
of indigenous forces, and where the security problem is much less acute
than in the eastern Mediterranean. As a result most of the Gulf states
had by the mid 1970s made it clear that they did not want a superpower naval presence in succession to the British, and that their
military relations with external powers should be confined to resource
transfers.

But the overall decline in military access throughout the region is
ultimately dependent on the development of a much greater sense of

security and a much greater degree of stability than has existed in the past. Such developments would seem remote. Inter-Arab rivalries, the problems of minorities, the question-marks over the future of conservative regimes, and above all the Arab-Israeli conflict, suggest that there is going to be continued demand or opportunity for external military involvement. This will be the case whatever happens in the Arab-Israeli conflict. In the absence of a settlement the risk of war remains, and in any major conflict the superpowers are liable to become at least indirectly involved, although the pattern of their involvement may prove different from that of the Six Day and Yom Kippur Wars. By the late 1970s it can be assumed that Israel will definitely have a nuclear capability, and the regional nuclear factor is liable to play an even more important role in any future conflict than it did in 1973. This consideration is made rather more ominous by the prospect that as economic resources are increasingly used to improve military capabilities, and as the erosion of the technological gap between Arabs and Israelis begins to make the Arab superiority in numbers tell, the balance of power may eventually come to swing against Israel. One possible consequence of this may be that the burden of initiating minatory diplomacy in order to rescue its client may shift from the Soviet Union to the United States, and that the United States may find the problem of Israeli security increasingly onerous.

Even if there is a settlement, it will almost certainly need to be underwritten by some form of external military guarantee, in order to help reduce the sense of insecurity which is likely to remain for the immediate future among both Arabs and Israelis. What form this guarantee would take, whether or not it would involve parties other than the superpowers,[9] and how the problem of providing security for any Palestinian state would be solved, remain open questions. So does the problem of whether or not guarantees would increase or decrease the risks for the superpowers. That would depend very much on the nature of the settlement. A viable settlement might involve little more than an institutionalisation of the de facto guarantees for the survival of the major parties which the superpowers have already long provided, while substantially decreasing the risk that these cheques would in future be called upon to be honoured. But if the superpowers, or indeed others, found themselves called upon to underwrite an unviable agreement, as did the British, Greeks and Turks in the case of the treaty of guarantee which accompanied the establishment of the independent republic of Cyprus, then a potentially dangerous situation may have been created.

There is also the question of whether external powers will wish to continue to pursue a military policy in the region. The mid 1970s in fact witnessed a slight increase in the number of secondary military actors. Large numbers of Cuban advisers became involved in Syria and South Yemen as well as in Africa, while North Korean and North Vietnamese pilots were active in the Egyptian and Syrian air forces. There was also evidence of a resurgence of French interest in the region, most notably in the offer of a French peacekeeping force for the Lebanon in May 1976. But the key issue concerns the attitude of the superpowers. The Soviet Union is clearly in a much better military position to support such a policy than it was ten or fifteen years earlier. Whereas in the 1950s Soviet minatory diplomacy was confined to vaguely worded threats to send 'volunteers' and to exercises along the Turkish and Iranian borders, by the early 1970s the Soviet Union was able to mount a major airlift to the Middle East and to deploy sufficient warships into the Mediterranean to cause very real concern in Washington over American freedom of action under crisis conditions. That concern can only be increased following the commissioning in 1976 of the first of three Soviet aircraft carriers. Nevertheless it is possible that the uncertain political dividends reaped on a large, and on occasion very dangerous, investment in the Arab-Israeli conflict may dispose Soviet policymakers, as far as this dispute at least is concerned, towards caution and the need for a settlement. That was certainly the impression that the Soviet Union was seeking to convey in the spring of 1977, at a time when the prospects for a settlement appeared, in relative terms at least, unusually favourable. Not only was Mr Brezhnev prepared to outline fairly detailed proposals for a settlement which took some account of Israeli security interests, but he also indicated Soviet willingness to consider American proposals for a limitation of arms transfers to the region.[10]

The Americans too appeared anxious to reduce the scale of their military policy in the Middle East. There seemed little doubt that the containment of Soviet power and the survival of Israel would remain priority objectives and that, the experience of Vietnam notwithstanding, there would be no dramatic shift of American policy towards the direction of isolationism. But by 1977 concern over the level of American resource transfers had spread from Congress to the Administration,[11] while Washington was also aware that an Arab-Israeli settlement was now more than ever imperative. Yet the superpowers had of course only imperfect control over the situation in the region. Whether they could co-operate in reducing the scale and danger of their military involvement in the Middle East remained to be seen, and would depend not least on the influence which Moscow and Washington would be prepared to exercise over their clients and on their willingness to develop the detente relationship.

Notes

1. Cf. American difficulties in Turkey following the Congressionally-imposed arms embargo in 1975.
2. At the time of the Soviet intervention in the War of Attrition, the Israelis, while believing that they might be able to win the occasional dogfight by dint of superior training and aircraft, were acutely aware that they could not win the war. It may however be unwise to draw any general conclusions from this single instance involving a branch of the armed forces which had long been afforded high priority in the Soviet Union.
3. *Economist*, 4 May 1957.
4. Mohamed Heikal, *The Road to Ramadan*, pp.56-7.
5. The evidence suggests that Washington is what has been described as a 'one-crisis' capital, and that the foreign policy machinery is not structured to allow continuous attention to be given at the necessary decision-making level to one problem for an indefinite period of time. Without, that is, an indefinite crisis of unignorable dimensions. There is also the problem that, in the words of a former Administration official, 'creative policy that initiates as well as reacts .. requires enormous efforts'. Robert J. Pranger, *American Policy for Peace in the Middle East*, p.56.
6. Another success for Soviet revisionist military policy is probably the Yemen. Soviet military resource transfers were one of the factors which contributed to the eventual British withdrawal from the Aden base and the collapse of the South Arabian Federation.
7. The most obvious example of this is the October 1973 Alert Crisis, but N.B. also the rejection of a more low-key approach proposed by Secretary of State Rogers and others during the September 1970 Jordan crisis.
8. This is of course based on the assumption that there are no major developments in countermeasures against such weapons. For evidence of this possibility see Richard Burt, *New Weapons Technologies: Debates and Directions*, pp.11-12.
9. According to a statement on the Middle East issued by the EEC in June 1977, the Nine are 'ready to consider participating in guarantees in the framework of the United Nations'.
10. Speech to the Soviet Trade Union Congress, *Times*, 22 March 1977.
11. In May 1977 the Carter Administration announced a set of guidelines intended to reduce American arms exports. These included the banning of development or modification of advanced weapons systems solely for export, the prohibition of co-production agreements for 'significant weapons' and a declaration that the United States would not introduce into a region 'newly-developed advanced weapons systems which would create a new or significantly higher combat capability'. Specific assurances were however given regarding American arms supplies to Israel, and the above guidelines were subject to the proviso that they would not apply when 'countries friendly to the United States must depend on advanced weaponry to offset quantitative and other disadvantages in order to maintain a regional balance'.

BIBLIOGRAPHY

Books and Pamphlets

Abir, Mordechai *Oil, Power and Politics: Conflict in Arabia, The Red Sea and the Gulf,* London, Frank Cass, 1974.

Adomeit, Hannes *Soviet Risk-Taking and Crisis Behaviour: from Confrontation to Coexistence,* London, International Institute for Strategic Studies, 1973.

Bar-Zohar, Michael *The Armed Prophet: A Biography of Ben-Gurion,* London, Arthur Barker, 1967.

Becker, Abraham *The Super Powers in the Arab-Israeli Conflict,* Santa Monica, Rand P 5167, 1973.

Beling, Willard A. (ed.) *The Middle East: Quest for an American Policy,* New York, State University of New York Press, 1974.

Bohlen, Charles *Witness to History, 1929-69,* London, Weidenfeld & Nicolson, 1973.

Brandon, Henry *The Retreat of American Power,* London, Bodley Head, 1972.

Bulloch, John *The Making of a War: The Middle East from 1967 to 1973,* London, Longman, 1974.

Burdett, Winston *Encounter with the Middle East,* New York, Atheneum, 1969.

Cable, James *Gunboat Diplomacy: Political Applications for Limited Naval Force,* London, Chatto & Windus, 1971.

Carlton, David and Scharff, Carlo (eds.) *International Terrorism and World Security,* London, Croom Helm, 1975.

Confino, Michael and Shamir, Shimon (eds.) *The USSR and the Middle East,* New York, John Wiley, 1973.

Crosbie, Sylvia Kowitt *A Tacit Alliance: France and Israel from Suez to the Six Day War,* Princeton, N.J., Princeton University Press, 1974.

Dayan, Moshe *Story of My Life,* London, Weidenfeld & Nicolson, 1976.

Draper, Theodore *Israel and World Politics: Roots of the Third Arab-Israeli War,* London, Secker & Warburg, 1968.

Eisenhower, Dwight D. *Waging Peace: 1956-61,* London, Heinemann, 1965.

Evron, Yair *The Middle East: Nations, Super Powers and Wars,* London, Elek, 1973.

Freedman, Robert O. *Soviet Policy towards the Middle East since 1970,* New York, Praeger, 1975.

George, Alexander L. and Smokes, Richard *Deterrence in American Foreign Policy: Theory and Practice,* New York, Columbia University Press, 1974.

Glassman, Jon D. *Arms for the Arabs: The Soviet Union and War in the Middle East,* Baltimore, John Hopkins University Press, 1975.

Golan, Galia *Yom Kippur and After,* Cambridge, Cambridge University Press, 1977.

Golan, Matti *The Secret Conversations of Henry Kissinger: Step-by-Step Diplomacy in the Middle East,* Bantam, 1976.

Griffith, William E. (ed.) *The World and the Great Power Triangles,* Cambridge, Mass., M.I.T. Press, 1975.

Hammond, Paul Y. and Alexander, Sidney S. (eds.) *Political Dynamics in the Middle East,* New York, Elsevier, 1972.

Heikal, Mohamed *The Road to Ramadan,* London, Collins, 1975.

Herzog, Major-General Chaim, *The War of Atonement,* London, Weidenfeld & Nicolson, 1975.

Howe, Jonathan Turnbull *Multicrises: Seapower and Global Politics in the Missile Age,* Cambridge, Mass., M.I.T. Press, 1971.

Hunter, Robert *The Soviet Dilemma in the Middle East,* Parts I and II, London, International Institute for Strategic Studies, 1969.

Hurewitz, J.C. *Soviet-American Rivalry in the Middle East,* New York, Academy of Political Science, 1969.

International Institute for Strategic Studies, *Conflict in Africa,* London, 1972.

International Institute for Strategic Studies, *Strategic Survey.*

International Institute for Strategic Studies, *The Military Balance.*

International Institute for Strategic Studies, *The Middle East and the International System: I The Impact of the 1973 War, II Security and the Energy Crisis,* 1975.

Ismael, Tareq Y. *The Middle East in World Politics,* Syracuse, Syracuse University Press, 1974.

Johnson, Lyndon Baines *The Vantage Point: Perspectives of the Presidency, 1963-69,* New York, Holt, Rinehart & Winston, 1971.

Jukes, Geoffrey *The Indian Ocean in Soviet Naval Policy,* London, International Institute for Strategic Studies, 1972.

Kalb, Marvin and Bernard *Kissinger,* London, Hutchinson, 1974.

Kohler, Foy, Goure, Leon and Harvey, Mose L. *The Soviet Union and the October 1973 Middle East War,* Miami, University of Miami, 1974.

Laqueur, Walter *Confrontation: The Middle East and World Politics,*

London, Abacus, 1974.

Laqueur, Walter *The Road to War,* London, Weidenfeld & Nicolson, 1968.

Lederer, Ivo and Vucinich, Wayne S. (eds.) *The Soviet Union and the Middle East: The Post World War II Era,* Stanford, Hoover Institution Press, 1974.

Lenczowski, George *Soviet Advances in the Middle East,* Washington DC, American Enterprise Institute, 1971.

Luttwak, Edward *The Political Uses of Seapower,* Baltimore, John Hopkins University Press, 1975.

McClintock, Robert *The Meaning of Limited War,* Boston, Houghton Mifflin, 1967.

McGwire, Michael *Soviet Naval Developments: Capabilities and Contexts,* New York, Praeger, 1973.

McGwire, Michael, Booth, Ken and McDonnell, John (eds.) *Soviet Naval Policy: Objectives and Constraints,* New York, Praeger, 1975.

Mackintosh, J.M. *Strategy and Tactics of Soviet Foreign Policy,* London, Oxford University Press, 1962.

McLaurin, R.D. *The Middle East in Soviet Policy,* Lexington, Lexington Books, 1975.

Macmillan, Harold *Riding the Storm, 1956-59,* London, Macmillan, 1971.

Maull, Hanns *Oil and Influence: The Oil Weapon Examined,* London, International Institute for Strategic Studies, 1975.

Murphy, Robert *Diplomat Among Warriors,* London, Collins, 1964.

O'Ballance, Edgar *The Electronic War in the Middle East,* London, Faber, 1974.

Peres, Shimon *David's Sling: The Arming of Israel,* London, Weidenfeld & Nicolson, 1970.

Pranger, Robert J. *American Policy for Peace in the Middle East, 1969-71: Problems of Principle, Manoeuvre, and Time,* Washington, American Enterprise Institute, 1971.

Ro'i, Yaacov *The USSR and Egypt in the Wake of Sadat's 'July Decision',* Tel Aviv, Israel Press, 1974.

Safran, Nadav *From War to War: The Arab-Israeli Confrontation, 1948-1967,* New York, Pegasus Books, 1969.

Schiff, Zeev *October Earthquake: Yom Kippur 1973,* Tel Aviv, University Publishing Projects, 1974.

Sella, Amnon *What will the Next War be Like,* Jerusalem, Hebrew University, 1975.

Slonim, Shlomo *US-Israeli Relations, 1967-1973: A Study in the

Convergence and Divergence of Interests, Jerusalem, Hebrew University, 1974.

Stookey, Robert W. *America and the Arab States: An Uneasy Encounter,* New York, John Wiley, 1975.

Sunday Times Insight Team *Insight on the Middle East War,* London, Deutsch, 1974.

Sunday Times Insight Team *The Yom Kippur War,* London, Deutsch, 1975.

SIPRI *The Arms Trade with the Third World,* Stockholm, Almquist & Wiksell, 1971.

SIPRI *Oil and Security,* Stockholm, Almquist & Wiksell, 1974.

Tahtinen, Dale R. *Arms in the Persian Gulf,* Washington, American Enterprise Institute, 1974.

US Congress Hearings, Senate Committee on Foreign Relations, 'Early warning system in Sinai', 1975.

US Congress House of Representatives Committee on Foreign Affairs, Subcommittee on National Security Policy and Scientific Developments, 'The Indian Ocean: political and strategic future', 1971.

US Congress House of Representatives Committee on Foreign Affairs, Subcommittee on the Near East and South Asia, 'New perspectives on the Persian Gulf', 1973.

US Congress House of Representatives Committee on Foreign Affairs, Subcommittee on the Near East and South Asia, 'The Persian Gulf 1974: money, politics, arms and power', 1974.

US Congress House of Representatives Committee on Foreign Affairs, Subcommittee on the Near East and South Asia, 'Proposed expansion of US military facilities in the Indian Ocean', 1974.

US Congress House of Representatives Committee on Foreign Affairs, Subcommittees on Europe and the Near East, 'Soviet involvement in the Middle East and the Western response', 1971.

Váli, Ferenc *The Turkish Straits and NATO,* Stanford, Hoover Institution Press, 1972.

Wall, Patrick (ed.) *The Indian Ocean and the Threat to the West,* London, Stacey International, 1975.

Weintal, Edward and Bartlett, Charles *Facing the Brink: An Intimate Study of Crisis Diplomacy,* New York, Scribner, 1967.

Whetten, Lawrence L. *The Arab-Israeli Dispute: Great Power Behaviour,* London, International Institute for Strategic Studies, Winter 1976-7.

Whetten, Lawrence L. *The Canal War: Four Power Conflict in the Middle East,* Cambridge, Mass., M.I.T. Press, 1974.

Articles

Adomeit, Hannes 'Soviet policy in the Middle East: problems of analysis', *Soviet Studies,* April 1975.

Ahmad, Eqbal and Caploe, David 'The logic of military intervention', *Race and Class,* Winter 1976.

Bell, Coral 'Middle East: crisis management during detente', *International Affairs,* October 1974.

Berry, John A. 'Oil and Soviet policy in the Middle East', *Middle East Journal,* Spring 1972.

Binder, David 'Israel and the bomb', *Middle East International,* May 1976.

Brecher, Michael 'Israel and the Rogers peace initiative', *Orbis,* Summer 1974.

Burrell, R.M. 'Opportunity knocks for the Kremlin's drive east', *New Middle East,* July 1972.

Burrell, R.M. 'Strategic aspects of the energy crisis', *Brasseys Annual,* 1974.

Buzan, Barry 'The status and future of the Montreux Convention', *Survival,* November-December 1976.

Campbell, John C. 'Middle East oil: American policy and superpower interaction', *Survival,* September-October 1973.

Cline, Ray S. 'Policy without intelligence', *Foreign Policy,* Winter 1974-5.

Cottrell, A.J. and Burrell, R.M. 'Soviet naval competition in the Indian Ocean', *Orbis,* Winter 1975.

Cottrell, A.J. and Joshua, Wynford 'The US-Soviet strategic balance', *Brasseys Annual,* 1974.

Daedalus, special issue 'The oil crisis in perspective', Fall 1975.

Dimant-Kass, Ilana 'The Soviet military and Soviet policy in the Middle East, 1970-73', *Soviet Studies,* October 1974.

Draper, Theodore 'From 1967-1973: the Arab-Israeli Wars', *Commentary,* December 1973.

Eran, Oded and Singer, Jerome 'Exodus from Egypt and the threat to the Kremlin leadership', *New Middle East,* November 1972.

Golan, Galia 'Soviet aims and the Middle East War', *Survival,* May-June 1974.

Griffith, William E. 'The fourth Middle East War, the energy crisis and US policy', *Orbis,* Winter 1974.

Heikal, Mohamed 'Soviet aims and Egypt', *Al Ahram,* 30 June 1972, reprinted *Survival,* September-October 1972.

Hunter, Robert 'In the middle of the Middle East', *Foreign Policy,* Winter 1971-2.

Ignatus, Miles (pseud.) 'Seizing Arab oil', *Harpers Magazine,* March 1975.

Journal of Palestine Studies 'The military balance of power in the Middle East: an American view', Spring 1972.

Kennedy, Edward 'The Persian Gulf: arms race or arms control', *Foreign Affairs,* October 1975.

Kerr, Malcolm H. 'Nixon's second term: political prospects in the Middle East', *Journal of Palestine Studies,* Spring 1973.

Klare, Michael 'Gunboat diplomacy, lightning war and the Nixon doctrine: US military strategy in the Arabian Gulf', *Race and Class,* Winter 1976.

Klinghoffer, Arthur Jay 'Soviet oil politics and the Suez Canal', *World Today,* October 1975.

Laqueur, Walter and Luttwak, Edward 'Kissinger and the Yom Kippur War', *Commentary,* September 1974.

Lenczowski, George 'Egypt and the Soviet exodus', *Current History,* January 1973.

McDermott, Anthony 'Sadat and the Soviet Union', *World Today,* September 1972.

Mangold, Peter 'Force and Middle East oil: the post war record', *Round Table,* January 1976.

Ofer, Gur 'The economic burden of Soviet involvement in the Middle East', *Soviet Studies,* January 1973.

Oren, Stephen 'Syria's options', *World Today,* November 1974.

Pajak, Robert F. 'Soviet arms and Egypt', *Survival,* July-August 1975.

Pajak, Robert F. 'Soviet military aid to Iraq and Syria', *Strategic Review,* Winter 1976.

Quandt, William B. 'The Middle East conflict in US strategy', *Journal of Palestine Studies,* Autumn 1971.

Ra'anan, Uri 'The Soviet-Egyptian "rift" ', *Commentary,* June 1976.

Ramazani, Rouhollah K. 'Emerging patterns of regional relationships in Iran's foreign policy', *Orbis,* Winter 1975.

Rostow, Eugene 'America, Europe and the Middle East', *Commentary,* February 1974.

Rostow, Eugene 'The Middle East crisis in the perspective of world politics', *International Affairs,* April 1970.

Rouleau, Eric 'Egypt from Nasser to Sadat', *Le Monde,* 9 August 1972, reprinted *Survival* November-December 1972.

Russell, Jeremy 'Energy considerations in Comecon policies', *World Today,* February 1976.

Safran, Nadav 'Engagement in the Middle East', *Foreign Affairs*, October 1974.

Safran, Nadav 'How long will Sadat last? Moscow's not-so-secret wish', *New Middle East*, March-April 1972.

Safran, Nadav 'The war and the future of the Arab-Israeli conflict', *Foreign Affairs*, January 1974.

Schoenbaum, David 'Jordan: the forgotten crisis', *Foreign Policy*, Spring 1973.

Sheehan, Edward R.F. 'How Kissinger did it: step-by-step diplomacy in the Middle East', *Foreign Policy*, Spring 1976.

Slonim, Shlomo 'American-Egyptian rapprochement', *World Today*, February 1975.

Smart, Ian 'The superpowers and the Middle East', *World Today*. January 1974.

Tucker, Robert W. 'Oil: the issue of American intervention', *Commentary*, January 1975.

Wright, Sir Denis 'The changed balance of power in the Persian Gulf', *Asian Affairs*, October 1973.

Yodfat, A.Y. 'Arms and influence in Egypt: the record of Soviet military assistance since June 1967', *New Middle East*, July 1969.

Zumwalt, Elmo R. 'The lessons for NATO of recent military experience', *Atlantic Community Quarterly*, Winter 1974-5.

INDEX

Printed in the USA/Agawam, MA
February 28, 2013